JUDGING BY THE BOOK:
A Legal and Literary Analysis of Fact Finding

Gilles Renaud
Ontario Court of Justice
Landon Legal Library Press
Cornwall, Ontario

Library and Archives Canada Cataloguing in Publication
Gilles Renaud

ISBN 978-1-926747-66-8

To communicate with the publisher if required at judgenecessity@live.ca

Printed in Canada
www.firstchoicebooks.ca

Other books by the author

Judge 'Necessity'
Landon Legal Library Press, Cornwall, Ontario (fiction)

The Sentencing Code of Canada: Principles and Objectives
LexisNexis Inc., Markham, 2009.

L'évaluation du témoignage Un juge se livre
Les Éditions Yvon Blais, Cowansville, Québec, Spring 2008.

Demeanour Evidence on Trial: A Legal and Literary Criticism
Sandstone Academic Press, Melbourne, Australia 2008

Les Misérables on Sentencing
Sandstone Academic Press, Melbourne, Australia, (Summer 2007).

Advocacy: A Lawyers' Playbook
Thomson Carswell, Toronto (October 2006)

Speaking to Sentence: A Practical Guide
Thomson Carswell, Toronto (June 2005)

Principes de la détermination de la peine
Les Editions Yvon Blais Cowansville, (January 2004)

DEDICATION

Once again, I am honoured to dedicate this book to my sweetheart, my wife Sharon, and to our children and grandchild.

In addition, I wish to thank my in-laws, Douglas and Carol Miller, my brothers Paul and Michel, my brother-in-law Stephen and my sister-in-law Wendy, and my nieces and nephews for their love and support.

I am grateful to Thomson Carswell, Toronto and Les Editions Yvon Blais for allowing me to quote from copyright material and I express my thanks to Ms. Jilliean Bell and to Me Marie-Noelle Guay for their helpful assistance.

Finally, I take this opportunity to thank Brian W. Lennox, the former Chief Justice of the Ontario Court of Justice, for his encouragement over three decades of writing and re-writing.

TABLE OF CONTENTS

Chapter 5:

Judging Evidence of Demeanour (5-1 to 5-75)

Chapter 6:

Concerns in judicial fact finding and the assistance from literature (6-1 to 6-64)

9) Reversing the proposition: Credibility and malapropisms (7-31)
10) Reversing the proposition: One reveller gets arrested, a thousand get a police escort (7-32)
11) Reversing the proposing: To what were you paying attention? (7-33)
12) Reversing the proposition: The impaired sing song (7-34)
13) Reverse the proposition: Never admitting a mistake (7-35)
14) Reversing the proposition: We are not all the same - our experiences differ (7-36)
15) Reversing the proposition: Misunderstandings of what we subjectively perceive (7-37)
16) Reversing the proposition: Attacking written proof or "Where Is It Written"? (7-38 to 7-39)
17) Reversing the proposition: Look at it from the child's perspective (7-40)
18) Reversing the proposition: The witness no longer believes what she once did (7-41)
19) Reversing the proposition: Immaturity is not unknown in older individuals (7-42)
20) Reversing the proposition: Avoiding cultural 'flips' (7-43)
21) Reversing the proposition: Decisions based on facts as opposed to beliefs (7-44 to 7-45)
22) Reversing the proposition: The actions of a person may not reflect their thoughts (7-46 to 7-48)
23) Reversing the proposition: For some, an obvious answer need not be expressed directly (7-49)
24) Reversing the proposition: What of apparent contradictions? (7-50)
25) Reversing the proposition: Cross-examining of record (7-51 to 7-52)
26) Reversing the proposition: The use of interpreters (7-53 to 7-55)
27) Reversing the proposition: Do not accept at face value the words spoken (7-56 to 7-58)
28) Reversing the proposition: "Old Enough to Know Better" implies that some are not (7-59)
29) Reversing the proposition: Mothers (and all other relatives) are not very objective witnesses (7-60 to 7-63)
30) Reversing the proposition: Turning Queen's evidence not limited to those motivated by noble intentions (7-64)
31) Reversing the proposition: Innocent persons, not just guilty ones, may give a poorly detailed alibi (especially when not given sufficient time to think) (7-65)
32) Reversing the proposition: We do not all react the same way to tragedy – the Nurse Nelles principle (7-66 to 7-67)

Chapter 10:

Index

Thanks owed to Marc Simenon

I wish to acknowledge in particular the signal assistance provided by Marc Simenon and the Clorion Company in permitting me to quote at length from the wonderful works of Georges Simenon including the following:

Maigret et le corps sans tête	Maigret à l'école
Maigret au Picratt's	L'escalier de fer
Les nouvelles enquêtes de Maigret	Maigret chez le ministre
Signé Picpus	Les dossiers de l'Agence O
Le locataire	Les témoins
L'homme qui regardait passer les trains	Les caves du Majestic
Maigret chez le ministre	Le pendu de Saint-Pholien
La guinguette à deux sous	L'affaire Saint-Fiacre
Le passager du Polarlys	Chez les Flamands
Le fou de Bergerac	L'Ombre chinoise
Le charretier de la Providence	Pietr le Letton
La Nuit du Carrefour	Les 13 coupables
Monsieur Gallet, décédé	L'Outlaw
Au Rendez-Vous des Terre-Neuvas	La danseuse du Gai-Moulin
La tête d'un homme	La guinguette à deux sous
Le Relais d'Alsace	Liberty Bar
Feux rouges	Le petit docteur

I wish to underline that Georges Simenon Limited has granted me permission to reproduce passages from these wonderful books and short stories on many occasions and that the quality of my analysis has been substantially enhanced by these references.

Table of Cases

(The references are to the chapter and paragraph number: thus, 9-32 refers to chapter 9, paragraph 32)

Chapter 1
An introduction to judging

[1-1]   Judges as a class and on an individual basis lack the most fundamental tool of all in the discharge of their daily duty of fact finding: the capacity to discern truth from falsehood in the assessment of testimony advanced by strangers in the course of a trial. Unlike the mythical Shelpesht, a character created by the wondrous imagination of Yves Thériault, one of French Canada's most prolific and celebrated writers, who discovers two forms of wild grass, the first which permits one to know who is telling the truth while the second endows the holder with the power to ferret out those who lies,[1] the members of the judiciary must rely on their common sense, their knowledge of human nature and the guidance found in the case law on truth telling.

[1-2]   Accordingly, the goal of this text is to foster a greater understanding of the jurisprudence on the assessment of testimonial credit and reliability while advancing, by far it is hoped, the foundation for our understanding of human nature chiefly as a result of a thorough review of the world of literature. In this vein, every judge and every advocate is familiar with the following instruction of the Supreme Court of Canada on the evaluation of testimony, as set out in the majority judgment of Chief Justice Dickson in R. v. Corbett, [1988] S.C.J. No. 40, [1988] A.C.S. no 40, [1988] 1 S.C.R. 670, [1988] 1 R.C.S. 670, 85 N.R. 81, [1988] 4 W.W.R. 481, 28 B.C.L.R. (2d) 145, 41 C.C.C. (3d) 385, 64 C.R. (3d) 1, 34 C.R.R. 54:

> [21] [...] In deciding whether or not to believe someone who takes the stand, the jury will quite naturally take a variety of

---

[1]   Refer to the fable entitled "L'herbe de tendresse", found in Yves Thériault's collection of fables bearing the same title, vlb éditeur: Montréal, 1983, at page 54.

factors into account. <u>They will observe the demeanour of the witness as he or she testifies, the witness' appearance, tone of voice, and general manner</u>. Similarly, the jury will take into account any information it has relating to the witness' habits or mode of life. There can surely be little argument that a prior criminal record is a fact which, to some extent at least, bears upon the credibility of a witness. Of course, the mere fact that a witness was previously convicted of an offence does not mean that he or she necessarily should not be believed, but it is a fact which a jury might take into account in assessing credibility. [Emphasis supplied]

[1-3]   The purpose of this book is to draw greater attention to the precise elements highlighted above, notably the demeanour of a witness with particular emphasis on the related issues of the appearance, tone of voice and general manner, in the overall analysis of what is generally understood to be the credibility and reliability of the person who testified. In so doing, this text will pursue and further refine the work I have undertaken in three prior related books: <u>Advocacy A Lawyer's Playbook</u>,[2] <u>Demeanour Evidence On Trial: A Legal and Literary Criticism</u>[3] and <u>L'évaluation du témoignage: Un juge se livre</u>.[4]   Once again, what is remarkable about my undertaking is that I look as much, if not more, to the world of literature in order to graft skin and flesh upon the dry skeleton of black letter law in this field of study.   Indeed, I am of the signal conviction that one cannot possibly succeed in drawing upon one's life experience or upon common sense without calling in aid a substantial stack of books penned by fiction writers.

---

[2]   Toronto: Thomson Carswell, 2006.
[3]   Melbourne: Sandstone Academic Press, 2007.
[4]   Cowansville, Québec: Yvon Blais, 2008.

[1-4]   Allow me to elaborate upon my baseline belief. I begin once again by making reference to an undisputed authority on the principles which direct judges in their quotidian function: identifying truth from lies, the case of *Faryna v. Chorny*, [1952] 2 D.L.R. 354, (1951), 4 W.W.R. (N.S.) 171 (B.C.C.A.), *per* O'Halloran, J.A. at paragraphs 9-11:

> [9] If a trial Judge's finding of credibility is to depend solely on which person he thinks made the better appearance of sincerity in the witness box, we are left with a purely arbitrary finding and justice would then depend upon the best actors in the witness box. On reflection it becomes almost axiomatic that the appearance of telling the truth is but one of the elements that enter into the credibility of the evidence of a witness. Opportunities for knowledge, powers of observation, judgment and memory, ability to describe clearly what he has seen and heard, as well as other factors, combine to produce what is called credibility, and cf. Raymond v. Bosanquet (1919), 50 D.L.R. 560 at p. 566, 59 S.C.R. 452 at p. 460, 17 O.W.N. 295. A witness by his manner may create a very unfavourable impression of his truthfulness upon the trial Judge, and yet the surrounding circumstances in the case may point decisively to the conclusion that he is actually telling the truth. I am not referring to the comparatively infrequent cases in which a witness is caught in a clumsy lie.

> [10] The credibility of interested witnesses, particularly in cases of conflict of evidence, cannot be gauged solely by

the test of whether the personal demeanour of the particular witness carried conviction of the truth. The test must reasonably subject his story to an examination of its consistency with the probabilities that surround the currently existing conditions. In short, the real test of the truth of the story of a witness in such a case must be its harmony with the preponderance of the probabilities which a practical and informed person would readily recognize as reasonable in that place and in those conditions. Only thus can a Court satisfactorily appraise the testimony of quick-minded, experienced and confident witnesses, and of those shrewd persons adept in the half-lie and of long and successful experience in combining skilful exaggeration with partial suppression of the truth. Again a witness may testify what he sincerely believes to be true, but he may be quite honestly mistaken. For a trial Judge to say "I believe him because I judge him to be telling the truth", is to come to a conclusion on consideration of only half the problem. In truth it may easily be self-direction of a dangerous kind.

[11] The trial Judge ought to go further and say that the evidence of the witness he believes is in accordance with the preponderance of probabilities in the case and, if his view is to command confidence, also state his reasons for that conclusion. The law does not clothe the trial Judge with a divine insight into the

heart and minds of the witnesses,[5] and a Court of Appeal must be satisfied that the trial Judge's finding of credibility is based not on one element only to the exclusion of others, but is based on all the elements by which it can be tested in the particular case. [Emphasis added]

[1-5]   It is as a result of this self-evident recognition that "The law does not clothe the trial Judge with a divine insight into the heart and minds of the witnesses", that this book seeks to call in aid the world's great works of fiction in order that the most eminent psychologists of the English-speaking world be enlisted to assist in the arduous function of fact finding.

[1-6]   If the question be asked, "What do novelists have to contribute to the law", the answer is the following: No less an authority on the law of evidence than Dean Wigmore opined: 'The lawyer [and the judge] must know human nature. He [or she] must deal understandingly with its types and motives. These he cannot all find close around... For this learning he [or she] must go to fiction which is the gallery of life's portraits.'"[6]   In fact, eminent judges have resorted to the world of literature, no greater example being known than the judgment of Lord Atkin which he drew against the background

---

[5]   O'Halloran J.A. had made the same remark in an earlier criminal case: R. v. Pressley (1948), 94 C.C.C. 29 at p. 34, 7 C.R. 342 (B.C.C.A.).

[6]   See "A List of One Hundred Legal Novels" (1922), 17 Ill. Law Rev. 26, at p. 31.   See also W.H. Hitchler, "The Reading of Lawyers" in (1928), 33 Dick. L. Rev. 1-13, at pp. 12-12: "The lawyers must know human nature. [They] must deal with types. [They] cannot find all them around... Life is not long enough. The range of [their] acquaintances is not broad enough. For this learning, they must go to fiction..." Reference may also be made to R. v. Armco Canada Ltd. (1975), 6 O.R. (2d) 521 (H.C.J.), at page 569 and R. v. Baker, [1990] O.J. No. 1617 (Prov. Ct.).

of the London Blitz and yet His Lordship did not hesitate at calling in aid what might otherwise be described as a whimsical or childish image, that of the rotund but not robust fellow, Humpty Dumpty! Is it not telling that of all the orthodox or traditional images that could have been selected to mark his disdain for one method of construction, Lord Atkin chose to make reference to his fallen fairytale figure?[7] In Liversidge v. Sir John Anderson (1942), A.C. 206, at pp. 244-245, quoting from Lewis Carroll's Through the Looking Glass, c. vi, His Lordship remarked, "I know of only one authority which might justify the suggested method of construction: 'When I use a word', Humpty Dumpty said in rather a scornful tone, 'it means just what I choose it to mean, neither more nor less...'"[8]

[1-7]   The structure of this text may be expressed as follows. This initial section has sought to identify certain of the main obstacles to the fact finding function of judges, and to point to the assistance that may be gained from the world of literature.

---

[7]   See also the House of Lords judgment, Investors v. West Bromwich, [1997] H.L.J. No. 27, at para. 57, the Australian High Court decision of Stevens v. Brodribb et al. (1986), 160 C.L.R. 16, at para. 4, the Australian Federal Court at para. 7 of Smoker v. Pharmacy, (1994), 53 F.C.R. 287, 36 A.L.D. 1. In Canada, 33 examples have been discovered, notably R. v. Grillo, [1987] A.J. No. 1340 (Q.B.), at para. 20, Montreal Trust Co. v. T.S. Engineering Inc., [1986] B.C.J. No. 1902 (S.C.), at p. 21 and Manitoba Provincial Judges' Assn. V. Manitoba (1995), 125 D.L.R. (4th) 149 (Man. C.A.), at para. 77, note 64.

[8]   Review A.G. of B.C. v. Smith, [1966] 2 C.C.C. 311 (B.C.C.A.), at pp. 324-325 with respect to the lengthy citation of the March Hare at the Mad Hatter's Tea Party, found in Alice in Wonderland [New York: Clarkson N. Potter, 1960, p. 95. Those readers who are found of Alice in Wonderland may read with profit "A Lawyer's 'Alice'", by Glanville L. Williams in (1945-47) 9 Cambridge L.J. 171-184. See also "This Other Eden: Lord Denning's Pastoral Vision" in (1994) 14 Oxford J. of Legal Studies 25-55, at p. 27.

The second chapter provides guidance on judgment writing and on the sufficiency of reasons. Chapter 3 will review in detail the salient elements of credibility in the exercise of testifying, as opposed to the sister element of reliability, and as opposed to the allied notion of demeanour evidence, a highly controversial aspect of judging. Each of these two issues will be discussed separately, in chapters 4 and 5 respectively. Thereafter, Chapter 6 will examine the topic of concerns in judicial fact finding and the assistance to be gained from literature in answering these questions. In effect, the goal is to further analyze the extent to which literature assists in judging, with a thorough review of the importance for a judge of looking at both sides of an issue. Chapter 7 bears the title, "Good counsel's role in judging: The duty of imagination and effort" and is devoted to the significant contribution which counsel must play in assisting the Court in assessing both sides of any issue of fact or question of credibility, reliability and demeanour. Chapter 9 is devoted to note taking and judgment writing while the penultimate one, entitled "Chapter 9) Some guidance on judging cross-examination", seeks to assist the Bench and Bar to address emerging issues in cross-examination, notably the limits on the practice to protect children. Chapter 10, the brief concluding chapter, reminds the reader of the wondrous possibilities that fiction may provide to judges in their fact finding functions.

[1-8] In concluding this introductory chapter, I wish to underscore that although the contents of this book are not equally divided between traditional and non-traditional elements of judging, it has been drawn with a view to addressing each and every aspect of the duty of the trial judge enhanced by significant references to literature with the ultimate purpose of ensuring the production of wise and well reasoned judgments.

Chapter 2
Instruction on the sufficiency of reasons for judgment

Part A) Instruction on the sufficiency of reasons for judgment

1) Duty of procedural fairness in criminal law and reasons for judgment

[2-1] As an introduction to this chapter, it will be of assistance to refer to para. 10 of *R. v. R.E.M.*, [2008] 3 S.C.R. 3, is apposite in this vein:

> [10] … There is no absolute rule that adjudicators must in all circumstances give reasons. In some adjudicative contexts, however, reasons are desirable, and in a few, mandatory. As this Court stated in *R. v. Sheppard*, [2002] 1 S.C.R. 869, 2002 SCC 26, at para. 18, quoting from *Baker v. Canada* (Minister of Citizenship and Immigration), [1999] 2 S.C.R. 817, at para. 43 (in the administrative law context), 'it is now appropriate to recognize that, in certain circumstances, the duty of procedural fairness will require the provision of a written explanation for a decision'. A criminal trial, where the accused's innocence is at stake, is one such circumstance. [Emphasis added]

[2-2] Subsequently, McLachlin C.J.C. wrote: "[14] In summary, the law has progressed to the point where it may now be said with confidence that a trial judge on a criminal trial where the accused's innocence is at stake has a duty to give reasons…"

2) Reasons for judgment serve the function of informing the parties why the decision was made

[2-3]   As we read at para. 11(1) of *R. v. R.E.M.*, [2008] 3 S.C.R. 3:

> [11] The authorities establish that reasons for judgment in a criminal trial serve three main functions:
>
>> 1. Reasons tell the parties affected by the decision why the decision was made. As Lord Denning remarked, on the desirability of giving reasons, 'by so doing, [the judge] gives proof that he has heard and considered the evidence and arguments that have been adduced before him on each side: and also that he has not taken extraneous considerations into account': The Road to Justice (1955), at p. 29. In this way, they attend to the dignity interest of the accused, an interest at the heart of post-World War II jurisprudence: M. Liston, 'Alert, alive and sensitive': Baker, the Duty to Give Reasons, and the Ethos of Justification in Canadian Public Law", in D. Dyzenhaus, ed., The Unity of Public Law (2004), 113, at p. 121. No less important is the function of explaining to the Crown and to the victims of crime why a conviction was or was not entered.

[2-4]   Para. 15 of *R. v. R.E.M.* reads as follows:

The Test for Sufficient Reasons

[15] This Court in *Sheppard* and subsequent cases has advocated a functional context-specific approach to the adequacy of reasons in a criminal case. The reasons must be sufficient to fulfill their functions of explaining why the accused was convicted or acquitted, providing public accountability and permitting effective appellate review.

[2-5]   In this vein, it will be useful to reproduce in full paras. 22 and 23 as they point to the flawed reasoning in the case of *Sheppard.*

[22] The charge in *Sheppard* was the theft of two windows. The only evidence connecting the accused to the windows came from an estranged girlfriend who had vowed to 'get him'. The trial judge convicted with these formulaic words:

Having considered all the testimony in this case, and reminding myself of the burden on the Crown and the credibility of witnesses, and how this is to be assessed, I find the defendant guilty as charged.

[23] The reasons said nothing about the facts. They said nothing about the credibility of the witnesses. And they said nothing about the law on the offence. They repeated stock phrases of what a

trial judge is expected to do, but did not show that he had done it. There was nothing in the reasons to tell the accused why the trial judge was convicting him. There was nothing to tell the public why the conviction had been entered. And there was nothing to tell the Court of Appeal whether the trial judge's findings and reasoning were sound. The reasons were clearly inadequate from a functional perspective.

3) Reasons for judgment serve the function of public accountability

[2-6] Para. 11(2) of *R. v. R.E.M.*, [2008] 3 S.C.R. 3 addresses this issue in these terms:

> [11] The authorities establish that reasons for judgment in a criminal trial serve three main functions:
>
> > 2. Reasons provide public accountability of the judicial decision; justice is not only done, but is seen to be done. Thus, it has been said that the main object of a judgment 'is not only to do but to seem to do justice': Lord Macmillan, "The Writing of Judgments" (1948), 26 Can. Bar Rev. 491, at p. 491.

[2-7] Refer to the above noted discussion under the rubric of "2) Reasons for judgment serve the function of informing the parties why the decision was made" for the text of para. 15 of *R.E.M.*

4) Reasons for judgment permit effective appellate review

[2-8] This issue is discussed at para. 11(3) of *R. v. R.E.M.*, [2008] 3 S.C.R. 3:

> [11] The authorities establish that reasons for judgment in a criminal trial serve three main functions:
>
>> [3] Reasons permit effective appellate review. A clear articulation of the factual findings facilitates the correction of errors and enables appeal courts to discern the inferences drawn, while at the same time inhibiting appeal courts from making factual determinations 'from the lifeless transcript of evidence, with the increased risk of factual error': M. Taggart, "Should Canadian judges be legally required to give reasoned decisions in civil cases" (1983), 33 U.T.L.J. 1, at p. 7. Likewise, appellate review for an error of law will be greatly aided where the trial judge has articulated her understanding of the legal principles governing the outcome of the case. Moreover, parties and lawyers rely on reasons in order to decide whether an appeal is warranted and, if so, on what grounds.

[2-9] Refer as well to the rubric "Reasons for judgment serve the function of public accountability", which sets out the contents of para. 15 of *R. v. R.E.M.*

5) Reasons for judgment and credibility findings

[2-10] Of note, two recent judgments of the Supreme Court of Canada on the subject of credibility from the perspective of the duty of the trial judge to provide reasons for judgment in this vein are *R. v. H.S.B.*, [2008] 3 S.C.R. 32 and *R. v. R.E.M.*, [2008] 3 S.C.R. 3.

[2-11] As we read at para. 2 of *H.S.B.*,

> [2] ... A trial judge's reasons for judgment do not need to meet a standard of perfection. So long as the trial judge fulfills the purposes of giving reasons — to explain the decision to the parties, to provide public accountability and to permit meaningful appellate review — a court of appeal is not justified in interfering with the verdict on the ground of insufficiency of reasons. The purposes of giving reasons are fulfilled where the reasons for judgment, read in context, establish a logical connection between the verdict and the basis for it — in other words, the reasons must explain why the judge made his or her decision. A detailed description of the judge's process in arriving at the verdict is unnecessary. The trial judge's reasons met this standard. It follows that no error of law has been established and that there was no basis for the British Columbia Court of Appeal's order for a new trial.

[2-12] Of further assistance are the following observations:

> [8] As explained in *R.E.M.*, a trial judge's reasons serve three main functions — to explain the decision to the parties, to

provide public accountability and to permit effective appellate review. These functions are fulfilled if the reasons for judgment explain the basis for the decision reached. <u>The question is not whether a different verdict could have been reached on the evidence</u>. Nor is the question whether the reasons detail every step of the reasoning process or refer to every piece of evidence or argument led by counsel. The task for the appellate court is simply to ensure that, read in the context of the entire record, <u>the trial judge's reasons demonstrate that he or she was alive to and resolved the central issues before the court</u>. [Emphasis added]

[2-13] Para. 15 of *R. v. R.E.M.* reads as follows:

The Test for Sufficient Reasons

[15] This Court in *Sheppard* and subsequent cases has advocated a functional context-specific approach to the adequacy of reasons in a criminal case. The reasons must be sufficient to fulfill their functions of explaining why the accused was convicted or acquitted, providing public accountability and permitting effective appellate review.

[2-14] In the final analysis: "… It is thus reasonable to infer from the reasons that, despite any errors in the complainant's testimony, there remained a body of credible evidence capable of proving the offences beyond a reasonable doubt. The trial judge's reasons thus explain the basis for the verdict reached. In meeting this standard, the trial judge's reasons fulfilled their purposes…" Refer to para. 15 of *R. v. H.S.B.*

6) Reasons for judgment and focusing the judge away from first impressions

[2-15] This issue is discussed at para. 12 of *R. v. R.E.M.*, [2008] 3 S.C.R. 3:

> [12] In addition, reasons help ensure fair and accurate decision making; the task of articulating the reasons directs the judge's attention to the salient issues and lessens the possibility of overlooking or under-emphasizing important points of fact or law. As one judge has said: 'Often a strong impression that, on the basis of the evidence, the facts are thus-and-so gives way when it comes to expressing that impression on paper' (*United States v. Forness*, 125 F.2d 928 (2d Cir. 1942), at p. 942)... [Emphasis added]

[2-16] Refer as well to the rubric "Reasons for judgment serve the function of public accountability", which sets out the contents of para. 15 of *R. v. R.E.M.*

7) The 'path' taken by the trial judge must be clear but no need to point to each landmark

[2-17] *R. v. R.E.M.*, [2008] 3 S.C.R. 3 provides clear guidance on the duty of the trial judge to record in the reasons the path taken to the conclusion reached, but insists on the fact that each landmark need not be described.

> [24] The Court of Appeal in this case took the phrase 'the path taken by the trial judge through confused or conflicting evidence' to mean that the trial judge must detail the precise path that led from disparate pieces of evidence to his conclusions on credibility and guilt. In

other words, it insisted on the very 'verbalization of the entire process engaged in by the trial judge in reaching a verdict' rejected in *Morrissey* (p. 525). *Sheppard* does not require this. The 'path' taken by the judge must be clear from the reasons read in the context of the trial. But it is not necessary that the judge describe every landmark along the way.

[25] The functional approach advocated in *Sheppard* suggests that what is required are reasons sufficient to perform the functions reasons serve -- to inform the parties of the basis of the verdict, to provide public accountability and to permit meaningful appeal. The functional approach does not require more than will accomplish these objectives. <u>Rather, reasons will be inadequate only where their objectives are not attained;</u> otherwise, an appeal does not lie on the ground of insufficiency of reasons. This principle from *Sheppard* was reiterated thus in *R. v. Braich*, [2002] 1 S.C.R. 903, 2002 SCC 27, at para. 31:

> [31] The general principle affirmed in *Sheppard* is that "the effort to establish the absence or inadequacy of reasons as a freestanding ground of appeal should be rejected. A more contextual approach is required. The appellant must show not only that there is a deficiency in the reasons, but that this deficiency has occasioned prejudice to the

exercise of his or her legal right to an appeal in a criminal case" (para. 33). The test, in other words, is whether the reasons adequately perform the function for which they are required, namely to allow the appeal court to review the correctness of the trial decision. [Emphasis in original.]

[2-18] Consider as well the comments consigned at para. 56: "The trial judge should not be found to have erred in law for failing to describe every consideration leading to a finding of credibility, or to the conclusion of guilt or innocence. Nor should error of law be found because the trial judge has failed to reconcile every frailty in the evidence or allude to every relevant principle of law. Reasonable inferences need not be spelled out." The Court goes on to illustrate its meaning in this fashion: "For example if, in a case that turns on credibility, a trial judge explains that he or she has rejected the accused's evidence, but fails to state that he or she has a reasonable doubt, this does not constitute an error of law; in such a case the conviction itself raises an inference that the accused's evidence failed to raise a reasonable doubt."

[2-19] Finally, note is taken of the following comment, consigned at para. 64: "Nor did the trial judge's failure to mention some of the accused's evidence render the reasons for judgment deficient. The foregoing discussion of the law establishes that a trial judge is not obliged to discuss all of the evidence on any given point, provided the reasons show that he or she grappled with the substance of the live issues on the trial." In the opinion of the Court, "It is clear from the reasons that the trial judge considered the accused's evidence carefully, and indeed accepted it on some points. In these circumstances, failure to mention some aspects of his evidence does not constitute error…"

8) Focus is on the substance, not the form, in the sufficiency analysis

[2-20] Para. 31 of *R. v. R.E.M.*, [2008] 3 S.C.R. 3 repeats the assistance put forth by our highest Court in *R. v. Gagnon*, [2008] 1 S.C.R. 788 as follows:

> [31] More recently, in *R. v. Dinardo*, [2008] 1 S.C.R. 788, 2008 SCC 24, the Court, per Charron J., rejected a formalistic approach. The case turned on credibility. The trial judge's reasons failed to articulate the alternatives to be considered in determining reasonable doubt as set out in *R. v. W. (D.)*, [1991] 1 S.C.R. 742. Charron J. stated that only the substance, not the form, of *W. (D.)* need be captured by the trial judge, then went on to say:
>
> > [23] In a case that turns on credibility, such as this one, the trial judge must direct his or her mind to the decisive question of whether the accused's evidence, considered in the context of the evidence as a whole, raises a reasonable doubt as to his guilt.

9) Reasons for judgment poorly expressed

[2-21] The recent judgment in the case of *R. v. R.E.M.*, [2008] 3 S.C.R. 3, makes repeated references to the fact that a poorly expressed judgment may still be functionally correct. As we read at para. 53: "... the Court in *Sheppard* also stated: 'The appellate court is not given the power to intervene simply because it thinks the trial court did a poor job of expressing itself' (para. 26). To justify appellate intervention, the Court makes clear, there must be a functional failing in the reasons..."

10) There is no "watch me think" function in the crafting of reasons for judgment

[2-22] As a follow-up to the prior rubric on the substance of a judgment, I note that Chief Justice McLachlin relied heavily on the instruction consigned by Justice Doherty in the Court of Appeal for Ontario's decision of *R. v. Morrissey* 22 O.R. (3d) 514 in the case of *R. v. R.E.M.*, [2008] 3 S.C.R. 3. Hence, paras. 17 and 18 of that latter judgment read as follows:

> [17] These purposes are fulfilled if the reasons, read in context, show why the judge decided as he or she did. <u>The object is not to show how the judge arrived at his or her conclusion, in a 'watch me think' fashion</u>. It is rather to show why the judge made that decision. ... the description in <u>Morrissey</u> of the object of a trial judge's reasons is apt. Doherty J.A. in *Morrissey*, at p. 525, [para. 29] puts it this way: 'In giving reasons for judgment, the trial judge is attempting to tell the parties <u>what</u> he or she has decided and <u>why</u> he or she made that decision' (Emphasis added). What is required is a logical connection between the 'what' -- the verdict -- and the 'why' -- the basis for the verdict. The foundations of the judge's decision must be discernable, when looked at in the context of the evidence, the submissions of counsel and the history of how the trial unfolded.
>
> [18] Explaining the 'why' and its logical link to the 'what' does not require the trial judge to set out every finding or conclusion in the process of arriving at the

verdict. Doherty J.A. in *Morrissey*, at p. 525, [para. 30] states:

> [30] A trial judge's reasons cannot be read or analyzed as if they were an instruction to a jury. Instructions provide a road map to direct lay jurors on their journey toward a verdict. <u>Reasons for judgment are given after a trial judge has reached the end of that journey and explain why he or she arrived at a particular conclusion. They are not intended to be, and should not be read, as a verbalization of the entire process engaged in by the trial judge in reaching a verdict.</u> [Emphasis by Chief Justice McLachlin.]

11) Barely sufficient reasons for judgment: Test for

[2-23] Chief Justice McLachlin provided a valuable reference in this vein at para. 34 of *R. v. R.E.M.*, [2008] 3 S.C.R. 3 when she quoted from *R. v. Walker*, [2008] 2 S.C.R. 245.

[2-24] In effect, we were reminded that "... the issue was whether the trial judge's reasons had adequately detailed the path to the verdict. Binnie J., writing for the Court, held that while the reasons 'fell well short of the ideal', they were not so impaired that the Crown's right of appeal was impaired (para. 27)." Of note, Binnie J. stated at para. 20: "Reasons are sufficient if they are responsive to the case's live issues and the parties' key arguments. Their sufficiency should be measured not in the abstract, but as they respond to the substance of what was in issue".

12) Verbalizing reasons for believing a witness

[2-25] Para. 49 of *R. v. R.E.M.*, [2008] 3 S.C.R. 3 discusses the thorny issue of the ability of a judge to articulate why a witness is or is not believed. Thus,

> [49] While it is useful for a judge to attempt to articulate the reasons for believing a witness and disbelieving another in general or on a particular point, the fact remains that the exercise may not be purely intellectual and may involve factors that are difficult to verbalize. Furthermore, embellishing why a particular witnesss's evidence is rejected may involve the judge saying unflattering things about the witness; judges may wish to spare the accused who takes the stand to deny the crime, for example, the indignity of not only rejecting his evidence and convicting him, but adding negative comments about his demeanour. <u>In short, assessing credibility is a difficult and delicate matter that does not always lend itself to precise and complete verbalization</u>. [Emphasis added]

13) Sparing a witness from being criticized

[2-26] Refer to the discussion consigned under the rubric "Verbalizing reasons for believing a witness".

14) The hurly burly of the trial court and reasons for judgment

[2-27] In closing this Part, I note that there is direct recognition in the judgment of Chief Justice McLachlin in *R. v. R.E.M.*, [2008] 3 S.C.R. 3, that the duty to give reasons must be understood within the functional requirements of a busy judge's responsibilities. Hence, "… At the same time, *Sheppard* acknowledged the constraints of time and the

general press of business in criminal trial courts and affirmed that the degree of detail required may vary with the circumstances and the completeness of the record." Refer to para. 13.

[2-28] A recent example of the expression of this rule is found in *R. v. Houle*, a judgment of Lalonde J. of the Superior Court, file number 07-16039, rendered on July 27, 2009. As we read at para. 45:

> [45] Clearly there are sufficient reasons given in the trial judge's Reasons for Judgment. On a reading of the Reasons you know why the Appellant was convicted and the Reasons provide public accountability and meaningful review. Trial judges at the Ontario Court level have many decisions to give inside of one work week. In this case this was a one-day trial with two witnesses, the trial judge gave his reasons from the bench and it was entirely appropriate for him to do so in order to give his decision quickly in such a high traffic, high volume court.

Chapter 3
The fundamental elements of judging credibility

1) Introduction: The right of the trier of fact to assess credibility

[3-1] Little authority other than the case of *Olmstead v. Vancouver-Fraser Park District*, [1975] 2 S.C.R. 831, 51 D.L.R. (3d) 416, 3 N.R. 326 is required in this regard. As is well known, Justice de Grandpré opined as follows, at para. 14:

> [14] There is no doubt that the jury are entitled to believe certain witnesses and disbelieve others. They also have the right to choose only part of the evidence of any witness. These rights belonging to the jury permit them to discard plaintiff's own evidence on facts, about which other relevant evidence is adduced, at variance with his own [...]

[3-2] This rule governs trials and actions heard by a single judge as well, who is both judge of law and trier of fact.

2) Differentiating between credibility and reliability

[3-3] At the outset, it will be of assistance to review a number of the principles which govern the assessment and evaluation of credibility in order to illuminate the path of reasoning which a judge must follow in addressing this fundamental aspect of fact finding. A first judgment to be considered in any case is, of course, *Faryna v. Chorny*, [1952] 2 D.L.R. 354, (1951) 4 W.W.R. (N.S.) 171 (B.C.C.A.) but the review of this judgment will be deferred to later in the chapter in order to allow room for consideration of the judicial progeny which Justice O'Hallaran's judgment has spawned. The first question to be addressed is how to distinguish between the question of the credibility to be assigned to a witnesses' testimony, if any, and the credit (if any) to be assigned to that individual's reliability.

[3-4] Accordingly, reference is now made to <u>Bairaktaris and</u> <u>9047-7993 Québec inc. c. Bouras and Naim</u>, [2002] J.Q. no 4148 (Sup. Ct.), at para. 32 to answer this preliminary question as the judgment is valuable in differentiating as between issues of sincerity and accuracy:

> "[Translation] Credibility of witnesses [32] The credibility of witnesses is evaluated in the light of the following principles: A) "<u>Testimonial evidence can raise</u> <u>veracity and accuracy concerns</u>. The former relate to the witness's sincerity, that is his or her willingness to speak the truth as the witness believes it to be. The latter concerns relate to the actual accuracy of the witness's testimony. The accuracy of a witness's testimony involves consideration of the witness's ability to accurately observe, recall and recount the events in issue. When one is concerned with a witness's veracity, one speaks of the witness's credibility. When one is concerned with the accuracy of a witness's testimony, one speaks of the reliability of that testimony. Obviously a witness whose testimony on a point is not credible cannot give reliable testimony on that point. The evidence of a credible, that is honest, witness, may, however, still be unreliable. [Footnote 3 refers to *R. v. Morrissey* (1995), 97 C.C.C. (3d) 193, at 205, per Doherty JA. (Ont. C.A.).] [Emphasis added]

3) Reasons for judgment and credibility findings

[3-5]   As discussed earlier, two recent judgments of the Supreme Court of Canada on the subject of credibility from the perspective of the duty of the trial judge to provide reasons for judgment in this vein are *R. v. H.S.B.,* [2008] 3 S.C.R. 32 and *R. v. R.E.M.,* [2008] 3 S.C.R. 3.

[3-6]   As we read at para. 2 of *H.S.B.,*

> [2] ... A trial judge's reasons for judgment do not need to meet a standard of perfection. So long as the trial judge fulfills the purposes of giving reasons — to explain the decision to the parties, to provide public accountability and to permit meaningful appellate review — a court of appeal is not justified in interfering with the verdict on the ground of insufficiency of reasons. The purposes of giving reasons are fulfilled where the reasons for judgment, read in context, establish a logical connection between the verdict and the basis for it — in other words, the reasons must explain why the judge made his or her decision. A detailed description of the judge's process in arriving at the verdict is unnecessary. The trial judge's reasons met this standard. It follows that no error of law has been established and that there was no basis for the British Columbia Court of Appeal's order for a new trial.

[3-7]   Of further assistance are the following observations:

> [8] As explained in *R.E.M.*, a trial judge's reasons serve three main functions — to explain the decision to the parties, to provide public accountability and to permit effective appellate review. These functions are fulfilled if the reasons for judgment explain the basis for the decision reached. <u>The question is not whether a different verdict could have been reached on the evidence.</u> Nor is the question whether the reasons detail every step of the reasoning process or refer to every piece of evidence or argument led by counsel. The task for the appellate court is simply to ensure that, read in the context of the entire record, <u>the trial judge's reasons demonstrate that he or she was alive to and resolved the central issues before the court</u>. [Emphasis added]

4) Assessing credibility is not a science

[3-8]   Chief Justice McLachlin reminds us at para. 28 of *R. v. R.E.M.*, [2008] 3 S.C.R. 3 of the guidance our highest Court provided on this issue in *R. v. Gagnon*, [2006] 1 S.C.R. 621:

> [28] In *R. v. Gagnon*, [2006] 1 S.C.R. 621, 2006 SCC 17, this Court allowed a Crown appeal of an appellate decision in which an error of law had been found on the basis of insufficiency of reasons. The majority, per Bastarache and Abella JJ., found that the appellate court had ignored the trial judge's unique position to see and hear witnesses. It had instead substituted its own assessment of credibility for the trial judge's view by impugning the

reasons for judgment for not explaining why a reasonable doubt was not raised. Bastarache and Abella JJ. observed, at para. 20:

> [20] Assessing credibility is not a science. It is very difficult for a trial judge to articulate with precision the complex intermingling of impressions that emerge after watching and listening to witnesses and attempting to reconcile the various versions of events. That is why this Court decided, most recently in H.L., that in the absence of a palpable and overriding error by the trial judge, his or her perceptions should be respected. [Emphasis added]

[3-9] Although what follows is somewhat redundant, since the Supreme Court thought it wise to reproduce at para. 48 much of its earlier guidance, I think it advisable to do the same:

> 3. Findings on Credibility

> [48] The sufficiency of reasons on findings of credibility -- the issue in this case -- merits specific comment. The Court tackled this issue in *Gagnon*, setting aside an appellate decision that had ruled that the trial judge's reasons on credibility were deficient. Bastarache and Abella JJ., at para. 20, observed that '[a]ssessing credibility is not a science.' They went on to state that it may be difficult for a trial judge 'to articulate with precision the complex intermingling of impressions that emerge after watching and listening to

witnesses and attempting to reconcile the various versions of events', and warned against appellate courts ignoring the trial judge's unique position to see and hear the witnesses and instead substituting their own assessment of credibility for the trial judge's.

5) Findings of credibility are findings of fact, not of law

[3-10] Bairaktaris and 9047-7993 Québec inc. c. Bouras and Naim, [2002] J.Q. no 4148 (Sup. Ct.) is also of interest in making plain that findings of credibility are assigned to the judges of fact and not to the judicial officers in a judge and jury case. In this vein, note para. 32(c):

> C) Credibility must always be the product of the judge or jury's view of the diverse ingredients it has perceived at trial, combined with experience, logic and an intuitive sense of the matter: see R. v. B. (G.) (1988), 65 Sask. R. 134 (C.A.), at p. 149, per Wakeling J.A., affirmed [1990] 2 S.C.R. 3. Credibility is a matter within the competence of lay people. [Footnote 5 reads: R. v. Marquard, [1993] 4 R.C.S. 223, p. 248.

6) Credibility and the trial judge' unique position to watch and listen to witnesses

[3-11] Chief Justice McLachlin reminds us at para. 28 of R. v. R.E.M., [2008] 3 S.C.R. 3 of the guidance our highest Court provided on this issue in R. v. Gagnon, [2006] 1 S.C.R. 621:

> [28] In R. v. Gagnon, [2006] 1 S.C.R. 621, 2006 SCC 17, this Court allowed a Crown appeal of an appellate decision in which an error of law had been found on the basis of insufficiency of reasons. The

majority, per Bastarache and Abella JJ., found that the appellate court had ignored the trial judge's unique position to see and hear witnesses. It had instead substituted its own assessment of credibility for the trial judge's view by impugning the reasons for judgment for not explaining why a reasonable doubt was not raised. Bastarache and Abella JJ. observed, at para. 20:

> [20] Assessing credibility is not a science. It is very difficult for a trial judge to articulate with precision the complex intermingling of impressions that emerge after watching and listening to witnesses and attempting to reconcile the various versions of events. That is why this Court decided, most recently in *H.L.*, that in the absence of a palpable and overriding error by the trial judge, his or her perceptions should be respected. [Emphasis added]

[3-12]   In the ultimate analysis, in the opinion of the Supreme Court of Canada,

> [68] ... the Court of Appeal focussed on omitted details and proceeded from a sceptical perspective. Having concluded that the accused's denial was plausible, it proceeded to examine the case from that perspective, asking whether the reasons disclosed that the trial judge had properly applied the reasonable doubt standard. In doing so, it fell into the trap identified in Gagnon of ignoring the trial judge's unique position to see and hear

witnesses, and instead substituted its own
assessment of credibility for the trial
judge's view by impugning the reasons for
judgment for not explaining why a
reasonable doubt was not raised.
[Emphasis added]

[3-13] I refer the reader to Chapter 5 devoted to demeanour evidence in which I question the importance which is assigned to this element of testimonial value.

7) Acceptance or rejection of all or part of the testimony

[3-14] *R. v. R.E.M.*, [2008] 3 S.C.R. 3 is of interest in that the Supreme Court of Canada reproduced the traditional guidance given to trial judges which makes it plain that credibility findings need not be a sum zero game.

[3-15] As we read at para. 65:

> [65] The trial judge's alleged failure to reconcile his generally positive findings on the complainant's evidence with the rejection of some of her evidence did not render the reasons deficient. As juries are routinely instructed, it is open to the trier of fact to accept some of the evidence of a witness, while rejecting other evidence of the same witness. The trial judge explained that the fact that many of the incidents testified to happened many years before and the fact that the complainant was a child at the time might well explain certain inconsistencies. In fact, he did explain why he rejected some of her evidence. [Emphasis added]

8) Findings of facts are at best an opinion

[3-16] We would do well to pause to point out that a finding of fact is at best an opinion by the trier of fact as to what did occur, which is why it is not binding on other fact finders. In this vein, note is taken of *R. v. P.G.G.*, [1987] N.B.J. No. 1171, 82 N.B.R. (2d) 410, 208 A.P.R. 410 (C.A.) at para. 9:

> [9] In most cases it is necessary for a judge to decide whether to accept or reject evidence, or portions of the evidence, of a witness. But only in the most extreme cases should it be necessary for a judge to call a witness a liar. [...] Accusations of perjury are, in my view, unnecessary and should be avoided. The power to speak withering words, when a person may not answer, is one that ought to be used with prudence and caution. <u>When a judge makes a finding with respect to a person's credibility, it is not a finding of fact but an expression of his opinion, limited to the facts established on the record in that particular case.</u> [Emphasis added]

9) Findings of credibility depend upon logic, intuition and life's experiences

[3-17] Having explained that findings of credibility are findings of facts entrusted to lay persons, it is not surprising that the corollary proposition is that such findings are tributary to a person's logic, intuition and experiences of life.

10) A caveat is necessary: The Court is a strange place!

[3-18] It is necessary to qualify the last noted proposition as it must be understood by all fact finders, be they professionally trained or selected by means of the jury lottery, that the Court

room is a strange often intimidating place and that this form of atmosphere may result in somewhat unusual responses touching upon peripheral or apparently unrelated issues. The classic example involves the witness who cannot recall his date of birth or place of residence.

[3-19] In this vein, consider the wise words of Trainor J. in *Vanderbyl v. Insurance Corporation of British Columbia*, [1993] B.C.J. No. 1007, [1993] 6 W.W.R. 725, 79 B.C.L.R. (2d) 156 (Sup. Ct.), at para. 20:

> [20] In both civil and criminal proceedings when sitting with a jury it is the responsibility of the trial judge to instruct them on the course they should follow when dealing with the testimony of witnesses. Those instructions apply, as well, to the task facing a judge sitting without a jury. I usually say something to a jury along the following lines [...] Bear in mind that a courtroom is a strange place for most people, and remember that the testimony of each of the witnesses must be regarded in the light of all of the circumstances, including what other persons have said.

11) Credibility findings do not depend upon a rigid formula

[3-20] It will be of assistance to pause in order to note that the existence of the well recognized principles identified to date, and there are more to follow, ought not to be envisaged as forming part of what might be described as a talismanic expression more in keeping with a rote formula than with a principled approach to fact finding. Far from it, the Courts are unanimous in decrying any attempt to establish a rigid formula in such endeavours as this would run counter to the need to address the logic of what is advanced by the witness in light of that person's age, intellect and capacity to observe, among

other factors. In effect, if there is any orthodox approach, it is that no orthodox view is mandated.

[3-21] In this light, note the comments consigned by Justice Brien at para. 23 and 24 of *R. v. S.W.C.*, [1994] N.B.J. No. 588, 163 N.B.R. (2d) 106 (Prov. Ct.) contrasting rigid but necessary formulas in jury fact finding with the absence of such rigidity for matters of credibility:

> [23] This court is mindful of the instruction of Cory J. in *R. v. W. (D.)* (1991) 63 C.C.C. (3d) 397, at p. 409 where he set out a formula for instruction to a jury on the question of credibility:
>
>> "First, if you believe the evidence of the accused, obviously you must acquit. Secondly, if you do not believe the testimony of the accused but you are left in reasonable doubt by it, you must acquit.
>> [...]
>> Thirdly, even if you are not left in doubt by the evidence of the accused, you must ask yourself whether, on the basis of the evidence which you do accept, you are convinced beyond a reasonable doubt by that evidence of the guilt of the accused."
>
> [24] Much has been written on the guidelines to be followed by a trial judge in the assessment of credibility of witnesses. Unlike the stated issue above, there is no formula to be followed. Clearly, the court may consider a number of factors in such assessments some of

which include power of observation, power of recollection, demeanour on the stand, consistency of conduct, and degree of impartiality. [Emphasis added]

[3-22] Consider as well the guidance found in *Brethour v. Law Society of British Columbia*, [1950] B.C.J. No. 110, [1951] 2 D.L.R. 138 (C.A.), at para. 15:

[15] The credibility of interested witnesses, particularly in cases of conflict of evidence, must reasonably be subjected to an examination of the consistency of their stories with the probabilities that surround the currently existing conditions. In short, the real test of the truth of a story of a witness in such a case must be its harmony with the preponderance of the probabilities which a practical and informed person would readily recognize as reasonable in that place and under those conditions. A Court of Appeal must be satisfied that the finding of credibility in the tribunal of first instance is based, not on one element only to the exclusion of others, but is based on all the elements by which it can be tested in the particular case. [Emphasis added]

12) In assessing credibility, be mindful of apparent sincerity

[3-23] *Trojan Technologies, Inc. v. Suntec Environmental Inc.*, [2004] F.C.J. No. 636, 2004 FCA 140, 239 D.L.R. (4th) 536, 320 N.R. 322, 31 C.P.R. (4th) 241, a judgment of Rothstein, Sexton and Pelletier JJ.A., includes these observations at para. 21

[21] [...] <u>If a trial Judge's finding of credibility is to depend solely on which person he thinks made the better appearance of sincerity in the witness box, we are left with a purely arbitrary finding and justice would then depend upon the best actors in the witness box.</u> On reflection it becomes almost axiomatic that the appearance of telling the truth is but one of the elements that enter into the credibility of the evidence of a witness. Opportunities for knowledge, powers of observation, judgment and memory, ability to describe clearly what he has seen and heard, as well as other factors, combine to produce what is called credibility [...] <u>A witness by his manner may create a very unfavourable impression of his truthfulness upon the trial Judge, and yet the surrounding circumstances in the case may point decisively to the conclusion that he is actually telling the truth. I am not referring to the comparatively infrequent cases in which a witness is caught in a clumsy lie.</u> [Emphasis added]

[3-24] In this vein, consider a passage drawn from the immortal Victor Hugo on the question of what guidance, if any, may be found in the visual cues that a witness may communicate unwittingly during the giving of testimony. For example, he teaches that the appearance of a person may never be taken into account. Consider the following passages: "The fire-light fell on him; he was hideous; it was a sinister apparition";[9] "There are some men whom you need only look at to distrust them ... The shadow they have in their

---

[9]   <u>Les Misérables</u>, Chapter XII, p. 60.

glance denounces them."[10] Hugo does insist on the fact on occasion it may be proper to look to the visage to see the heart, "... that word which God has nevertheless written on the brow of every man: Hope!"[11] or the mind: "Javert had nothing in his mind which he did not also have in his face..."[12] On the subject of the look on one's face, note the following passage from <u>Arcadian Adventures With the Idle Rich</u>, by Stephen Leacock, found in the chapter entitled "A Little Dinner with Mr. Lucullus Fyshe": "[as] he got further and further away from the topic of money, which was what he really wanted to come to; and the Duke rose from his conversations with a look of such obvious distress on his face that everybody realized that his anxiety about England was killing him."

[3-25]   Note as well that a person may appear stoic, the face displaying no emotion, and yet be deeply and seriously troubled.[13]

[3-26] In the final analysis, the difficulty with this precise element of fact finding is that it may not be easily reviewed by an appellate tribunal as it does not rest upon anything which is objectively verifiable. No transcript will contain anything close to the type of information generally available to sustain the other propositions discussed in this chapter.

13) Honesty and integrity in the evaluation of credibility

[3-27] Having reviewed briefly the importance of not assigning too much importance to the apparent sincerity of a witness, attention is now drawn to the question of the weight to be assigned to the honesty and integrity of a witness. A first case

---

[10]   <u>Les Misérables</u>, Chapter XXI, p. 18. For a light-hearted view of how appearances may deceive, note Polonius' advice to his son: "For the apparel oft proclaims the man". <u>Hamlet</u>, Act I, sc. iii, l. 72.

[11]   See Chapter XIV, p. 76 of <u>Les Misérables</u>.

[12]   See Chapter XXVI, p. 156 of <u>Les Misérables</u>.

[13]   Refer to Chapter XXV, p. 145 of <u>Les Misérables</u>.

is drawn from the sphere of family law, *Grieve v. Grieve*, [1990] N.B.J. No. 730, 109 N.B.R. (2d) 304, 29 R.F.L. (3d) 8 (Q.B.). As we read at para. 10:

> [10] Such contradictory evidence should be resolved as noted by O'Halloran, J.A. in *Weeks v Weeks*, [1955] 3 DLR 704 (B.C.C.A.) as follows:

>> <u>In such a case a court must look for the balanced truth in the corroborative evidence if such exists</u>, and in any event measure all the evidence perspectively by the test of its consistency with the preponderance of probabilities in the surrounding circumstances ...

>> The issue of what weight or credibility should be attached to the evidence of the parties is very important in this case. As Riddell, J.A. stated in *Wallace v. Davis* (1926), 31 O.W.N. 202:

>>> ... <u>the credibility of a witness in the proper sense does not depend solely on his honesty in expressing his views</u>. It depends also upon his opportunity for exact observation, his capacity to observe accurately, the firmness of his memory to carry in his mind the facts as observed, his ability to resist the influence, frequently unconscious of interest to modify his recollection, his

ability to reproduce in the witness-box the facts observed, the capacity to express clearly what was in his mind - all these are to be considered in determining what effect to give to the evidence of any witness. (Cited in Sopinka & Lederman, The Law of Evidence in Civil Cases, p. 528.) [Emphasis added]

14) The interest or stake a witness may have in the case's outcome

[3-28] At this stage in the discussion, it will be opportune to call in aid directly the seminal guidance provided by Justice O'Hallaran at para. 10 of *Faryna v. Chorny*, [1952] 2 D.L.R. 354, (1951) 4 W.W.R. (N.S.) 171 (B.C.C.A.):

> [10] The credibility of interested witnesses, particularly in cases of conflict of evidence, cannot be gauged solely by the test of whether the personal demeanour of the particular witness carried conviction of the truth. The test must reasonably subject his story to an examination of its consistency with the probabilities that surround the currently existing conditions. [Emphasis added]

[3-29] Of note, this passage was was expressly approved by the Ontario Court of Appeal in *Phillips v. Ford Motor Co. of Canada* (1971) 2 O.R. 637 at page 645, as noted at para. 71 of *Vilamar S.A. v. Sparling*, [1987] R.J.Q. 2186, [1987] Q.J. No. 2708 (Sup. Ct.).

15) The real test of the truth of testimony: its harmony with preponderance of probabilities

[3-30] Once again, reference is made to Justice O'Halloran's eloquent and influential judgment in *Faryna v. Chorny*, [1952] 2 D.L.R. 354, (1951) 4 W.W.R. (N.S.) 171 (B.C.C.A.), at para. 10, with respect to a passage not quoted immediately above:

> [10] [...] In short, the real test of the truth of the story of a witness in such a case must be its harmony with the preponderance of the probabilities which a practical and informed person would readily recognize as reasonable in that place and in those conditions. Only thus can a Court satisfactorily appraise the testimony of quick-minded, experienced and confident witnesses, and of those shrewd persons adept in the half-lie and of long and successful experience in combining skilful exaggeration with partial suppression of the truth. Again a witness may testify what he sincerely believes to be true, but he may be quite honestly mistaken. For a trial Judge to say "I believe him because I judge him to be telling the truth", is to come to a conclusion on consideration of only half the problem. In truth it may easily be self-direction of a dangerous kind. [Emphasis added]

16) The real test ought not to be the demeanour when testifying, with little else being evaluated

[3-31] In this regard, reference must be made to Justice Finlayson's forceful observations as to the frailties of demeanour evidence as being a sound badge of demonstrating the presence of such 'preponderance' in the case of *R. v. Norman*, [1993] O.J. No. 2802, 16 O.R. (3d) 295, 68 O.A.C. 22, 87 C.C.C. (3d) 153, 26 C.R. (4th) 256 (C.A.) at para. 47:

[47] I do not think that an assessment of credibility based on demeanour alone is good enough in a case where there are so many significant inconsistencies. The issue is not merely whether the complainant sincerely believes her evidence to be true; it is also whether this evidence is reliable. Accordingly, her demeanour and credibility are not the only issues. The reliability of the evidence is what is paramount. So far as Mrs. Goebel is concerned, her evidence is inherently hard to credit, and should have been subjected to closer analysis. For the purposes of this case, I adopt what was said by O'Halloran J.A., speaking for the British Columbia Court of Appeal in *Faryna v. Chorny* (1951), 4 W.W.R. (N.S.) 171 at p. 174, [1952] 2 D.L.R. 354 [...]

O'Halloran J.A. pointed out later at p. 175 that "[t]he law does not clothe the trial judge with a divine insight into the hearts and minds of the witnesses". He had also made this latter remark in an earlier criminal case: *R. v. Pressley* (1948), 94 C.C.C. 29 at p. 34, 7 C.R. 342 (B.C.C.A.).

[3-32] Consider as well the well reasoned opinion of Justice Gomery in *Vilamar S.A. v. Sparling*, [1987] R.J.Q. 2186, [1987] Q.J. No. 2708 (Sup. Ct.), at para. 70: "The credibility of a witness is not tested solely by his demeanour in the witness box. His version of the facts should also be consistent with the evidence as a whole, and should not be so unreasonable and far-fetched as to require the court to abandon all notions of common sense [...]"

17) The duty to identify the element which satisfies the 'preponderance' element

[3-33] Briefly stated, it seems consonant with the Court's duty to consign reasons to identify the salient if not decisive element which permits the trier of fact to conclude that, in fact, what the witness stated is in harmony "[...] with the preponderance of the probabilities which a practical and informed person would readily recognize as reasonable in that place and in those conditions."

[3-34] Accordingly, it will be apposite to quote Lord Wright in Grant v. Australian Knitting Mills, Ltd., [1935] All E.R. 209 (P.C.) who insisted that there had to be a basis for an inference at pages 213 - 214:

> ...This, however, does not do justice either to the process of reasoning by way of probable inference which has to do so much in human affairs or to the nature of circumstantial evidence in law courts. Mathematical, or strict logical, demonstration is generally impossible: juries are in practice told that they must act on such reasonable balance of probabilities as would suffice to determine a reasonable man to take a decision in the grave affairs of life. Pieces of evidence, each by itself insufficient, may together constitute a significant whole, and justify by their combined effect a conclusion....

[3-35] This citation was found at para. 12 of *Jiang v. Canada (Minister of Citizenship and Immigration,* [2006] F.C.J. No. 621, 2006 FC 499.

[3-36] Note as well a passage from para. 21 of *Trojan Technologies, inc. v. Sunter Environmental Inc.,* [2004] F.C.J. No. 636, 2004 FCA 140, 239 D.L.R. (4th) 536, 320 N.R. 322:

"[…] The trial Judge ought to go further and say that evidence of the witness he believes is in accordance with the preponderance of probabilities in the case and, if his view is to command confidence, also state his reasons for that conclusion […]"

18) Rejecting non-contradicted testimony based on a lack of harmony with the element of preponderance

[3-37] The foregoing discussion ought not to lead to the conclusion that non-contradicted testimony ought to be accepted and acted upon for such a finding cannot be reached if the suggested result fails to accord with the preponderance element that has been discussed. By way of limited example, consider the judgment of Justice Noël in *Najera v. Canada (Minister of Citizenship and Immigration)*, [2002] F.C.J. No. 1514 at para. 21:

> [21] It is established law that unless the inferences were "so unreasonable", the Court should not intervene. In this case, most of the issues on credibility were based on implausibility findings for which the CRDD gave clear reasons. A Board may reject a testimony which is uncontradicted if that evidence does not accord with the probabilities affecting the whole case [see: *Alizadeh v. Canada (M.E.I.)*, [1993] F.C.J. No. 11 (C.A)]. In that respect, the British Columbia Court of Appeal stated in *Faryna v. Chorny*, [1952] 2 D.L.R. 354, that "the real test of the truth of the story of a witness in such a case must be its harmony with the preponderance of the probabilities which a practical and informed person would readily recognize as reasonable in that place and in those conditions". [Emphasis added]

[3-38] Consider again the well reasoned opinion of Justice Gomery in *Vilamar S.A. v. Sparling*, [1987] R.J.Q. 2186, [1987] Q.J. No. 2708 (Sup. Ct.), at para. 70: "The credibility of a witness is not tested solely by his demeanour in the witness box. His version of the facts should also be consistent with the evidence as a whole, and should not be so unreasonable and far-fetched as to require the court to abandon all notions of common sense [...]" Justice Gomery added:

> [72] In appreciating testimony, a court is entitled not only to believe or not to believe the version of the facts the witness is relating, it may also come to the conclusion that the truth is completely contrary to what he or she is asserting, if the circumstances permit such an inference to be drawn. In La Corporation municipale des Cantons Unis de Stoneham et Tewkesbury v. Ouellet, [1979] 2 S.C.R. 172, Mr. Justice Beetz says at page 195:
>
>> In a civil proceeding, where the rule is that of a preponderance of the evidence and the balance of probabilities, when a party testifies and is not believed it is possible for the trial judge to regard his assertions and denials and his denials as admissions, taking into account contradictions, hesitations, the time the witness takes to answer, his expression, circumstantial evidence and the evidence as a whole. The witness' answers then tend to establish the opposite of what the witness wants the judge to think. Thus, when respondent stated that the Wright

brothers made insulting remarks concerning the municipal authorities, and denied a suggestion that it was in fact he who made these statements to the two brothers in order to discredit the municipal authorities, the trial judge was entitled to consider, whatever the reply, whether the suggestion had its effect, and he was entitles to draw deductions from it unfavourable to respondent. [Emphasis added]

19) Rationality and common sense in assessing credibility

[3-39] *Toora v. Canada (Minister of Citizenship and Immigration*, [2006] F.C.J. No. 1057, 2006 FC 828, 300 F.T.R. 7, is of interest for the information consigned at para. 43:

[43] It is trite law that the Board, in assessing a claimant's credibility, may reject testimony if it does not tally with the balance of probabilities that characterize the case as a whole, and may refer to rationality and common sense, as was held in *Antonippillai v. Canada (Minister of Employment and Immigration)*, [1999] F.C.J. No. 382 (QL), at paragraph 9:

[9] There is no question that the Board has all the necessary discretion to assess the credibility of the testimony of people who claim refugee status, and may have regard to a multitude of factors in so doing. <u>The Board may base its findings on internal</u>

contradictions, inconsistencies and evasive statements, which are the "heartland of the discretion of triers of fact", and <u>other extrinsic factors such as rationality, common sense and judicial notice</u>, but those findings must not be made in a perverse or capricious manner or without regard for the material before the Board: *Sbitty v. Canada (M.C.I.)*, (IMM-4668-96, December 12, 1997), *Shahamati v. M.E.I.*, (F.C.A.) (A-388-92, March 24, 1994).

20) Improbability as a basis for rejecting credibility

[3-40] A further judgment of the Federal Court which is apposite is that of <u>Petrova v. The Minister of Citizenship and Immigration</u>, [2004] F.C.J. No. 613, 2004 FC 506, 251 F.T.R. 43, at paras. 29 and 30:

> [29] <u>As the primary finder of fact the Board is entitled to reject even uncontradicted evidence if it is not "consistent with the probabilities affecting the case as a whole</u>." Moreover, the Board is entitled to make an adverse finding of credibility based upon the implausibility of the Applicant's story alone (*Faryna v. Chorny*, [1952] 2 D.L.R. 354 (B.C.C.A.) at 356). [Emphasis added]
>
> [30] The jurisprudence is clear that the Board can make findings based on implausibilities, common sense and rationality. A heavy burden lies on the Applicant to rebut the Board's finding that she lacked credibility (*Kahandani v. M.C.I.*, [1999] F.C.J. No. 1769, (T.D.) […].

[3-41] A further example of the concerns which arise when apparently uncontradicted evidence being rejected as improbable and thus, as not "consistent with the probabilities affecting the case as a whole" is found in *Valadkhani v. The Minister of Citizenship and Immigration*, [2005] F.C.J. No. 1418, 2005 FC 1152, especially at paras. 17-20:

> [17] The Board concluded that the Events were a fabrication. It decided, because it knew that the Applicant was unhappy and unwell and had all her daughters and family in Canada, that she had been motivated, after she arrived, to use Canada's refugee system to improve her personal situation.
>
> [18] <u>The difficulty lies in the fact that this conclusion was not based on inconsistencies or contradictions in the Applicant's story. She described the Events in an identical manner at all points in the refugee process</u>. As well, the Board did not identify any specific implausibilities. The Board knew that it was not making a traditional credibility finding and, in this regard, it said:
>
> > Counsel contends that the principal claimant's story is not inherently implausible. I have considered all of the evidence in this claim and, although there are no inconsistencies and contradictions, the story, in my opinion, does not ring true. A decision-maker does not necessarily have to accept a witness's testimony, which is uncontradicted, if that evidence does not accord with the

probabilities affecting the case as a whole. In *Faryna v. Chorny*, [...] the Court of Appeal stated that the real test of the truth of a story must be in harmony with the preponderance of the probabilities which a practical and informed person would readily recognize as reasonable in that place and in those conditions. In my opinion, the preponderance of evidence before me suggests the principal claimant left Iran on account of a desire to live apart from her husband and be close to family members in Canada.

[...]

[20] In my view it was open to the Board to conclude that the "Events" had not occurred in the particular circumstances of this case. Accordingly, the Decision was not patently unreasonable and the application will be dismissed. [Emphasis added]

21) Issues in credibility cases: Consistency

a) Introduction to consistency as a badge of credibility

[3-42] As a matter of common sense, it is often thought that credit ought to be awarded to an account with is advanced consistently and denied when this constancy in the telling is absent, as noted in a number of the citations reviewed thus far. An additional authority of note is found in Justice Hill's judgment in R. v. N.K.D., [1997] O.J. No. 3877 (Sup. Ct.), at para. 33:

[33] It is generally recognized that some differences or discrepancies in a witness' testimony, in particular when compared to prior statements of that witness out of court, may well be indicative of a truthful witness -- one who has not provided a scripted and rehearsed account, but rather one which suffers only from certain human frailties, for example, the product of a dulled memory, confusion from the stress of being a witness or other cause too insufficient to significantly affect the witness' credibility and reliability.

[34] In particular, in a case such as this, every reasonable allowance must be provided the complainant for such evidentiary discrepancies on account of passage of time and the stresses of the court proceeding itself. As well, one must be sensitive to the difficulties experienced by complainants regarding precise recall as to time and detail in instances of multiple occasions of abuse. I note as well, quite apart from the criminality alleged, that the complainant in this case was, in any event, under psychological pressures arising from the arranged marriage, the separation between her and her husband in the D.'s residence, and the revelation once in Canada that her husband had had a prior marriage.

[35] In considering the significance of prior inconsistent statements of a complainant, it is necessary to reflect upon the materiality of the differences, the number of such inconsistencies, and such explanations as may be provided for the discrepancies.

[3-43] Note as well the Court's unfavourable references to a party's inconsistency in testifying about material issues in the citation which follows: "The testimony of the wife regarding various investments contains a number of serious inconsistencies with her own prior sworn statements at discoveries. As well her evidence is inconsistent with various documents including a list of assets prefaced with her name in her own handwriting (Ex. R27) and bank and income tax records. She asks the court to believe evidence that she herself and her father have contradicted under oath [...]" Refer to para. 11 of *Grieve v. Grieve*, [1990] N.B.J. No. 730, 109 N.B.R. (2d) 304, 29 R.F.L. (3d) 8 (Q.B.).

[3-44] Para. 29 of *R. v. R.W.B.,* [1993] B.C.J. No. 758, 24 B.C.A.C. 1 (C.A.) is also of assistance:

> [29] In this case there were a number of inconsistencies in the complainant's own evidence and a number of inconsistencies between the complainant's evidence and the testimony of other witnesses. While it is true that minor inconsistencies may not diminish the credibility of a witness unduly, a series of inconsistencies may become quite significant and cause the trier of fact to have a reasonable doubt about the reliability of the witness' evidence. There is no rule as to when, in the face of inconsistency, such doubt may arise but at the least the trier of fact should look to the totality of the inconsistencies in order to assess whether the witness' evidence is reliable. This is particularly so when there is no supporting evidence on the central issue, which was the case here. [Emphasis added]

[3-45] In considering the latter judgment, Galligan J.A. opined: "[26] [...] I do not think the principle is different whether there is one or several inconsistencies. What is important is the

significance of the inconsistency. If the inconsistency is a significant one then the trial judge must pay careful attention to it when assessing the reliability of the witness's testimony. [Emphasis added] Refer to *R. v. M.G.*, [1994] O.J. No. 2086, 73 O.A.C. 356 (C.A.).

[3-46] Finally, note is taken again of <u>R. v. Genest</u>, [1990] A.Q. no. 1609, [1990] R.J.Q. 2387, 32 Q.A.C. 182, 61 C.C.C. (3d) 251 (C.A.) at page 281 C.C.C., para. E, wherein a witness was described by defence counsel as "[…] unsatisfactory in terms of honesty, veracity and impartiality, eminently weak in terms of the trustworthiness of her personal faculties of observation, retention, comprehension and communication and tainted with contradictions on essential facts […]" [Emphasis added]

b) Inconsistencies: Judged against the background of multiple alleged wrongful acts over many years

[3-47] *R. v. H.S.B.*, [2008] 3 S.C.R. 32 also reminds us that is open to a trial judge to not only accept the testimony of a complainant notwithstanding the presence of inconsistencies, but to find an accused person guilty notwithstanding these difficulties and a complete denial by the person charged.

[3-48] Indeed, as we read at para. 4, the trial judge found the accused guilty and upheld the four convictions after having re-opened the case to permit further evidence to support an alibi defence. "He found that inconsistencies in the complainant's evidence were about details peripheral to the sexual acts in question. He commented that some inconsistencies are to be expected in a case involving such a great number of incidents said to have occurred several times a week over a period of several years…"

[3-49] To be exhaustive, I note as well certain comments found at para. 9, 14 and 15:

[9] ... He then acknowledged the accused's argument that the complainant's evidence was contradictory and inconsistent, but went on to note that several specific allegations were not challenged on cross-examination. <u>He also explained his view that most inconsistencies were ancillary or peripheral to the fundamental question of whether the sexual abuse happened and that, in any case, the inconsistencies were excusable, given the high volume of incidents and the young age of the complainant when they occurred</u>. The trial judge considered in detail certain inconsistencies in the evidence regarding the complainant's disclosure to her family members about the abuse. He concluded that he was not left with a reasonable doubt on any of the four charges. [Emphasis added]

[14] ... It is also clear that the trial judge found the frailties in the complainant's evidence to be an understandable result of trying to remember events that happened in childhood and were, in any case, related to peripheral, not core, issues.

[15] The trial judge explained his view of why any errors in the complainant's testimony did not undermine her credibility as to the central issue of whether the offences were committed; he said that much of the testimony was unchallenged, that the inconsistencies and contradictions in her testimony were related to peripheral matters and that

frailties in her testimony were attributable to the difficulty of recalling childhood events. It is thus reasonable to infer from the reasons that, despite any errors in the complainant's testimony, there remained a body of credible evidence capable of proving the offences beyond a reasonable doubt. The trial judge's reasons thus explain the basis for the verdict reached. In meeting this standard, the trial judge's reasons fulfilled their purposes. That being so, the Court of Appeal was not entitled to substitute its own view of the complainant's credibility (specifically, its concerns about her credibility being capable of raising a reasonable doubt) in the guise of impugning the sufficiency of the reasons.

c) Inconsistencies and the youth of a witness

[3-50] *R. v. H.S.B.*, [2008] 3 S.C.R. 32 is of assistance in illustrating that certain inconsistencies in the evidence of a witness may be explained by reason of the youth of the person testifying at the relevant time. As observed by Chief Justice McLachlin at para. 4, the trial judge "... commented further that the complainant's young age at the relevant time, and the fact that the memories were bottled up for a long period, explained her confusion..."

[3-51] Refer as well to para. 9 which includes this comment: "... He also explained his view that most inconsistencies were ancillary or peripheral to the fundamental question of whether the sexual abuse happened and that, in any case, <u>the inconsistencies were excusable, given the high volume of incidents and the young age of the complainant when they occurred</u>." [Emphasis added]

[3-52] Further, para. 10 makes reference to the finding of the trial judge that "… the frailties in the complainant's evidence were explicable as the natural distortion that occurs when events from childhood are recounted at an older age…"

[3-53] Further yet, para. 14 reports the view of the Court: "… It is also clear that the trial judge found the frailties in the complainant's evidence to be an understandable result of trying to remember events that happened in childhood and were, in any case, related to peripheral, not core, issues."

[3-54] Finally, in respect of *R. v. H.S.B.*, para. 15 informs us of the following:

> [15] The trial judge explained his view of why any errors in the complainant's testimony did not undermine her credibility as to the central issue of whether the offences were committed; he said that much of the testimony was unchallenged, that the inconsistencies and contradictions in her testimony were related to peripheral matters and that frailties in her testimony were attributable to the difficulty of recalling childhood events….

[3-55] Turning our attention now to *R. v. R.E.M.*, [2008] 3 S.C.R. 3 it is of interest that the Supreme Court of Canada did not criticize the trial judge in any respect for making allowances in his fact finding for the passage of time as between the complainant's perception of events when a youth and her subsequent testimony.

[3-56] As we read at para. 65:

> [65] The trial judge's alleged failure to reconcile his generally positive findings on the complainant's evidence with the

rejection of some of her evidence did not render the reasons deficient. As juries are routinely instructed, it is open to the trier of fact to accept some of the evidence of a witness, while rejecting other evidence of the same witness. <u>The trial judge explained that the fact that many of the incidents testified to happened many years before and the fact that the complainant was a child at the time might well explain certain inconsistencies</u>. In fact, he did explain why he rejected some of her evidence. [Emphasis added]

[3-57] Earlier, para. 59 recorded that "The trial judge found the complainant to be a credible witness and accepted most of her evidence, while rejecting some portions that had been contradicted by other evidence. He discussed the reasons for these conclusions in some detail, noting that the complainant was a child at the time of most of the incidents, and that they had occurred a long time before. Some errors in her evidence were understandable, he concluded."

d) Details in testimony and credibility

[3-58] Para. 9 of the reasons for judgment of Chief Justice McLachlin in *R. v. H.S.B.*, [2008] 3 S.C.R. 32 advances our understanding of the potential importance of a witness including a great deal of detail in the course of testifying. Thus: "In the trial judge's first set of reasons, he recounted in part what he called the 'extremely detailed' evidence given by the complainant…" In other words, the Supreme Court of Canada found no error on the part of the trial judge in looking to this fact in reaching a favourable view of the credibility of the witness.

[3-59] Thereafter, para. 12 includes remarks to the effect that the fundamental objection raised by the Court of Appeal "… to the trial judge's reasons for judgment was that they failed to explain why errors in details of the complainant's evidence did not undermine her credibility…" In response to this concern,

the Supreme Court held: "[13] In demanding that the trial judge relate each of the errors in the complainant's evidence to his ultimate finding that in general she was a credible witness, the Court of Appeal overlooked the central question — did the reasons disclose the basis for the convictions, when considered in light of the issues at trial and the record as a whole? In my view, the answer to this question is affirmative."

[3-60] McLachlin C.J.C. went on to add these observations:

> [14] The trial judge had to determine whether the evidence as a whole proved the allegations beyond a reasonable doubt. This issue turned largely on the trial judge's findings with respect to the credibility of the complainant and the accused. It is clear from the trial judge's reasons for judgment that his verdict resulted from his acceptance of the complainant's evidence as to whether the incidents occurred, from his rejection of the accused's defence of lack of opportunity from his finding that the accused was not a credible witness and that the evidence as a whole did not leave him with a reasonable doubt. It is also clear that the trial judge found the frailties in the complainant's evidence to be an understandable result of trying to remember events that happened in childhood and were, in any case, related to peripheral, not core, issues.

e) Duty to challenge contradictions and inconsistencies

[3-61] It is noteworthy that the Supreme Court of Canada judgment in *R. v. H.S.B.* includes these comments on the duty to challenge adverse testimony: "[9] ... [The trial judge] then acknowledged the accused's argument that the complainant's

evidence was contradictory and inconsistent, but went on to note that several specific allegations were not challenged on cross-examination..." [Emphasis added]

[3-62] Finally, note a passage from para. 15: "The trial judge explained his view of why any errors in the complainant's testimony did not undermine her credibility as to the central issue of whether the offences were committed; he said that much of the testimony was unchallenged..."

f) Are the contradictions and inconsistencies fundamental or secondary?

[3-63] Para. 9 of *R. v. H.S.B.*, [2008] 3 S.C.R. 32 consigns these useful observations:

> [9] ... [The trial judge] then acknowledged the accused's argument that the complainant's evidence was contradictory and inconsistent, but went on to note that several specific allegations were not challenged on cross-examination. He also explained <u>his view that most inconsistencies were ancillary or peripheral to the fundamental question of whether the sexual abuse happened</u> ... [Emphasis added]

[3-64] Of interest, para. 11 records the view of the trial judge that the "... frequency and duration of the incidents unreliable... He found, moreover, that the frequency and duration of the incidents were secondary to the main issue as to whether the abuse in fact took place...." Of note, though it set aside the findings of guilt, "The Court of Appeal agreed that much of the complainant's testimony was consistent and uncontradicted, and that several of the inconsistencies and contradictions that did exist were 'not of great moment' (para. 22)." Refer to para. 12.

[3-65] Further yet, para. 14 records that "... the trial judge found the frailties in the complainant's evidence ... were, in any case, related to peripheral, not core, issues" while para. 15 states: "... the inconsistencies and contradictions in her testimony were related to peripheral matters..."

g) Inconsistencies due to witness being chagrined

[3-66] R. v. Stirling, [2008] 1 S.C.R. 272, a judgment of Bastarache J. for the unanimous Court, includes an example at para. 3 of a trial judge having discounted certain inconsistencies in the testimony of a witness by reason of the fact that the person had received certain medication shortly before first speaking to the police. As we read at para. 3:

> [3] ... Mr. Stirling argues that the following passages indicate that the trial judge misused the prior consistent statements:
>
>> In weighing and considering all of his evidence, with the benefit of his many previous statements, I find there is a consistent pattern of not recalling many details of the driving up to the collision, but of stating clearly he was in the back seat, that Mr. [Bateman] sat beside him, that Mr. [Hamilton] was in the front seat, and on a number of occasions that the accused was the driver. In my view, the previous inconsistencies as to other details are understandable given the circumstances in which he gave many of the previous statements, including the fact that while at the hospital he was under the influence of medication and/or suffering from serious injury, along with the other effects of a terrible collision, including the death of two friends... [Emphasis added]

22) Issues in credibility cases: Memory

a) Introduction

[3-67] As noted repeatedly, para. 9 of the judgment of O'Halloran J.A. in *Faryna v. Chorny*, [1952] 2 D.L.R. 354, (1951) 4 W.W.R. (N.S.) 171 (B.C.C.A.) at 356-357 includes a reference to the memory of a witness as being an important element in the analysis of that individual's credibility. In many ways, it should more properly be analyzed as an element of reliability. In this vein, note R. v. Genest, [1990] A.Q. no. 1609, [1990] R.J.Q. 2387, 32 Q.A.C. 182, 61 C.C.C. (3d) 251 (C.A.) at page 281 C.C.C., para. E, wherein a witness was described by defence counsel as "[...] unsatisfactory in terms of honesty, veracity and impartiality, eminently weak in terms of the trustworthiness of her personal faculties of observation, retention, comprehension and communication and tainted with contradictions on essential facts [...]" Nonetheless, longstanding practice appears to require it to be discussed under the heading of credibility and, accordingly, the following references to literature are apt.

[3-68] Firstly, consideration should be given to the well-regarded comment, "The Average, Nervous, Inadequate, Inarticulate, In Short, Typical' Accused's Defence", 22 C.R. (4th) 253, written by Mr. Alan D. Gold and to the fact that this gifted counsel and author does not mention directly the issue of memory. In particular, the concerns that arise when a witness for any party in any situation has difficulty in recalling matters when first asked for information, but who later purports to enjoy a good memory of the event. For example, what of the potential alibi witness who is interviewed by the police and who did not recall where the defendant was on a precise date when first questioned, but who later professes to remember the matter, having given it some thought? In such cases, is it credible to suggest that memory may improve with time? Is that not counterintuitive?

b) Two schools of thought

[3-69] There are two obvious schools of thought about memory of important matters. On the one hand, it is believed that one ought not to forget such events and any purported ability to recall matters after an initial period of difficulty should be evaluated with grave reservations. As made plain in the world of dramatic fiction penned by Shakespeare, people should enjoy the faculty possessed by lachimo who stated, 'Why should I write this down, that's riveted, Screw'd to my memory, [Cymbeline, Act 11, sc. ii, 1. 43]. Consider also Ophelia who remarked 'Tis in my memory lock.d...' [Hamlet, Act 1, sc. iii, 1. 84]. On the other hand, in everyday affairs, it appears that most non-fictional individuals are subject to fading memories, as commented upon in W. Somerset Maugham's 'The Colonel's Wife': 'The world moves so quickly and people's memories are so short.' [The Complete Short Stories, Book 2, Doubleday & Co., N.Y., 1952, p. 603].

[3-70] In either case, is there any support for the purported ability of some to have forgotten something apparently, and yet to be able to recall it subsequently? It is suggested that you judges may wish to explain why you accept one scenario, let us say involving the "drinking buddy" who did not remember, at first, the number of beverages consumed, by reference to other short stories penned by Maugham, as opposed to the writings of Shakespeare. Indeed, there is a persistent theme in Maugham's writings, which are far more contemporary than mine, to the effect that memory way well be unavailable unless and until triggered by a thought, a word, a picture, a smell. And, further unless the memory is 'activated' in this way, it remains unavailable. Finally, his writings suggest that memory does not simply flow back without effort; it may be unreliable until such time as adequate thought and reflection has occurred.

[3-71] For example, in "A Woman of Fifty" Maugham wrote: "I dozed off, but before I fell into the blessedness of deep sleep,

my subconscious, released from the effort at striving at recollection, I suppose, grew active and I was suddenly wide awake, for I remembered..." Other examples include from "The Bum": "But the cruel stripe had whipped my memory and suddenly I remembered", and from "A Casual Affair": "With his name there flashed back into my memory all my recollections of him." A further example taken from "Mirage" is the following: "Then from somewhere in the depths of my memory a faint hint crept into the rim, as it were of consciousness, as on a rising tide the water slides up the sand and then withdraws to advance with the next wave in a fuller volume". Lastly, consider "I had not the least notion of what he was talking about. He reminded me of our interview, he repeated to me what we had said, and gradually, out of the night, a dim recollection of the incident came back to me." See "The Happy Man".[14]

[3-72] Consider as well the guidance from Mark Twain on the issue of whether a judge expects a person to have forgotten "moving events". In support of the belief that this ought not to occur, reference may be made to The Prince and the Pauper, Ch. IV, p. 22. The young Duke of Wales was so impressed by the hardship he saw that he was moved to say, "I will keep this diligently in my remembrance..." Note as well Chap. XV, p. 122: "Above forty witnesses have proved the storm; and sooth one might have had a thousand, for all had reason to remember it, with all had suffered by it." Lastly, "That which I have seen, in that one little moment, will never go out from my memory, but will abide there; and I shall see it all the days, and dream of it all the nights, till I die." See Chap. XXVII, p. 222.

---

[14]   Consider as well Stephen Leacock's splendid Arcadian Adventures With the Idle Rich, at Chapter 1, "A Little Dinner with Mr. Lucullus Fyshe", on the subject of refreshing the memory of an individual touching upon a subject which ought to be recalled easily: "The president, therefore, had said yes to Mr. Fyshe's invitation with alacrity, and had taken a look through the list of his more incompetent professors to refresh his memory."

c) The triggering of memories

[3-73] On the subject of what might trigger "hidden memories", note the following quotation which supports the view that memory may be triggered; another way of saying it may be refreshed. "'Tis strange how my memory doth wanton with me these days', says Tom. 'But mind it not – I mend space – a little clue doth often serve to bring me back again the things and names which had escaped me.'" See Prince, Ch. XIV, p. 106. See also Pudding'head Wilson, at Ch. III, p. 26 on the question of reviving a memory: "She began to muse; she was trying to gather out of her memory the dim particulars of some tale she had heard sometime or other."

[3-74] Finally, touching upon the subject of a "failing memory", Ch. VIII, p. 50 of Prince, contains a passage which may be brought to the attention of a witness, as a gentle prod to suggest that they also may be suffering from a failing memory: "Why, so in sooth I did; I do remember it... What did I with it!... I am very feeble... So oft these days my memory play the traitor with me..."

d) Memory and credibility: 'Bottling-up' of recall

[3-75] Para. 4 of the reasons for judgment of Chief Justice McLachlin in *R. v. H.S.B.*, [2008] 3 S.C.R. 32 includes the comment that the trial judge was of the view "... that the complainant's young age at the relevant time, and the fact that the memories were bottled up for a long period, explained her confusion..."

23) Issues in credibility cases: Misleading the Court

[3-76] *R. v. H.S.B.*, [2008] 3 S.C.R. 32 consigns this conclusion of the trial judge as reproduced by Chief Justice McLachlin: "... the complainant was a credible witness, not deliberately trying to mislead the court..." In other words, although para. 4 makes reference to inconsistencies in the complainant's testimony and that she experienced memory

problems, the trial judge found her credible as she did not seek to impair the work of the Court by a conscious effort to put forward incorrect information.

24) Credibility lacking 'in general': An example

[3-77] *R. v. H.S.B.*, [2008] 3 S.C.R. 32 includes the following summary by Chief Justice McLachlin of one aspect of the fact finding of the trial judge: "… Rejecting the evidence of the accused, the trial judge found that he was not a credible witness 'in general', and that he was prone to exaggeration." Refer as well to para. 11 and to para. 14 wherein we read "… his verdict resulted from … his finding that the accused was not a credible witness…"

25) Exaggerations and findings of credibility

[3-78] Refer to the discussion consigned under the rubric "Credibility lacking 'in general': An example".

26) Credibility and the mentally challenged witness

[3-79] The Supreme Court of Canada expressed the view, albeit in a somewhat oblique fashion, that certain concerns surrounding credibility may arise if the witness is mentally challenged. As we read at para. 33 of *R. v. R.E.M.*, [2008] 3 S.C.R. 3 reference is made to *R. v. Gagnon*, [2008] 1 S.C.R. 788. In particular, the opinion of Charron J. was noted as follows:

> [33] The Court found that the trial judge's reasons fell short of even this flexible standard. <u>There was evidence that the complainant was mentally challenged</u>, with a history of making up stories to get attention, and her testimony had wavered on the core issue of whether the accused had committed the assault in question. <u>The trial judge's failure to avert to these critical matters left the Court in doubt that he had directed his mind to the central issue of credibility</u>. [Emphasis added]

27) Credibility and a witness who has a history of making up stories

[3-80] Of relevance in this regard is para. 33 of *R. v. R.E.M.*, [2008] 3 S.C.R. 3 wherein reference is made to *R. v. Gagnon*, [2008] 1 S.C.R. 788, as noted above.

28) Credibility and a wavering witness

[3-81] Of relevance in this regard is para. 33 of *R. v. R.E.M.*, [2008] 3 S.C.R. 3 wherein reference is made to *R. v. Gagnon*, [2008] 1 S.C.R. 788, as noted above.

29) Findings of credibility and other evidence in the case

[3-82] Para. 50 of *R. v. R.E.M.*, [2008] 3 S.C.R. 3 includes these valuable observations on this subject:

> [50] What constitutes sufficient reasons on issues of credibility may be deduced from *R. v. Dinardo*, [2008] 1 S.C.R. 788, 2008 SCC 24, <u>where Charron J. held that findings on credibility must be made with regard to the other evidence in the case</u> (para. 23). This may require at least some reference to the contradictory evidence. However, as Dinardo makes clear, what is required is that the reasons show that the judge has seized the substance of the issue. 'In a case that turns on credibility ... the trial judge must direct his or her mind to the decisive question of whether the accused's evidence, considered in the context of the evidence as a whole, raises a reasonable doubt as to his guilt' (para. 23). Charron J. went on to dispel the suggestion that the trial judge is required to enter into a detailed account of the conflicting evidence: *Dinardo*, at para. 30.

30) Findings of credibility which are obvious

[3-83] Para. 51 of *R. v. R.E.M.*, [2008] 3 S.C.R. 3 reminds us that "The degree of detail required in explaining findings on credibility may also, as discussed above, vary with the evidentiary record and the dynamic of the trial. The factors supporting or detracting from credibility may be clear from the record. In such cases, the trial judge's reasons will not be found deficient simply because the trial judge failed to recite these factors."

31) Credibility findings favourable though some testimony is not accepted

[3-84] Para. 59 of *R. v. R.E.M.*, [2008] 3 S.C.R. 3 provides an useful example of how a trial judge (and, ultimately, the Supreme Court of Canada), may conclude that a witness was credible though part of his or her testimony is not accepted. As we read:

> [59] The trial judge found the complainant to be a credible witness and accepted most of her evidence, while rejecting some portions that had been contradicted by other evidence. He discussed the reasons for these conclusions in some detail, noting that the complainant was a child at the time of most of the incidents, and that they had occurred a long time before. Some errors in her evidence were understandable, he concluded.

[3-85] In addition, para. 61 makes plain that "... on most points, the trial judge accepted the evidence of the complainant and rejected that of the accused. This said, there were aspects of the complainant's evidence that he did not accept and aspects of the accused's evidence that he accepted..."

32) Acceptance of one witness' testimony may demonstrate implicit rejection of another's

[3-86] Para. 66 of *R. v. R.E.M.*, [2008] 3 S.C.R. 3 is of assistance in respect of the thorny issue of the explicit acceptance of testimony by one witness as being an implicit finding that the testimony of another witness has been rejected.

[3-87] As we note at para. 66:

> [66] Finally, the trial judge's failure to explain why he rejected the accused's plausible denial of the charges provides no ground for finding the reasons deficient. <u>The trial judge's reasons made it clear that in general, where the complainant's evidence and the accused's evidence conflicted, he accepted the evidence of the complainant.</u> This explains why he rejected the accused's denial. He gave reasons for accepting the complainant's evidence, finding her generally truthful and 'a very credible witness', and concluding that her testimony on specific events was 'not seriously challenged' (para. 68). <u>It followed of necessity that he rejected the accused's evidence where it conflicted with evidence of the complainant that he accepted. No further explanation for rejecting the accused's evidence was required.</u> In this context, the convictions themselves raise a reasonable inference that the accused's denial of the charges failed to raise a reasonable doubt. [Emphasis added]

[3-88] Of course, the difficulty is that the orthodox *W.D.* analysis, as per Cory J., in [1991] 1 S.C.R. 742 typically

rejects a contest of credibility as being a flawed method of analysis. In other words, to accept the testimony of one witness in preference to another without more is to fail to decide why the evidence of one is worthy of belief and why the other's is not.

[3-89] At all events, McLachlin C.J.C. held at para. 67: "... The central issue at trial was credibility. It is clear that the trial judge accepted all or sufficient of the complainant's ample evidence as to the incidents, and was not left with a reasonable doubt on the whole of the evidence or from the contradictory evidence of the accused. From this, he concluded that the accused's guilt had been established beyond a reasonable doubt. When the record is considered as a whole, the basis for the verdict is evident."

33) Opportunities for knowledge in the evaluation of credibility

[3-90] It will be easily recalled that the classic reference from the reasons of O'Halloran J.A. in *Faryna v. Chorny*, [1952] 2 D.L.R. 354, (1951) 4 W.W.R. (N.S.) 171 (B.C.C.A.) at 356-357 include this observation at para. 9: "[...] Opportunities for knowledge, powers of observation, judgment and memory, ability to describe clearly what he has seen and heard, as well as other factors, combine to produce what is called credibility [...]"

[3-91] In this vein, a sound example of credibility being found to be lacking for significant difficulties under this rubric is the judgment of Shore J. in *Froment v. The Minister of Citizenship and Immigration,* [2006] F.C.J. No. 1273, 2006 FC 1002, 299 F.T.R. 70. In effect, the Federal Court upheld the decision establishing that the appellant had contracted a marriage for a 'sham' purpose related to her desire to immigrate. In reaching this decision, the specialized administrative tribunal had assigned special weight to the following adverse findings, linked to this element of "opportunities for knowledge in the evaluation of credibility."

[10] The IAD [Immigration Appeal Division] rendered its decision on the basis of the numerous differences between the personal situations of the spouses and the little knowledge they had of each other. They do not speak the same language, as Ms. Froment speaks very little English and Mr. Malhi does not speak any French at all. Ms. Froment is ten years older than Mr. Malhi. They do not share the same religion, as Ms. Froment is a Christian and Mr. Malhi is a Sikh. Mr. Malhi knows very little about Ms. Froment's daughters, whom she cherishes above all else in life. At the interview at the Canadian consulate, he did not know their first names or birthdates. The IAD was also of the opinion that Mr. Malhi had not been forthcoming with Ms. Froment about his divorce from his first wife and his tenuous status in the United States. [Emphasis added]

[3-92] Citing Justice Shore's ultimate conclusions at para. 17 and 18 we read:

[17] The appropriate standard of review in this case is that of patent unreasonableness, since a question of fact is involved (*Khangura v. Canada (Minister of Citizenship and Immigration)*, [2000] F.C.J. No. 815 (QL), at paragraph 21; *Sanichara v. Canada (Minister of Citizenship and Immigration)*, 2005 FC 1015, [2005] F.C.J. No. 1272 (QL), at paragraph 11; *Singh v. Canada (Minister of Citizenship and Immigration)*, 2002 FCT 347, [2002] F.C.J. No. 461 (QL), at

paragraph 17; *Canada (Minister of Citizenship and Immigration) v. Savard*, 2006 FC 109, [2006] F.C.J. No. 126 (QL), at paragraph 12).

[18] As stated by Mr. Justice Luc Martineau in *Singh, supra*, at paragraph 18:

> The standard of judicial deference that applies to findings of fact and to the weight given to the evidence by the Appeal Division is quite high. Unless the contrary is shown, the Appeal Division is assumed to have considered all the evidence presented to it. The Appeal Division's decision in this regard must be interpreted as a whole and it should not be subject to microscopic examination. Accordingly, the reviewing Court should refuse to interfere with decisions which assess credibility, provided that the explanations given are rational or reasonable, or that the evidence on the record permits the Appeal Division to reach, as the case may be, a negative inference as to the credibility of an applicant or a witness. [Emphasis added]

34) Powers of observation in the evaluation of credibility

[3-93] As noted immediately above, the second of the listed elements of this precise sub-set found in the reasons of O'Halloran J.A. in *Faryna v. Chorny*, [1952] 2 D.L.R. 354,

(1951) 4 W.W.R. (N.S.) 171 (B.C.C.A.) at 356-357, para. 9, refers to "[...] powers of observation [...]"

[3-94] In light of this guidance, reference is made to the following comments, consigned in *Bairaktaris and 9047-7993 Québec inc. c. Bouras and Naim*, [2002] J.Q. no 4148 (Sup. Ct.), at para. 32(b):

> [32] [...] It is a matter in which so many human characteristics, both the strong and the weak, must be taken into consideration. The general integrity and intelligence of the witness, <u>his power to observe</u>, his capacity to remember and his accuracy in statement are important. It is also important to determine whether he is honestly endeavouring to tell the truth, whether he is sincere and frank or whether he is biased, reticent and evasive. All these questions and others may be answered from the observation of the witness's general conduct and demeanour in determining the question of credibility [Footnote 4 refers to the following authority: *White v. The King*, [1947] S.C.R. 268, at page 272] [Emphasis added]

[3-95] Returning to the judgment of Trainor J. in *Vanderbyl v. Insurance Corporation of British Columbia*, [1993] B.C.J. No. 1007, [1993] 6 W.W.R. 725, 79 B.C.L.R. (2d) 156 (Sup. Ct.), para. 20 includes these helpful remarks:

> [20] In both civil and criminal proceedings when sitting with a jury it is the responsibility of the trial judge to instruct them on the course they should follow when dealing with the testimony of witnesses. Those instructions apply, as

well, to the task facing a judge sitting without a jury. I usually say something to a jury along the following lines,

> When you think about the evidence of a witness concern yourself about their opportunity to observe. What chance did they have to observe whatever it was about which they are testifying? What are their powers of observation? Generally what kind of an individual are they? Are they the kind of person that you can rely on to give you an accurate account? You have to make that decision on the basis of their general evidence and your impression of the individual as they gave you their evidence.

35) Judgment in the evaluation of credibility

[3-96] Returning yet again to the enumeration found at para. 9 of the judgment of O'Halloran J.A. in *Faryna v. Chorny*, [1952] 2 D.L.R. 354, (1951) 4 W.W.R. (N.S.) 171 (B.C.C.A.) at 356-357, we read "[...] Opportunities for knowledge, powers of observation, judgment and memory, ability to describe clearly what he has seen and heard, as well as other factors, combine to produce what is called credibility [...]" The emphasized passage is a fairly easily understood and somewhat dangerous proposition in that the word 'judgment' is at once too broad in scope and quite narrow in terms of what an appellate court may review. Nevertheless, 'judgment' in the evaluation of credibility is a constant value and one reference in this vein will suffice. *Bairaktaris and 9047-7993 Québec inc. c. Bouras and Naim*, [2002] J.Q. no 4148 (Sup. Ct.), at para. 32(b) reminds us of the following: "[...] It is a matter in which so many human characteristics, both the strong and the weak, must be taken into consideration. The

general integrity and intelligence of the witness, his power to observe, his capacity to remember and his accuracy in statement are important [...]" Stated otherwise, are the conclusions reached by the witness sound and do they appear to present a well reasoned thought process free of bias and over-simplification?

36) Ability to describe in the evaluation of credibility

[3-97] "[...] Opportunities for knowledge, powers of observation, judgment and memory, ability to describe clearly what he has seen and heard, as well as other factors, combine to produce what is called credibility [...]" The passage which is underlined, consigned at para. 9 of the judgment of O'Halloran J.A. in *Faryna v. Chorny*, [1952] 2 D.L.R. 354, (1951) 4 W.W.R. (N.S.) 171 (B.C.C.A.) at 356-357 reminds us that the powers of recall of a witness constitute one side of a two sided coin in that a superb memory will count for very little if a witness cannot fairly set out what it is that is retained due to a number of reasons, notably confusion or nervousness. In this instance, it will do to recall the judgment in *Bairaktaris and 9047-7993 Québec inc. c. Bouras and Naim*, [2002] J.Q. no 4148 (Sup. Ct.), at para. 32(b): "[...] It is a matter in which so many human characteristics, both the strong and the weak, must be taken into consideration. The general integrity and intelligence of the witness, his power to observe, his capacity to remember and his accuracy in statement are important [...]" [Emphasis added]

37) The spontaneous nature of responses in the evaluation of credibility

[3-98] Implicit in much of the foregoing discussion is the importance and weight which may be assigned to the manner of testifying, not from the perspective of demeanour which appears to be a limited concept better described as the question of a person's appearance while testifying which does not form part of the Court's record, but rather the manner of responding to questions which is available to an appellate

tribunal if it chooses to listen to the audio tape of the proceedings.

[3-99] Consider the observations of Justice Martineau in the case of *The Minister of Citizenship and Immigration and Soltesz*, [2002] F.C.J. No. 606, 2002 FCT 467, at para. 8:

> [8] Third, credibility assessments depend on a variety of factors which are better left to the Board which has the benefit of hearing the witnesses. Furthermore, <u>even if there are some inconsistencies this does not mean that this will automatically command a negative inference. The spontaneous character of the answers given during the examination</u>, the details given concerning alleged incidents, the claimant's removal, etc. <u>are also important</u>. The Board's findings of fact and inferences concerning the credibility should not be disturbed unless they are perverse, capricious or patently unreasonable. Sharlow J., as she then was, in *Gonzalez v. Canada (Minister of Citizenship and Immigration)* [1999] F.C.J. 805 stated as follows:
>
> > In my view, it was open to the CRDD to assess the plausibility of the applicant's conduct as it did, <u>by considering her story, and the manner in which it was told</u> and tested in the course of the hearing, against the backdrop of other evidence and its own understanding of human behaviour. [Emphasis added]

[3-100] Often, a Court is concerned that apparently logical information adduced in testimony is given in what might best be described as a scripted fashion, amounting to a pat recitation of a scenario seemingly fully assimilitated but devoid of a spontaneous character such that well grounded fears arise that it is no better than a rehearsed concoction or distortion of what really took place. In this vein, it will profit to recall the remarks consigned at para. 12 of *Goa v. Canada*

(Minister of Citizenship and Immigration, [2001] F.C.J. No. 1364, 2001 FCT 978:

> [12] Although I was not present at the October 12, 2000 hearing and thus, did not have the benefit of seeing the applicant as the Board did, I have no hesitation in concluding, <u>on a reading of the transcript, that the claimant did not testify in a forthright manner</u>. Consequently, the Board's remarks to the effect that the <u>applicant's answers sounded wooden and rehearsed, do not surprise me</u>. The applicant was unable to convince me that in so concluding, the Board made a reviewable error. [Emphasis added]

[3-101] In many instances, spontaneity is twinned with sincerity as seen in para. 25 of *Doucet v. Halifax Insurance Co.*, [2001] N.B.J. No. 121 (Q.B.).

38) Hesitations in the assessment of the spontaneous character of testimony

[3-102] Quite possibly the most arduous element in the evaluation of the spontaneous nature of testimony is the presence of hesitations by the witness while answering questions from opposing counsel, especially if few such hesitations were in evidence when answering the question of "friendly" counsel. The traditional authority cited in this respect is that of Lord Shaw of Dunfermline who penned the following remarks in *Clarke v. Edinburgh and District Tramways Company Limited*, [1919] S.C. 35 (H.L.), at page 37: "[…] witness without any conscious bias towards a conclusion may have in their demeanour, in their manner, <u>in their hesitation</u>, in the nuance of their expression, in even the turns of the eyelid, left an impression [upon the trier of fact]". [Emphasis added]

[3-103] Noteworthy as well are the comments reproduced in *Xu v. Minister of Citizenship and Immigration,* [2003] F.C.J. No. 1762, 2003 FC 1383 at para. 10: "The Board found [...] the applicant was hesitant in answering questions. The applicant's counsel attributed her demeanor and hesitancy to the fact that the applicant was eight months pregnant, however, the Board did not accept this explanation [...]" [Emphasis added]

[3-104] To digress for a moment to enter the world of literature, consider an example drawn from Arcadian Adventures With the Idle Rich, by Stephen Leacock. Chapter 3, "The Arrested Philanthropy of Mr. Tomlinson", includes this passage on demeanour evidence touching upon hesitations:

> But most of all, the electric department interested the Wizard of Finance. And this time his voice lost its hesitating tone and he looked straight at Dr. Boomer as he began, "I have a boy--"
> "Ah!" said Dr. Boomer, with a huge ejaculation of surprise and relief; "you have a boy!"
> There were volumes in his tone. What it meant was, "Now, indeed, we have got you where we want you," and he exchanged a meaning look with the professor of Greek.

39) Exaggerations in the evaluation of credibility

[3-105] Having reviewed at length a number of potential badges of credibility and, by parity of reasoning, a number of obstacles to the assignment of credit, it will be of assistance at this stage to discuss briefly certain more limited concerns, at least in terms of ultimate scope, in the objective presentation of testimony by witnesses. A first example is taken from *Smith v. Agnew; Smith v. Wawanesa Mutual Insurance Co.,* [2005]

N.B.J. No. 137, 2005 NBCA 36, 282 N.B.R. (2d) 95, 19 C.C.L.I. (4th) 164, at para. 7:

> [7] The trial judge made the following key findings of fact and credibility:
>
> 1. Mr. Smith was not a credible witness. Most significantly, his account of post-accident problems was, to a significant extent, lacking in credibility. He "deceived his doctors and the Court" in respect of some of the symptoms associated to conditions that he tried to link to the accident. <u>More generally, his evidence featured "exaggerations, inconsistencies, omissions and rationalizations</u> [...] [Emphasis added]

[3-106] Not surprisingly, the Court of Appeal accepted the findings of the trial judge as consigned at paras. 16 and 17:

> [16] Mr. Smith challenges the trial judge's adverse finding on the issue of his credibility on the ground that it is disharmonious with "the preponderance of the probabilities which a practical and informed person would readily recognize as reasonable in that place and in those conditions": *Faryna v. Chorny*, [1952] 2 D.L.R. 354 (B.C.C.A.), per O'Halloran, J.A., at page 357. See, as well, *Hvalfangerselskapet Polaris A/S v. Unilever Ltd.* (1933), 46 Ll. L. Rep. 29 (H.L.), per Lord Atkin and *Yuill v. Yuill*, [1945] P. 15, per Lord Green.
>
> [17] There is simply no merit whatsoever to this contention. The finding in question is rooted in the trial judge's assessment of

Mr. Smith's demeanor while testifying. It also reflects her considered judgment as to the significance of various features of Mr. Smith's testimony both on discovery and at trial in the determination of his reliability as a witness. Bluntly put, the impugned finding is beyond reproach.

40) Omissions in the evaluation of credibility

[3-107] Given the lengthy treatment of the question of exaggerations immediately above, suffice it to refer again a passage from *Smith v. Agnew; Smith v. Wawanesa Mutual Insurance Co.*, [2005] N.B.J. No. 137, 2005 NBCA 36, 282 N.B.R. (2d) 95, 19 C.C.L.I. (4th) 164, at para. 7, cited at para. 3-105.

41) The global approach to the evaluation of credibility

[3-108] The Supreme Court of Canada has often guided judges in the evaluation of credibility by insisting on the need for a global or comprehensive assessment of all of the disparate elements which make up a positive or negative finding of credibility. Most recently, in *R. v. Gagnon*, [2006] S.C.J. No. 17, [2006] 1 S.C.R. 621, 266 D.L.R. (4th) 1, 347 N.R. 355, 207 C.C.C. (3d) 353, 37 C.R. (6th) 209, it framed the following guidance on this issue:

> [10] There is general agreement on the test applicable to a review of a finding of credibility by a trial judge: the appeal court must defer to the conclusions of the trial judge unless a palpable or overriding error can be shown. It is not enough that there is a difference of opinion with the trial judge (*Schwartz v. Canada*, [1996] 1 S.C.R. 254, at paras. 32-33; *H.L. v. Canada (Attorney General)*, [2005] 1

S.C.R. 401, 2005 SCC 25, at para. 74). A succinct <u>description of the overall approach</u> appears in *R. v. Burke*, [1996] 1 S.C.R. 474, at para. 4, where this Court stated that "it is only where the Court has considered all of the evidence before the trier of fact and determined that a conviction cannot be reasonably supported by that evidence that the court can ... overturn the trial court's verdict". <u>With respect to the credibility of witnesses, the same standard applies.</u> In *R. v. Lavoie*, [2003] Q.J. No. 1474 (QL), at para. 37, Nuss J.A. of the Quebec Court of Appeal stated that a trial judge's assessment of the credibility of witnesses "will not be disturbed unless it can be demonstrated that he committed a palpable and overriding error" (citing *Housen v. Nikolaisen*, [2002] 2 S.C.R. 235, 2002 SCC 33). [Emphasis added]

[11] In this case, the majority in the Court of Appeal expressly declined to find the verdict unreasonable, thereby confirming that the verdict was available on the record. Instead, it based its analysis on a conclusion that the trial judge's reasons, like those in *R. v. Sheppard*, [2002] 1 S.C.R. 869, 2002 SCC 26, were [TRANSLATION] "insufficient" (para. 91) and that she had therefore committed an error in law. Yet it is clear from its reasons that what was troubling the majority was not the sufficiency of her reasons but the trial judge's findings of credibility. In particular, the majority disagreed with her conclusions about the credibility of the accused, and, contrary to her findings,

appears to have concluded that the evidence of the accused ought to have raised a reasonable doubt. Ignoring both this Court's dictum in *Burke* and the unique position a trial judge enjoys in being able to see and hear the witnesses, the majority chose instead to substitute its own assessment of credibility for that of the trial judge by impugning her reasons, saying she did not sufficiently explain why the evidence did not raise a reasonable doubt. We disagree.

[3-109] Recall as well that the Federal Court of Appeal quoted with approval the judgment of *Faryna v. Chorny*, [1952] 2 D.L.R. 354, (1951), 4 W.W.R. (N.S.) 171 (B.C.C.A.), *per* O'Halloran, J.A. at paragraph 11: "[...] The law does not clothe the trial Judge with a divine insight into the hearts and minds of the witnesses. And a Court of Appeal must be satisfied that the trial Judge's finding of credibility is based not on one element only to the exclusion of others, but is based on all the elements by which it can be tested in the particular case."

[3-110] A further useful reference drawn from the Federal Court of Appeal is that of *Cana Construction Co. v Canada (M.N.R.)*, [1996] F.C.J. No. 827, [1996] 3 C.T.C. 11, 96 D.T.C. 6370, at para. 4:

[4] The Tax Court Judge essentially based his conclusions of fact on the testimony of one very much interested witness which he accepted, in my view, without weighing it against a critical examination of the whole of the evidence (see *Faryna v. Chorny*, [1952] 2 D.L.R. 354 (B.C.C.A.); *Schwartz v. The Queen* (1996) 96 D.T.C. 6103 (S.C.C.). Such a critical examination could not have led

him to conclude as he did that the
Appellant had agreed to pay the wages of
the employees of its subcontractor
(Vidalin). [Emphasis added]

42) Findings of credibility are only made at the conclusion of the trial

[3-111] A necessary corollary proposition to the above noted proposition requiring a global approach is that a finding of credibility must only be reached at the end of the proceedings when all of the evidence, testimonial and documentary, may be scrutinized on the whole. It is an obvious conclusion that to proceed otherwise risks undermining the appearance of trial fairness leaving aside the real concern that the Court will make a premature and possibly unfounded judgment. In this vein, the opinion of Justice Pelletier of the Federal Court of Appeal in the case of *Trojan Technologies, Inc. v. Suntec Environmental Inc.*, [2004] F.C.J. No. 636, 2004 FCA 140, 239 D.L.R. (4th) 536, 320 N.R. 322, 31 C.P.R. (4th) 241 is worth repeating:

> [22] I take the thrust of this passage to be that the assessment of credibility is not simply a matter of the judge's opinion as to which witness "made the better appearance of sincerity". It also involves an examination of the witness' testimony and "of its consistency with the probabilities that surround the currently existing conditions". A judge's finding of credibility therefore must not be based on "one element only to the exclusion of others, but on all the elements by which it can be tested in the particular case". In cases such as this, one of the elements, though not to the exclusion of all others, is the impression created by the witness giving his evidence in chief and under

cross-examination. <u>This is why the jurisprudence is so consistent in holding that credibility issues, broadly defined, should be decided after trial</u>. [Emphasis added]

43) The 'clumsy lie' in the evaluation of credibility

[3-112] In closing, although one might be excused for believing that the question of the "[...] comparatively infrequent cases in which a witness is caught in a clumsy lie", as noted by O'Halloran, J.A. at para. 10 of *Faryna v. Chorny*, [1952] 2 D.L.R. 354, (1951), 4 W.W.R. (N.S.) 171 is a straightforward one, it may be that a far more nuanced approach is required. Indeed, the case books are replete with examples of apparently clumsy lies which, on the ultimate analysis made at the conclusion of the whole of the case, may be found to have been either simple errors or mistakes not by the witness but by the finder of fact. For reasons of limitations of space, only one example is required. In the case of *Xu v. Canada (Minister of Immigration and Citizenship)*, [2003] F.C.J. No. 1762, 2003 FC 1383, the Court found that the administrative tribunal had erred in finding that the claimant was obviously not telling the truth when she claimed to be a Christian. As we read at para. 12:

> [12] The Board furthermore found that the applicant had not proved, on a balance of probabilities, that she was a Christian. The Board came to this conclusion because, when asked what "season" it was in the calendar year, the applicant stated that it was Easter. Moreover, she did not know anything about Lent or Palm Sunday. The applicant later submitted a document from her church in Canada, wherein it was explained that the church does not observe Palm Sunday or use the phrase "seasons of the Church".

However, the Board stated, "since the claimant alleges that she has been practicing Christian [sic] in China since 1998 and had spread the gospel to others, surely she would be aware of Lent and Palm Sunday." The Board ruled that the claimant's association with a church in Canada was an attempt to bolster her claim, and found that she was not a believer of Christianity in China.

[3-113] In the opinion of the Federal Court, as expressed at para. 40 and follows, was quite critical of this finding of an obvious fabrication:

[40] In its reasons, the Board noted at page 5 of its decision "[s]he did not know anything about Lent, which is celebrated universally in all Churches." The Board grounded its finding of lack of credibility in the applicant's lack of knowledge of specific Christian practices.

[...]

[42] In my view, on the facts of this case, it was not open to the Board to conclude that Lent is celebrated universally in all churches. The applicant testified that her church did not celebrate Lent. The lack of knowledge about Lent and Palm Sunday were the central basis for finding that the applicant was not credible in her claim to be a Christian.

[43] The Board's findings regarding the applicant's identity as a Christian weighed heavy in its ultimate assessment of credibility. Furthermore, the Board's non-

credibility finding was central to the
outcome of this case. I find that the Board
has made a reviewable error. [Emphasis
added]

44) The role of common sense in the evaluation of credibility

[3-114] In a manner of speaking, all of the elements discussed
thus far comprise a huge tapestry of 'common sense' in that it
is expected, as a matter of logic or of common sense that a
witness will not be tainted with the concerns which follow,
enumerated by defence counsel in R. v. Genest, [1990] A.Q.
no. 1609, [1990] R.J.Q. 2387, 32 Q.A.C. 182, 61 C.C.C. (3d)
251 (C.A.) at page 281 C.C.C., para. e: "[…] unsatisfactory in
terms of honesty, veracity and impartiality, eminently weak in
terms of the trustworthiness of her personal faculties of
observation, retention, comprehension and communication
and tainted with contradictions on essential facts […]"

[3-115] The Supreme Court of Canada has provided valuable
guidance in this regard in cases such as *Olmstead v.
Vancouver-Fraser Park District*, [1975] 2 S.C.R. 831, 51
D.L.R. (3d) 416, 3 N.R. 326. In sum, the jury held that
defendant was liable for the injuries complained of by the
plaintiff but the trial judge declined to find any negligence on
the part of the defendant. A passage from para. 6 will suffice
to situate the respective positions: "I am of the opinion that the
jury did not follow any of the principles outlined by O'Halloran,
J.A. in the *Faryna* case (supra) but 'accepted and rejected the
evidence of the witnesses in whole or in part' without giving
any consideration to consistency, harmony or logic. In my
view, there should be, as a matter of law, some point at which
this method of finding the facts should be considered wholly
unreasonable and perverse and should be viewed as a means
of securing a verdict for the plaintiff on sympathetic grounds.
That point, in my opinion, was reached in this case."

[3-116] For the Court, Justice de Grandpré opined as follows, at paras. 14 and 15:

> [14] There is no doubt that the jury are entitled to believe certain witnesses and disbelieve others. They also have the right to choose only part of the evidence of any witness. These rights belonging to the jury permit them to discard plaintiff's own evidence on facts, about which other relevant evidence is adduced, at variance with his own [...]

> [15] In the present instance, the jury, therefore, had the right to conclude as they did that plaintiff took a running dive into the water and did not do a standing dive when at the edge of the water as he repeatedly maintained during his evidence. On that point, the jury could rely as they did on the evidence of one of plaintiff's companions, namely Chase, who stated that he heard plaintiff run into the water and take a splash [...]

[3-117] In the result, the Supreme Court of Canada held that the triers of fact had erred in finding that the preponderance of testimony favoured an interpretation that held the defendant liable for the injuries sustained and this intervention by our highest Court took place even though it had not heard or seen a single witness owing to the fact that, as a matter of common sense, the plaintiff came to harm through no fault of anyone but himself.

45) Improbable results as a matter of common sense

[3-118] By parity of reasoning, improbable results will not be found to be in accord with common sense and will thus be rejected. For example, in *Goa v. Canada (Minister of*

Citizenship and Immigration), [2001] F.C.J. No. 1364, 2001 FCT 978 we read the following comments at paras. 7 to 12:

> [7] Consequently, the Board's concerns regarding the credibility of this evidence are, in my view, unassailable.
>
> [8] I now turn to the Board's concerns regarding the circumstances of the whereabouts of the applicant's teaching certificate. Although the Board's remarks, as drafted, would not win a prize for draftsmanship, they do convey that the Board was not impressed with the applicant's evidence. <u>I can only agree with the Board that the applicant's evidence on this point is, in all likelihood, not truthful</u>.
>
> [9] The applicant testified that her parents had sent her high school certificate to her by courier. According to the applicant, the courier was detained by the immigration authorities and her certificate was seized. She then states that the courier informed her of what happened. The applicant then goes on to state that she went to the airport to pick up her certificate, but was told by someone that the document would only be released should the Refugee Board request it. The applicant then states that she informed her counsel regarding what happened. Then, surprisingly, the applicant states that she does not know what advice her counsel gave her with respect to the certificate. Further on in her testimony, the claimant states that she had not been informed by the courier that her document had been

seized, but that she had been so informed later on by a friend who came to Canada on a visit from China.

[10] In my view, the applicant's testimony is simply not believable. Consequently, I can only agree with the comments made by the Board that the applicant was not being truthful.

[...]

[12] Although I was not present at the October 12, 2000 hearing and thus, did not have the benefit of seeing the applicant as the Board did, I have no hesitation in concluding, on a reading of the transcript, that the claimant did not testify in a forthright manner. Consequently, the Board's remarks to the effect that the applicant's answers sounded wooden and rehearsed, do not surprise me. The applicant was unable to convince me that in so concluding, the Board made a reviewable error. [Emphasis added]

[3-119] Consider as well the guidance found in the case of *Nderitu v. The Minister of Citizenship and Immigration*, [2005] F.C.J. No. 86, 2005 FC 72, at para. 34:

[34] Further, the Respondent notes that the Board can make an adverse credibility decision on the basis of contradictions and inconsistencies in the Applicant's story, or on the basis that it is simply implausible. (*Sheikh v. Canada (Minister of Employment and Immigration)*, [1990] 3 F.C. 238 (F.C.A.); *Leung v. Canada*

(Minister of Employment and Immigration)
(1990), 74 D.L.R. (4th) 313).

[3-120] To better orient the reader's comprehension, the following passages set out the grievances raised by the party whose credibility was found to be lacking due to an implausible account, a finding which was supported, in part, by what the losing party submitted:

> [27] The Applicant submits that the Board's Decision itself is confusing in that it impugns her credibility, then proceeds to use aspects of her story to find adequate state protection.

> [28] The Respondent counters with the argument that the Decision is not confusing. The Board completed its credibility assessment, and then proceeded with an analysis of state protection and IFA. The further assessment is common practice for the Board. The Respondent says that the Board, after giving reasons for its negative credibility assessment of the Applicant, then proceeded to analyse the availability of state protection and IFA. This practice is not inconsistent with the Board's credibility findings. Such an analysis is often conducted assuming the Applicant's allegations to be true, so that, at the end of the day, if the explicit credibility findings cannot stand, the Court can move on to review state protection and IFA findings.

[3-121] Noteworthy as well are the facts and findings in *Navarrete*   *v.*
The Minister of Citizenship and Immigration, [2006] F.C.J.

No. 878, 2006 FC 691, 294 F.T.R. 242, at para. 36-40, which were upset on appeal:

> [36] Before the Board, Mr. Navarrete did not produce corroborative evidence of phone contact and <u>none of the letters or cards he presented were accompanied by stamped envelopes</u>.
>
> [37] <u>Before the Board, Mr. Navarrete did not produce a lease</u> to demonstrate who was the actual tenant at his address. He produced a photograph of his 1999 vacation in the Dominican Republic. The Minister submitted evidence which indicated that the photograph was taken in January 1997 and not in December 1999.
>
> [38] The "… real test of the truth of the story of a witness in such a case must be its harmony with the preponderance of the probabilities which a practical and informed person would readily recognize as reasonable in that place and in those conditions." (*Faryna*, above)
>
> [39] In this case, the two sisters (Maria and Gleidys) married on the same day in Santo Domingo. Mr. Navarrete testified that in June or July 2000, Ms. Gleidys De Jesus told him not to tell Ms. Maria Roselina De Jesus that she too planned to get married on the same day in November 2000. Mr. <u>Navarrete testified that he did not find the matter of importance to him as he finds the family a little strange.</u> The Board accepted this explanation as "unusual but not unreasonable in all the circumstances." <u>Mr.</u>

> Navarrete's explanation is hardly in
> harmony with the evidence and is actually
> inconsistent with his own evidence – given
> that the Board also accepted his testimony
> that he really likes Ms. De Jesus' family
> and finds them "down to earth."

CONCLUSION

> [40] In making these erroneous findings
> without regard to the evidence, the Board
> erred in a reviewable manner pursuant to
> subsection 18.1(4)(*d*) of the *Federal
> Courts Act*, R.S.C. 1985, c. F-7, and in
> law pursuant to subsection 18.1(4)(*c*) of
> the same Act. Having relied on these
> erroneous findings to allow the appeal,
> the Board's decision is set aside and the
> matter is remitted for re-consideration by
> a differently constituted panel. [Emphasis
> added]

46) Common sense findings and a motive to lie

[3-122] We are indebted to Rowles J.A. for a lucid contribution
to this debate, as found at para. 28 of *R. v. R.W.B.,* [1993]
B.C.J. No. 758, 24 B.C.A.C. 1 (C.A.):

> [28] It does not logically follow that
> because there is no apparent reason for a
> witness to lie, the witness must be telling
> the truth. Whether a witness has a motive
> to lie is one factor which may be
> considered in assessing the credibility of
> a witness, but it is not the only factor to be
> considered. Where, as here, the case for
> the Crown is wholly dependant upon the
> testimony of the complainant, it is
> essential that the credibility and reliability

of the complainant's evidence be tested in the light of all of the other evidence presented. [Emphasis added]

47) External contradictions and common sense

[3-123] Although the issue of contradictions might easily have been discussed earlier when addressing the question of inconsistencies, it is thought preferable to address it at this stage as one of the pillars of a common sense findings. Simply put, one's testimony ought to be found to be in accord with other testimony and evidence and ought not to be contradictory to other 'known' facts, as a matter of common sense. A simple example would be an alibi advanced by an accused person which is not in keeping with the testimony of his two best friends as to the date and place of the accused's bachelor party. See the elaborate discussion of this type of question in R. v. Mayrand, [1989] A.Q. no. 1070, 25 Q.A.C. 208 (C.A.). In effect, this is not an obvious area of impeachment in a judgment as much will depend on the quality of the opposing testimony and any such contradictions are of less concern, on an analytical plane at the very least, than is the existence of internal contradictions for, as a matter of common sense, we expect persons to be able to be consistent in their accounts of their actions, especially in a setting as solemn as a trial court.

48) Internal contradictions and common sense

[3-124] Following upon the thoughts consigned immediately above, the preponderance element in fact finding may far more easily be met by the presence on the record of consistent accounts, and less likely met in the contrary situation.

[3-125] In considering the case law in this respect, it will be useful to note that the existence of internal contradictions is not necessarily a fatal element in any analysis of credibility, as has been seen, but must be assigned weight in accordance

with the nature and number of these elements of inconsistency.

[3-126] First, recall Justice Hill's judgment in R. v. N.K.D., [1997] O.J. No. 3877 (Sup. Ct.), at para. 33:

> [33] It is generally recognized that some differences or discrepancies in a witness' testimony, in particular when compared to prior statements of that witness out of court, may well be indicative of a truthful witness -- one who has not provided a scripted and rehearsed account, but rather one which suffers only from certain human frailties, for example, the product of a dulled memory, confusion from the stress of being a witness or other cause too insufficient to significantly affect the witness' credibility and reliability. [Emphasis added]
>
> [...]
>
> [35]   In considering the significance of prior inconsistent statements of a complainant, it is necessary to reflect upon the materiality of the differences, the number of such inconsistencies, and such explanations as may be provided for the discrepancies.

[3-127] Para. 29 of R. v. R.W.B., [1993] B.C.J. No. 758, 24 B.C.A.C. 1 (C.A.) is also of assistance:

> [29] In this case there were a number of inconsistencies in the complainant's own evidence and a number of inconsistencies between the complainant's evidence and the testimony of other witnesses. While it

is true that minor inconsistencies may not diminish the credibility of a witness unduly, a series of inconsistencies may become quite significant and cause the trier of fact to have a reasonable doubt about the reliability of the witness' evidence. There is no rule as to when, in the face of inconsistency, such doubt may arise but at the least the trier of fact should look to the totality of the inconsistencies in order to assess whether the witness' evidence is reliable. This is particularly so when there is no supporting evidence on the central issue, which was the case here. [Emphasis added]

[3-128] In considering the latter judgment, Galligan J.A. opined: "[26] [...] I do not think the principle is different whether there is one or several inconsistencies. What is important is the significance of the inconsistency. If the inconsistency is a significant one then the trial judge must pay careful attention to it when assessing the reliability of the witness's testimony. [Emphasis added] Refer to *R. v. M.G.*, [1994] O.J. No. 2086, 73 O.A.C. 356 (C.A.).

[3-129] Finally, note is taken again of R. v. Genest, [1990] A.Q. no. 1609, [1990] R.J.Q. 2387, 32 Q.A.C. 182, 61 C.C.C. (3d) 251 (C.A.) at page 281 C.C.C., para. E, wherein a witness was described by defence counsel as "[...] unsatisfactory in terms of honesty, veracity and impartiality, eminently weak in terms of the trustworthiness of her personal faculties of observation, retention, comprehension and communication and tainted with contradictions on essential facts [...]" [Emphasis added]

[3-130] Thus, the focus must be on the significance of any internal contradiction, though the number of contradictions emanating from one source cannot fail, as a matter of

common sense, to be telling after a certain threshold is achieved.

49) Reviewing common sense findings on appeal

[3-131] Justice Mosley identified the baseline concerns in such cases in *Henin v. Canada (Minister of Citizenship and Immigration)*, [2005] F.C.J. No. 958, 2005 FC 766, 45 Imm. L.R. (3d) 242, at para. 18:

> [18] It should be easier to have a plausibility finding overturned than a credibility finding because the Board is in no better position than the Court to make findings based on common sense: *Callejas v. Canada (Minister of Employment and Immigration)* [1994] F.C.J. No. 113 (T.D.); *Karikari v. Canada (Minister of Employment and Immigration)* [1994] F.C.J. No. 586 (T.D.); *Parizi v. Canada (Minister of Citizenship and Immigration)* [1994] F.C.J. No. 1977 (T.D.); *Singh v. Canada (Minister of Employment and Immigration)* (1993), 69 F.T.R. 142 (T.D.); *Soto y Giron v. Canada (Minister of Employment and Immigration)* [1992] F.C.J. No. 481 (F.C.A.).

[3-132] To repeat, an appellate tribunal labours under no disadvantage in such matters though it has not seen or heard the witnesses. To the same effect is *Vifansi v. Minister of Employment and Immigration*, [2003] F.C.J. No. 397, 2003 FCT 284, 230 F.T.R. 5, 27 Imm. L.R. (3d) 145, especially at para. 17: "The Respondent generally takes the position that the Board is mandated to assess credibility and unless its conclusions are patently unreasonable, its decision should stand. Relying on *Faryna v. Chorny*, [1952] 2 D.L.R. 354 (B.C.C.A.), the Respondent submits that the Board is entitled

to reject uncontradicted evidence if it is inconsistent with the probability findings affecting the case as a whole.

50) The concerns surrounding common sense: It is part of human nature for different persons to view similar events differently?

[3-133] Perhaps the best way of addressing this issue at the outset is to say that if common sense is common, which proposition is often put in doubt, it is far from obvious that different individuals sense matters the same way due to their disparate human nature. Put differently, the life experience discussed earlier is quintessentially an individual matter far removed from being common in nature. Or, as expressed famously in Hamlet, "[…] There are more things in heaven and earth, Horatio, Than are dreamt of in your philosophy […]". Refer to Act 1, sc. V., l. 166.

[3-134] Let us consider certain cases to then draw further attention to the world of literature. Firstly, the judgment in *Khan v. Canada (Minister of Citizenship and Immigration)*, [2005] F.C.J. No. 501, 2005 FC 403, at para. 19, *per* Blais J., as he then was:

> [19] The fact that the Board gathered all of the implausibilities it perceived, and rendered its decision based partly on these findings is entirely within its field of expertise, as it is within the Board's function to assess plausibility. As was stated by Justice Sharlow in *Gonzalez v. Canada (Minister of Citizenship and Immigration)*, [1999] F.C.J. No. 805:
>
>> In my view, it was open to the CRDD to assess the plausibility of the applicant's conduct as it did, by considering her story, and the manner in which it was told and

tested in the course of the hearing, against the backdrop of other evidence and its own understanding of human behaviour. The comments of O'Halloran J.A. in *Faryna v. Chorny*, [1952] 2 D.L.R. 354 at 357 (B.C.C.A.) reflect my view:

> In short, the real test of the truth of the story of a witness ... must be its harmony with the preponderance of the probabilities which a reasonable and informed person would readily recognize as reasonable in that place and in those conditions.

[...] As long as the inferences drawn by the tribunal are not so unreasonable as to warrant our intervention, its findings are not open to judicial review.

[3-135] Further guidance on the question of assessing human conduct is found at para. 57 of *Saliaj v. Canada (Minister of Citizenship and Immigration)*, [2004] F.C.J. No. 1506, 2004 FC 1247, to the same general effect:

> [57] <u>The Respondent also submits that the Panel was entitled to make plausibility findings based on its understanding of believable human conduct</u>. Sharlow J., in *Gonzalez*, had the following to say on this issue:

[27] In my view, it was open to the CRDD to assess the plausibility of the applicant's conduct as it did, by considering her story, and the manner in which it was told and tested in the course of the hearing, against the backdrop of other evidence and its own understanding of human behaviour. The comments of O'Halloran J.A. in *Faryna v. Chorny*, [1952] 2 D.L.R 354 at 357 (B.C.C.A) reflect my view:

> In short, the real test of the truth of the story of a witness ... must be its harmony with the preponderance of the probabilities which a reasonable and informed person would readily recognize as reasonable in that place and in those conditions.

[3-136] The obvious difficulty is that it is quite onerous to gather any degree of unanimity as to what, precisely, may be said to be the common sense view of a precise act or activity in light of what Justice McKeown described as the right of a Court to "[...] assess the plausibility of the applicant's conduct as it did, by considering her story, and the manner in which it was told and tested in the course of the hearing, against the backdrop of other evidence and its own understanding of human behaviour [...]" See para. 9 of *Li v. The Minister of Citizenship and Immigration*, [2002] F.C.J. No. 470, 2002 FCT 358.

[3-137] Turning now to the world of literature, Shakespeare is often quoted in this respect as being the greatest observer of humankind and thus, his plays are the mirror of the lives, events and souls of those who parade before the Courts to testify. This is not to say that the Bard is not criticised for his views, notably the opinion that "[...] men are merriest, when they are from home", words I couched on paper in writing <u>King Henry the Fifth</u>. Refer to Act 1, sc. 2, line 273.

[3-138] Nonetheless, all are familiar with judgments in which it was thought of assistance to decry the testimony of a witness by reason of the untoward protestations of innocence. Thus, one might cite with profit the "doth protest too much" comment contained in <u>Hamlet</u>, at Act III, sc. ii, 1. 235. This may serve to draw the focus of the inquiry away from the account to the manner of its presentation. For example, in <u>R. v. D. (G.C.),</u> [1988] O.J. No. 292 the trial judge appears to have assigned little weight to the defendant's testimony on the grounds that he "protested too much." Refer to para. 6, at p. 289. See also <u>Archibald v. Kuntz,</u> [1994] B.C.J. No. 199 (S.C.) (Q.L.), at para. 33: "But there is in this exhibition [of discomfort] almost an appearance that leads one to wonder whether or not it is just a bit too demonstrative. One is rather reminded of that line from Shakespeare about protesting too much."

[3-139] Further, Shakespeare's writings have served to warn judicial officers that if someone doth protest too much, it might reflect poorly on the listener's evaluation of the account. In the *Mikado*, by Gilbert and Sullivan, the contrary occurs: there is too much boasting. Ko-Ko tells the Emperor how well he himself performed in executing the prisoner, adding "A tough fellow he was, too – a man of gigantic strength. His struggles were terrific. It was a remarkable scene". The trouble starts when he is asked to describe the scene in detail."[15]

---

[15] See "The Criminal Credit as He Droppeth Him Down," Song No. 18, Act 2.

[3-140] At bottom, it is a question of understanding human nature and reference must thus be made to the wise words of Dean Wigmore: 'The lawyer [and judge] must know human nature. He [or she] must deal understandingly with its types and motives. These he cannot all find close around... For this learning he [or she] must go to fiction which is the gallery of life's portraits.'"[16]

51) The evaluation of credibility in the case of children

[3-141] The leading statement in this respect was penned by Justice McLachlin, now C.J.C., *in R. v. R.W.*, [1992] S.C.J. No. 56, [1992] 2 S.C.R. 122, 137 N.R. 214, 54 O.A.C. 164, 74 C.C.C. (3d) 134, 13 C.R. (4th) 257. It will suffice to reproduce paras. 24 and following:

> [24] The second change in the attitude of the law toward the evidence of children in recent years is a new appreciation that it may be wrong to apply adult tests for credibility to the evidence of children. One finds emerging a new sensitivity to the peculiar perspectives of children. Since children may experience the world differently from adults, it is hardly surprising that details important to adults, like time and place, may be missing from their recollection. Wilson J. recognized this in *R. v. B. (G.),* [1990] 2 S.C.R. 30, at pp. 54-55, when, in referring to submissions regarding the court of appeal judge's treatment of the evidence of the complainant, she said that

---

[16]   See "A List of One Hundred Legal Novels" (1922), 17 Ill. Law Rev. 26, at p. 31. Reference may also be made to R. v. Armco Canada Ltd. (1975), 6 O.R. (2d) 521 (H.C.J.), at page 569 and R. v. Baker, [1990] O.J. No. 1617 (Prov. Ct.).

[...] it seems to me that he was simply suggesting that the judiciary should take a common sense approach when dealing with the testimony of young children and not impose the same exacting standard on them as it does on adults. However, this is not to say that the courts should not carefully assess the credibility of child witnesses and I do not read his reasons as suggesting that the standard of proof must be lowered when dealing with children as the appellants submit. Rather, he was expressing concern that a flaw, such as a contradiction, in a child's testimony should not be given the same effect as a similar flaw in the testimony of an adult. I think his concern is well founded and his comments entirely appropriate. While children may not be able to recount precise details and communicate the when and where of an event with exactitude, this does not mean that they have misconceived what happened to them and who did it. In recent years we have adopted a much more benign attitude to children's evidence, lessening the strict standards of oath taking and corroboration, and I believe that this is a desirable development. The credibility of every witness who testifies before the courts must, of course, be carefully assessed but the standard of the "reasonable adult" is not necessarily appropriate in assessing the credibility of young children.

[25] As Wilson J. emphasized in *B. (G.)*, these changes in the way the courts look at the evidence of children do not mean that the evidence of children should not be subject to the same standard of proof as the evidence of adult witnesses in criminal cases. Protecting the liberty of the accused and guarding against the injustice of the conviction of an innocent person require a solid foundation for a verdict of guilt, whether the complainant be an adult or a child. What the changes do mean is that we approach the evidence of children not from the perspective of rigid stereotypes, but on what Wilson J. called a "common sense" basis, taking into account the strengths and weaknesses which characterize the evidence offered in the particular case.

[26] It is neither desirable nor possible to state hard and fast rules as to when a witness's evidence should be assessed by reference to "adult" or "child" standards -- to do so would be to create anew stereotypes potentially as rigid and unjust as those which the recent developments in the law's approach to children's evidence have been designed to dispel. Every person giving testimony in court, of whatever age, is an individual, whose credibility and evidence must be assessed by reference to criteria appropriate to her mental development,

understanding and ability to communicate. But I would add this. In general, where an adult is testifying as to events which occurred when she was a child, her credibility should be assessed according to criteria applicable to her as an adult witness. Yet with regard to her evidence pertaining to events which occurred in childhood, the presence of inconsistencies, particularly as to peripheral matters such as time and location, should be considered in the context of the age of the witness at the time of the events to which she is testifying.

52) Appellate review of findings of credibility as a general matter

[3-142] It will suffice in this respect to cite but one of a legion of judgments in this regard, that of *R. v. Gagnon*, [2006] S.C.J. No. 17, [2006] 1 S.C.R. 621, 266 D.L.R. (4th) 1, 347 N.R. 355, 207 C.C.C. (3d) 353, at para. 10:

> [10] There is general agreement on the test applicable to a review of a finding of credibility by a trial judge: the appeal court must defer to the conclusions of the trial judge unless a palpable or overriding error can be shown. It is not enough that there is a difference of opinion with the trial judge (*Schwartz v. Canada*, [1996] 1 S.C.R. 254, at paras. 32-33; *H.L. v. Canada (Attorney General)*, [2005] 1 S.C.R. 401, 2005 SCC 25, at para. 74). A succinct description of the overall approach appears in *R. v. Burke*, [1996] 1 S.C.R. 474, at para. 4, where this Court stated that "it is only where the Court has considered all of the

<u>evidence before the trier of fact and determined that a conviction cannot be reasonably supported by that evidence that the court can ... overturn the trial court's verdict". With respect to the credibility of witnesses, the same standard applies.</u> In *Lavoie v. R.*, [2003] Q.J. No. 1474 (QL), at para. 37, Nuss J.A. of the Quebec Court of Appeal stated that a trial judge's assessment of the credibility of witnesses "will not be disturbed unless it can be demonstrated that he committed a palpable and overriding error" (citing *Housen v. Nikolaisen*, [2002] 2 S.C.R. 235, 2002 SCC 33). [Emphasis added]

Chapter 4
The fundamental elements of judging reliability

1) Introduction

[4-1] To many minds, there is no real distinction between credibility and reliability while others, such as the writer, draw the following distinction: the notion of credit may embrace many subjective elements but reliability may be reduced to the fundamental notion that notwithstanding the basic honesty of the person who is testifying, the weight to be assigned to the evidence must be discounted, in whole or in part, for an objective reason such as the involvement of an intoxicant. Stated otherwise, no matter how much value one might otherwise wish to attribute to the observations of an honest witness, the fact that their faculties were impaired by alcohol abuse on the occasion in question serves to limit the reach of the reliability that such testimony is entitled to bear.

[4-2] In this chapter, the three main elements of reliability which a judge is called upon to assess and evaluate will be considered in turn, both from a legal and literary perspective. These are identification evidence, intoxication and bias.

2) Discussion

a) Introduction to identification evidence

[4-3] Scant authority is required in support of the general proposition that identification evidence is fraught with intrinsic frailties to such an extent that eyewitness testimony is considered to be inherently dangerous.[17] Indeed, the Law Reform Commission remarked:

---

[17] Refer to R. v. Miaponoose (1996), 2 C.R. (5th) 82, 30 O.R. (3d) 419, 93 O.A.C. 115, 110 C.C.C. (3d) 445 (C.A.). Consider also the further comments of the Court of Appeal in

... psychologists have shown that much of what one thinks one saw is really perpetual filling-in. Contrary to the belief of most laymen, and indeed some judges, the signals received by the senses and transmitted to the brain do not constitute photographic representations of reality. The work of psychologists has shown that the process whereby sensory stimuli are converted into conscious experience is prone to error, because it is impossible for the brain to receive a total picture of any event. Since perception and memory are selective processes, viewers are inclined to fill in perceived events with other details, a process which enables them to create a logical sequence. <u>The details people add to their actual perception of an event are largely governed by past experience and personal expectations</u>. Thus the final recreation of the event in the observer's mind may be quite different from reality.[18] [Emphasis supplied]

R. v. McIntosh (1997), 35 O.R. (3d) 97, 102 O.A.C. 210, 117 C.C.C. (3d) 385. On behalf of Labrosse and Austin, JJ.A., Mr. Justice Finlayson wrote, at page 394 [C.C.C.], para. 19: "We should all be reminded of the frailties of identification evidence." Note that in "The Mystery of Marie Roget", by Edgar Allan Poe, we find these observations at para. 52: "Nothing is more vague than impressions of individual identity. Each man recognizes his neighbour, yet there are few instances in which any one is prepared *to give a reason* for his recognition."

[18] Refer to R. v. Miaponoose (1996), 2 C.R. (5th) 82, 30 O.R. (3d) 419, 93 O.A.C. 115, 110 C.C.C. (3d) 445 (C.A.), at para. 11.

[4-4] It is thus obvious that identification evidence is inherently unreliable, and that the jury will be instructed accordingly prior to evaluating the testimony in question. Accordingly, in this initial section of chapter 3, attention will be drawn to a number of themes that might be considered with profit prior to drawing either the charge for the jury or the Court's reasons, if it is a judge alone trial, in the case of an honest but potentially unreliable or mistaken observer. In this context, the witnesses to be cross-examined are assumed to be conscientious and not the less than candid witnesses described by Mr. Justice Moldaver, now a member of the Court of Appeal for Ontario, in R. v. Anderson, [1994] O.J. No. 2059 (Gen. Div.).

[4-5] Moreover, the passages from the world of literature that follow may well have been influential in providing to the witness (if not the trier of fact) with a false belief in the reliability of identification evidence. Indeed, one noted novelist, Georges Simenon, appears to have been of the mistaken belief that persons do perceive and retain images of reality by means of what amounts to a photographic image. As we read in Maigret à l'école, Tout Simenon 7, Presses de la Cité, Paris, 1989, at page 225, one reads: "There are images that one records unwittingly, with the precision of a camera, and later on we may be able to recall them..." It is the duty of the Court to ensure that the trier of fact is not labouring under any faulty belief of this nature that may well have been influenced by the world of fiction.

[4-6] Of note, the themes that have been selected offer dual advice, both from the animating case law and from literature that may well serve to underscore the potential harm to the truth-seeking function that the Court must advance. The resulting guidance in this crucial area of the law should provide self-evident instruction on the question of how individuals "fill-in" the blanks of their perception and memory of events.[19]

---

[19]   Consider as well the original trial scene in A Tale of Two Cities, by Charles Dickens, in which the lawyer Carton

[4-7] In sum, it is suggested once again that the world of the fiction writer is an ideal source of common sense examples that may be considered when assessing the merits of purported identification evidence.

b) A discussion of the salient elements of identification evidence

i) The presence of a distinguishing feature

[4-8] Not uncommonly, the outcome of a prosecution may turn on the presence or absence of a single yet signal identifying feature. For example, what prosecuting counsel would not wish for a witness, described as completely self-assured, for whom misgivings are unknown, who is able to state with absolute certainty that the person observed had a remarkable birth-mark, under her left heel, as in the case of <u>Maigret in Montmartre</u>?[20] Noteworthy as well are the opening words in "The Man With The Scar", by W. Somerset Maugham, at page 18: "it was on account of the scar that I first noticed him…". In such a case, the Court may accept more readily the identification evidence advanced, as discussed briefly at para. 9 of <u>R. v. Ali and Houlder</u>, [2002] O.J. No. 4358 (C.A.). The Court drew particular attention to the description of the robber as having marks on the left hand side of his mouth and Mr. Ali had mole-like marks in the location she described. "This enhanced the worth of her evidence…."[21]

---

saves Charles Darney based on their uncanny resemblance. Refer to pages 221-222 of "The Law in Fiction" by Winifred Duke (1928), 37 <u>Juridical Review</u> 219-233.

[20]   Penguin Books, Harmondsworth, 1963, at page 82. Translated by D. Woodward from <u>Maigret au Picratt's</u>, Tout Simenon 5, Presses de la Cité, Paris, 1988, at page 288.

[21]   In the tale "The Fall of the House of Usher", Edgar Allan Poe records at para. 8 "… these features, with an inordinate expansion above the regions of the temple, made

[4-9] It is suggested that one concern of the trier of fact must surround how well this distinguishing aspect, let us say a mole, has been perceived. Counsel might well have asked a number of questions in order to demonstrate that the witness must have taken particular notice of such a feature. If, on the one hand, it becomes obvious that the witness can supply abundant details in the description to the point that the witness will profess to be able to recognize the mole standing alone, she may then have been led to concede that they could not have gained (and retained) an equally detailed memory of the other less distinctive features. At that point, a number of photos of moles (or of the particular physical trait in question) might have been produced and the witness invited to select the correct one. Not unlike the classic question asked of the witness who had a gun pointed at her head, likely the witness either stared at it or her assailant, but not both.

[4-10] On the other hand, if the witness is unable to point out anything precise about the unusual feature, she may be led to concede that all she can state with any certainty is that there was some kind of mole, or blemish, or pimple, or cut, etc. Counsel might well then have attempted to have her agree with the suggestion that what she recalls is that there was something distinctive, but that she cannot describe anything particular about that distinctive feature, if you will excuse the redundancy. At that point, it will have been suggested that she cannot recall anything else out of the ordinary about the person in question save for some kind of mark which is not unusual in general terms.

[4-11] At bottom, as will be discussed in greater detail, whether the witness is attempting to describe a tattoo[22], a

---

up altogether a countenance not easily to be forgotten." Recall as well the woeful countenance of Don Quixote.

[22]   See Feux rouges, Tout Simenon 6, Presses de la Cité, Paris, 1989, at page 774.

mouth like that of a frog,[23] unusual yellow shoes,[24] a scar,[25] a space between the teeth,[26] a harelip,[27] a beauty spot,[28] or marks caused by smallpox,[29] may it be said that the feature observed is so distinctive that it may be described without reference to any other aspect of the person in question? Is the witness able to select such a feature from a representative sampling? Is the witness able to say what was so distinctive about one "gap-tooth"[30] smile that it could not be mistaken for another? Is it a remarkable tattoo in which the whole may be described or is simply a less common but not particular form of the well-known "Mother" in the case of older individual, not

---

[23]   See Monsieur Gallet, décédé, Tout Simenon 16, Presses de la Cité, Paris, 1991, at page 25.

[24]   See The Sailors' Rendez-Vous, Penguin Books, Harmondsworth, 1970, at page 21. Translated by M. Ludwig from Au Rendez-Vous des Terre-Neuvas, Tout Simenon 16, Presses de la Cité, Paris, 1991, at page 654.

[25]   See Les 13 Énigmes, Tout Simenon 18, Presses de la Cité, Paris, 1991, at page 67.
[26]   See L'Outlaw, Tout Simenon 22, Presses de la Cité, Paris, 1992, at page 625.

[27]   See Le petit docteur, Tout Simenon 23, Presses de la Cité, Paris, 1992, at page 682.

[28]   See Les dossiers de l'Agence O., Tout Simenon 24, Presses de la Cité, Paris, 1992, at page 320.

[29]   See Maigret and the Hotel Majestic, Harvest/HBJ, Orlando, 1982, at p. 132. Translated by C. Hillier from Les caves du Majestic, Tout Simenon 23, Presses de la Cité, Paris, 1992, at page 381.

[30]   See again the book L'Outlaw, Tout Simenon 22, Presses de la Cité, Paris, 1992, at page 625.

to speak of the abundant wealth of commonplace tattoos that adorn the bodies of young people these days? If not, the Court will ultimately have to judge whether the witness was mistaken by reason of the fact that the feature observed is similar to a feature found on the person of the accused,[31] leaving aside entirely the issue of poor eyesight.[32]

ii) The absence of a distinguishing feature

[4-12] With respect to the obverse issue of the absence of a distinguishing feature, consider this example taken from fiction. The witness is asked, "Would you know him again?" He replies: 'I've only seen his back.' The further reply: "Backs are quite easy to recognize." He then states: 'I'm not sure. Perhaps."[33] If this witness is later called to testify and is heard to suggest that the accused's back resembles the person in question, the Court must consider whether this response is the

---

[31]   Refer to L'escalier de fer, Tout Simenon 6, Presses de la Cité, Paris, 1989, at page 743. In effect, the witness is hard pressed to explain what it is about the individual in question that allows him to be singled out from so many others.

[32]   In this respect, note the contributions found in Arcadian Adventures With the Idle Rich, by Stephen Leacock, at Chapter 5, "The Love Story of Mr. Peter Spillikins": "One must add to this that Mr. Spillikins, in spite of his large and bulging blue eyes, enjoyed the heavenly gift of short sight. As a consequence he lived in a world of amazingly beautiful women. And as his mind was focused in the same way as his eyes he endowed them with all the virtues and graces which ought to adhere to fifty-dollar flowered hats and cerise parasols with ivory handles."

[33]   See Maigret in Montmartre, Penguin Books, Harmondsworth, 1963, at page 13. Translated by D. Woodward from Maigret au Picratt's, Tout Simenon 5, Presses de la Cité, Paris, 1988, at page 235.

result of a normal desire to assist the authorities who must have other information suggesting guilt if the accused was charged. In this vein, the Court must weigh the testimony to see if it discloses nothing more than general observations or if the record includes what might be described as a high degree of assistance. For example, was the witness made to agree that by reason of the observations in question, there is no doubt but that it was a mature man, not a child and not an elderly person; that the person was neither quite slim nor obese; that the person was not dressed in an expensive suit or a t-shirt; that he wore a watch and did not smoke; that he was neither tall nor short, etc. to permit a firm conclusion as opposed to an uncertain one?

[4-13] As stated in L'escalier de fer, why should anyone take account of someone who looks like millions of others and who is not remarkable by the presence of a distinctive feature. Indeed, Les nouvelles enquêtes de Maigret sets out the comment that "... Jehan d'Oulmont had nothing particular about his features and thus people to whom his photograph was shown would promptly identify someone else."

[4-14] In effect, leaving aside the unusual case of objective identification evidence, for example, a bite-mark in an apple revealing not only the pattern of the teeth but a distinct dental impression, the Court must ask itself whether it is confident in cases in which no such truly distinguishing feature is present. One suspects that most witnesses will identify with the harried individual in Maigret in Montmartre who was asked "But you think you caught sight of him a few weeks ago. What did he look like?" and who remarked: "All you policemen seem to think that whenever one passes a man in the street one notices everything about him".[34]

---

[34] Penguin Books, Harmondsworth, 1963, at page 104. Translated by D. Woodward from Maigret au Picratt's, Tout Simenon 5, Presses de la Cité, Paris, 1988, at page 305.

[4-15] If we pause to think of the question, a general description taken from <u>Maigret and the Minister</u> that a person is "Middle-aged. Somewhat stouter than average..." amounts to very little but it may be conducive to a fertile cross-examination. How does the witness define middle age? Surely a 22-year-old defines it quite differently from the view of a 40-year-old or of a person born 60 years ago. How does s/he define "stouter than average"? In this respect, consider if the advocate attempted to underscore that one's view of the world depends on how little we know of it. In other words, whether the witness is a young male or female, their age and health may render them susceptible to quite negative views of others. Unlike some of the jury members, they may not be very sympathetic to middle age downward gravitational pulls and might have exaggerated the seemingly poor physical shape of the suspect.[35]

[4-16] In the same vein, a person's ability to identify an average person may be impaired by other factors, notably the number of other individuals who pass by and who share a common feature. For example, if an event occurred in a fitness centre, it may be difficult to distinguish between the Nike-clad Reebok-skirted Adidas-shod members milling about. If the event involved young skate boarders, or bicycle messengers, or Armani-suited articling students, or Boston Red Sox fans, it may be of assistance to consider whether the witness was asked to attempt to distinguish between these individuals by presenting photos of such groups in the courtroom. In such cases, do we really notice the individual features, the person should be asked, or the common qualities of clothing or hairstyle, etc? Think further of the example supplied by Simenon in <u>Le locataire</u>, at page 23: "[Translation: The attendant has provided your description. But he did not

_____

[35] See <u>Maigret and the Minister</u>, Heinemann/Octopus, London, 1978, at page 510. Translated by M. Budberg from <u>Maigret chez le ministre</u>, Tout Simenon 7, Presses de la Cité, Paris, 1989, at page 610.

enjoy a good look. What struck him mostly was your yellow slicker".[36]

iii) The quality of the opportunity to observe

§1) Glimpses

[4-17] The quality of the purported opportunity to obtain identification evidence is often of fundamental importance in light of the fact that occasionally, triers of fact will prefer to be afforded an "out" so to speak as it is human nature to be reluctant to castigate others or to criticize those who are no doubt honest and credible.[37] In other words, careful and competent counsel may have provided the means of rejecting the evidence but not the person offering it. "The primrose path" may provide such an out. Hence, if counsel is required to impeach the reliability of a well intentioned but mistaken witness in a case of identification evidence it may be appropriate to be guided by the words of Mr. Justice Muldoon in <u>Allen A. Rose v. Canada</u>, [1990] F.C.J. No. 176 (T.D.) (Q.L.):   "Good intentions, especially those which are composed only of words … are the stuff of that 'primrose path' so eloquently described by Shakespeare." See page 11 (Q.L.) and <u>Hamlet</u>, Act I, sc. iii, l. 50 and <u>Macbeth</u>, Act II, sc. iii, l. 19.

[4-18] In this respect, Mark Twain's fiction provides useful guidance to Courts involved in criminal litigation, notably by means of the beloved story of <u>The Prince and the Pauper</u> which is of signal assistance in this respect. As noted earlier, not infrequently, questions of law in an identification case

---

[36]   Tout Simenon, Volume 19, Paris: Presses de la Cité, 1992.
[37]   An excellent example is found in <u>Maigret and the Headless Corpse</u>, Avon, New York, 1971, at page 102. Translated by E. Ellenbough from <u>Maigret et le corps sans tête</u>, Tout Simenon 8, Presses de la Cité, Paris, 1989, at page 63.

revolve around the merits of testimony based on a "glimpse" of the subject.[38] As recorded at Ch. III, page 11 of <u>Prince</u>, "At a respectful distance were many country-folk, and people from the city, waiting for any chance glimpse of royalty that might offer." One can draw from this Twain's belief that, unlike the typical situation confronting witnesses, these potential witnesses are preparing to catch a glimpse. By contrast, most witnesses are surprised by the event and this may play a major role in the traditional reluctance of the Courts in assigning much if any weight to testimony involving such surprising situations. Counsel might have been successful in emphasizing this aspect to support the challenge to the so-called "fleeting" glance or glimpse identification evidence.

§2) Prolonged opportunities to observe

[4-19] Typically, a Court may be greatly impressed by a witness who enjoyed a prolonged opportunity to observe, or at least a superior opportunity than a mere glance or glimpse. In this respect it is noteworthy that Simenon was of the view that certain groups of employees, retired people who stare out of their windows all day long, waiters and "concierges" in particular, and so many other groups of whom there are too many examples to list, were unusually gifted in their opportunity to observe those about them. As observed in <u>Signé Picpus</u>: "Clerks in stores and maids are in the habit of taking note of cars that are unusual". Is it not a commonly experienced event to notice that many of these individuals are more than willing to admit that they are so preoccupied with carrying out their duties that they would be hard pressed to take particular notice of people unless something quite striking occurred?   In this respect, counsel is attempting to get the honest and fair witness to echo the comments of the "concierge" in <u>Maigret and the Hotel Majestic</u> when asked if she recognized the suspect: "Er... Frankly, I don't! I couldn't

---

[38]   The leading decision is <u>R. v. Turnbull et al.</u>, [1976] 3 All E.R. 549, 63 Cr. App. R. 132 (C.A.).

say for sure. I see so many people!"[39] A further example is taken from Les dossiers de l'Agence O.[40] The ticket attendant is unable to identify anyone, explaining that the events took place during the "grande presse", that is to say the rush hour.[41]

[4-20] Thus, it is evident that the opportunity to observe is critical in the evaluation of the merits of any identification evidence as illustrated by the following passage drawn from Arcadian Adventures With the Idle Rich, by Stephen Leacock, more precisely from Chapter 5, "The Love Story of Mr. Peter Spillikins": "[...] Mr. Spillikins, having seen the back of Mrs. Everleigh's head, had decided instantly that she was the most beautiful woman in the world; and that impression is not easily corrected in the half-light of a shaded drawing-room; nor across a dinner-table lighted only with candles with deep red shades; nor even in the daytime through a veil." At all events, counsel must attack (or support) the opportunity to observe.

---

[39]   See also Les nouvelles enquêtes de Maigret, Tout Simenon 24, Presses de la Cité, Paris, 1992, at page 958 wherein the dubious answer provided is: "Oh my! We see so many... Possibly?...".

[40]   See Les dossiers de l'Agence O., Tout Simenon 24, Presses de la Cité, Paris, 1992, at page 320.

[41]   To gain a good understanding of the dangers of 'confrontation', that is to say in the circumstances of an investigation wherein the police show the witness one person, see the aptly named book, Les témoins, Tout Simenon 7, Presses de la Cité, Paris, 1989, at page 690 and The Man Who Watched The Trains Go By, Penguin Books, Harmondsworth, 1986, at p. 137. Translated by S. Gilbert from L'homme qui regardait passer les trains, Tout Simenon 21, Presses de la Cité, Paris, 1992, at pages 662-663. The original version is more detailed in this respect.

The two extremes are illustrated as follows: One the one hand, as Twain penned in <u>The Prince and the Pauper</u>, Ch. XXV, page 200: "Quick-come to the light — let me scan thee well." On the other hand, Huck spoke of seeing the faces by the light of their cigars. See <u>Sawyer,</u> Ch. XXX, at page 227. If one did not come to the light, it seems that the challenge stood a better chance of success as opposed to a challenge undertaken in the context of better lighting.

iv) Identification based on uniforms or costumes

[4-21] Let us begin by reproducing once again a passage from Simenon's <u>Le locataire</u>, at page 23: "[Translation: The attendant has provided your description. But he did not enjoy a good look. What struck him mostly was your yellow slicker".[42] <u>The Prince and the Pauper</u> also makes plain the relative ease with which honest individuals may be mistaken in their identification when their attention is drawn to the costume or uniform, and not to the features, of someone they think they know. For example, note the following passage, at Ch. III, page 17: "A few minutes later the little Prince of Wales was garlanded with Tom's fluttering odds and ends, and the little Prince of Pauperdom was tricked out in the gaudy plumage of royalty. The two went and stood side by side before a great mirror, and lo, a miracle: there did not seem to have been any change made!"

[4-22] The notion that people may commit mistakes in recognition based on their expectation that certain individuals will be dressed in a certain fashion is seen in Twain's hilarious book, <u>Pudding'head Wilson</u>[43] as well. Fearful that her child will be sold "down the river", the slave Roxy switched his clothing with that worn by the Master's child. "She undressed

---

[42] Tout Simenon, Volume 19, Paris: Presses de la City, 1992.

[43] Reference is made to the 1966 edition published by the Airmont Publishing Company, Inc, New York, N.Y.

Thomas à Becket, stripping him of everything, and put the tow-linen shirt on him. She put his coral necklace on her own child's neck. Then she placed the children side by side, and after earnest inspection she muttered: 'Now who would b'lieve clo'es could do de like o' dat? Dog my cats if it ain't all I kin do to tell t' other fum which, let alone his pappy.'" See Ch. 3, page 25.[44]

[4-23] Thus, it is evident that one of the ways that counsel may challenge the purported identification of a person within a group, all of whom are dressed in a similar fashion, is to draw attention to the clothing as opposed to the features on the assumption that the witness observed as much of the former as the latter. Let us take for example a procession of young communicants. It is suggested that the witness should be asked to provide as much detail about her observations with a view to emphasizing how attention was drawn to the group. If the witness is able to describe the group in great detail, the questioning will then focus on that individual's ability and opportunity to notice one person in particular. It would be surprising, it is suggested, that any particular individual stood out, at least until such time as an event occurred. In addition, anecdotal evidence suggests strongly that a judge and counsel, both of whom are gowned, will often draw the comment from those who later meet them that they look quite different in ordinary clothes. No doubt the same difficulty will be noted by those observing medical personnel in white hospital coats, or workers who have donned uniforms or modes of dress that are remarkable for their appearance or, equally remarkable, totally drab in outlook. In the final

---

[44]   Twain loved to exploit the "twin theme", that is to say to have look-a-likes appear together and to craft intricate tales of mistaken identification and mistaken anticipations. For example, in Wilson, at Ch. 5, p. 41, he wrote: "Then entered the twins – the handsomest, the best dressed, the most distinguished-looking pair of young fellows the West had ever seen. One was a little fairer than the other, but otherwise they were exact duplicates."

analysis, the Court must be concerned with such factual controversies in assessing the weight to be assigned to such potential unreliable testimony.

[4-24] Finally, consider <u>Hamlet</u>, at Act 1, Sc. 1, l. 44-57:

> Barnardo: "Looks a' not like the king?" 1-1-44
> Horatio: "Together with that fair and warlike form In which the majesty of buried Denmark Did sometimes march?'''" 1-1-47
> Marcellus: "Is it not like the king?"
> Horatio: "As thou art to thyself. Such was the very armour he had on"…" 1-1-58

v) The quality of the in-court testimony: Leading questions and identification evidence

[4-25] Of interest, Twain anticipated the Court of Appeal for Ontario's decision in <u>R. v. Williams</u> (1982), 66 C.C.C. (3d) 234, at page 236. For the Court, Martin J.A. remarked that "…an answer on a critical issue elicited by a leading question is entitled to little, if any weight." Thus, in <u>The Prince and the Pauper</u>, we read: "The villain is in this room – cast thy old eyes about and see if thou canst say which he is." See Ch. XXVII, page 213. If one is told that the culprit is present, it is not surprising that the person accused, often seated in the prisoner's box, will be designated as the perpetrator of the earlier event. It is by reason of this fundamental view of human psychology that the exclamation of a witness to the effect of "That is the Man!" is entitled to so little weight.

Twain is also instructive in discussing the principle that no weight should be assigned to in-dock identification, known also as a "Thou Art the Man! I.D."[45], unless it is preceded by a fair identification parade or photo line-up. In this regard,

---

[45]   See Ch. 10, page 67, of <u>Pudd'nhead Wilson</u>: "…he felt as secret murderers are said to feel when the accuser says, 'Thou art the man!'"

consider Ch. XV, page 120 of <u>The Prince and the Pauper</u>: "...did foretell... a stranger with brown hair and clothed in a worn and common garb; and surely this prisoner doth answer woundily to the bill." As the story makes plain, it is self-evident that such purported identifications are without foundation, being based on nothing more than generalities. There is nothing to justify assigning any reliability to such opinions.

[4-26] In the same light, on occasion one is confronted in the courtroom with a witness who wishes that what he or she hopes or believes is the truth, often in cases of identifying persons or objects. Hence, "... he must be my boy!" is an excellent example. See <u>Prince</u>, ch. VIII, page 63.

vi) Habit and identification

[4-27] A further potential issue surrounding identification evidence concerns a person's habits. In this respect, one suspects that the author of <u>Cross and Tapper on Evidence</u> (Eighth Edition), Prof. Colin Tapper, has also been influenced by Mark Twain. He wrote in his text, "The fact that someone was in the habit of acting in a given way is relevant to the question whether he acted in that way on the occasion into which the court is inquiring."[46] Note that Twain emphasized at page 63 of Ch. X of <u>The Prince and the Pauper</u>, "... to test her doubts, she watched for her child's unwavering habit of casting his hand before his eyes with the palm turned outward – and he failed to do so."[47] In <u>Pudding'head Wilson</u>, we are told that "Habit is habit, and not to be flung out of the window by any man, but coaxed downstairs a step at a time". See Ch. VI, page 42.

---

[46]   See page 25, 1995, Butterworths, London.

[47]   Consider also how the fact that Muff Porter was seen washing himself was considered a suspicious circumstance as it "was not a habit with Potter." Refer to Ch. XI, page 93 of <u>Sawyer.</u>

vii) Identification evidence and historical prosecutions

[4-28] Turning to the issue of identification evidence of individuals who have aged since the events were said to have occurred, an important factor in 'historical' prosecutions, what guidance is found in these observations for the Court? "...nothing is altered; nothing but the people, at any rate; then years make a change in people; some of these I seem to know, but none know me."[48] Refer to The Prince and the Pauper, ch. XXV, pages 198-99. Some further guidance is found in Pudding'head Wilson, at p. Ch. 21, page 148: "Every human being carries with him from his cradle to his grave certain physical marks which do not change their character ... These marks are his signature ... This signature is not his face – age can change that beyond recognition; it is not his hair, for that can fall out; it is not his height, for duplicates of that exist; if is not his form, for duplicates of that exist also, whereas this signature is each man's very own [fingerprints]"[49]

viii) The strength of unchallenged testimony

[4-29] What of unchallenged identification evidence? Must the judge or trier of fact accept unchallenged testimony? Twain instructs us that this may well be a dangerous course of action at Ch. XXIII, page 188 of The Prince and the Pauper: "When

---

[48]   Consider as well Maigret and the Hotel Majestic, Harvest/HBJ, Orlando, 1982, at page 165. Translated by C. Hillier from Les caves du Majestic, Tout Simenon 23, Presses de la Cité, Paris, 1992, at page 396.

[49]   On the issue of the passage of time, note that in Maigret and the Minister, Heinemann/Octopus, London, 1978, at page 510, there is an interesting discussion about the difficulties in identifying people some years after an event. Translated by M. Budberg from Maigret chez le ministre, Tout Simenon 7, Presses de la Cité, Paris, 1989, at page 610.

the woman was called upon to testify before the justice of the peace, she swore that the small prisoner at the bar was the person who had committed the theft; there was none able to show the contrary, so the king stood convicted." She was mistaken, as we later discover.

ix) Voice identification

[4-30] The passage set out next is typical of voice identification evidence: "But thou needst not have misgivings. He is my sister's son; are not his voice, his face, his form, familiar to me from his cradle?" Ch. IV, page 42 of <u>Prince</u>. One of the challenges to voice identification that is not attempted often enough consists of preparing a number of voice 'foils' to read out a prepared text that resembles the voice identification in question. The witness will then be asked to select the defendant's voice from the selection of foils.

[4-31] In respect of voice identification, note that in "The Murders in The Rue Morgue", Edgar Allan Poe gives some instruction on the capacity of a witness to identify the language spoken by a person though it is not a language spoken by that person. As we read at para. 45, a Spaniard described a shrill voice as that of an Englishman and, more to the point, "... is sure of this. Does not understand the English language, but judges by the intonation." Subsequently, we see that in fact, no credit may be assigned to that identification in that the person simply concluded that it not being French, it had to be English. In Lethal Weapon II, Danny Glover and Mel Gibson try to identify the culprits' language, knowing only, according to their own understanding, that it is guttural. Surely this type of belief is not worthy of being called better than informed speculation, if that.

x) Fingerprints

[4-32] It will be instructive to note the guidance that Twain provided on the subject of fingerprints. Indeed, he is thought generally to have been the first novelists to have discussed the significance of fingerprints in identification evidence in his

Pudding'head Wilson novel. Pudd'nhead's mastery of this subject permitted him to win his first trial in brilliant fashion. See Ch. XXI, page 148.

[4-33] Turning to the issue of identification evidence of individuals who have aged since the events were said to have occurred, an important factor in 'historical' prosecutions, what guidance is found in these observations? "...nothing is altered; nothing but the people, at any rate; then years make a change in people; some of these I seem to know, but none know me." Refer to Prince, ch. XXV, pages 198-99. Some further guidance is found in Pudd'nhead Wilson, at page Ch. 21, page 148: "Every human being carries with him from his cradle to his grave certain physical marks which do not change their character ... These marks are his signature ... This signature is not his face – age can change that beyond recognition; it is not his hair, for that can fall out; it is not his height, for duplicates of that exist; if is not his form, for duplicates of that exist also, whereas this signature is each man's very own [fingerprints]"

xi) Overcoming initial difficulties with identification: the rehabilitation of 'challenged' testimony

[4-34] In "A Woman of Fifty", at page 4, we are informed that our mind may well be capable of recalling faces we have seen in the past, although we are unable to do so when first called upon so to do, by reason of the stress of being asked to "identify" someone too quickly. In other words, after the passage of time and some opportunity to relax, our memory may grow active, and permit recollection.

[4-35] In this respect, would the concerns respecting the failure to identify set out below, taken from R. v. Holmes, [2002] O.J. No. 4178 (C.A.), be distinguished on the grounds that the original attempt at identification occurred too soon after a traumatic event?

[4-36] Indeed, the orthodox position on the frailties of identification evidence is captured in the passages that follow. As discussed at para. 38, only one witness purported to identify Mr. Holmes as being in the vicinity of the fires, and she testified that at about 3:00 a.m. she observed a man run across the street near her house and walk past her parked car. A short time later the fire trucks, police and the police dog arrived. It must be noted that a few hours later, the witness viewed a photographic line-up that included a picture of the defendant. She tentatively identified someone other than Mr. Holmes as the person she saw run by her house.

[4-37] At the preliminary inquiry, she testified that she saw the man for "two seconds". By contrast, at trial, the witness testified that she saw the man for about two minutes. In the course of her examination-in-chief, the witness gave the following evidence:

> Q. That particular individual, do you think you saw him well enough that you would know him to see him again?
>
> A. At that time?
>
> Q. Yes.
>
> A. I thought I did, but…
>
> Q. And what about now?
>
> A. Now? Yes.
>
> Q. Do you see that individual?
>
> A. Yes, I do.
>
> Q. Could you point to him, please?
>
> A. Sitting right there.
>
> Q. Sorry, right where?
>
> A. Sitting right behind you.
>
> Q. Indicating the accused, sir.

[4-38] Of note, no objection was taken at trial to this evidence but on appeal, it was argued that this evidence should not have been admitted or that the trial judge should have instructed the jury to disregard it. Para. 39 sets out that

> The trial judge gave the jury a very strong charge on the danger of relying upon this evidence. He told the jury that this kind of dock identification has little evidentiary value and he explained why this is so. He concluded by directing the jury that if they were 'satisfied beyond a reasonable doubt' that the witness correctly identified the appellant as the person who ran across the street near her home, this was a piece of circumstantial evidence[50] that could be considered by the jury along with all of the other proven facts. The defence did not object to that part of the charge to the jury.

---

[50] With respect to the proposition that circumstantial evidence may deceive, refer to the passage "… blame his guards for Duncan's death – mark with blood the two sleepy guards", from *Macbeth* (1-7-65). In addition, note that page 87 of "Dickens and the Law", (1970), Vol. 1-3 <u>Auckland University Law Review</u> 78-88 includes guidance in this regard. "It is surprising how often Dickens uses legal imagery. It is evident in his writing from the beginning, and is most striking when used in an entirely non-legal context. Writing, for example, of his jesting suspicion that the chimney sweeps who traditionally danced in the streets on May day were no longer true sweeps because they were too big for the job, he says: "This is strong presumptive evidence, but we have positive proof – the evidence of our own senses." <u>Sketches By Boz</u>, Chapter 20, "The First of May.

[4-39] Although a new trial was ordered on another ground, some comments were advanced in any event. "I need not decide whether, in view of the lack of objection at trial and the very strong warning given by the trial judge, there was any reversible error. However, it seems to me that the prejudicial effect of the in-dock identification outweighed its probative value and on the new trial, if exclusion of this evidence is sought by the defence, the trial judge should exclude that part of [the] testimony." Refer to para. 40.

[4-40] In the ultimate analysis, might not the Crown have argued that the trial identification was reliable, as the witness had had time to permit her stress from the moment to subside?

[4-41] Further, reference may be made to the lengthy passages found at pages 26-27 of "The Bum", setting out how the mind works in its attempt to recall faces. Again, it appears to the novelist that allowance must be made for this thought process prior to seeking to ask a witness to select someone in an identification parade of some kind.

3) Conclusion

[4-42] Identification evidence of someone previously unknown in either a situation of stress or, not surprisingly, in a situation in which nothing appears to have occurred that is noteworthy, is inherently frail and must be challenged vigorously to ensure that no miscarriage of justice will ensue. It is the duty of counsel to pursue such issues forcibly lest findings of guilt be based on a lesser and unjust standard of proof, as was illustrated by Simenon in Maigret and the Minister: "If he answers to the description I've given you, if he smokes cigars and meddles in politics there's every chance he's my man."

d) The question of bias as an impediment to reliable testimony

i) Introduction

[4-43] By way of introductory comment to the discussion surrounding bias in the assessment of the reliability of testimony, consider the following passage from <u>Arcadian Adventures With the Idle Rich</u>, by Stephen Leacock, taken from Chapter 5, "The Love Story of Mr. Peter Spillikins", which might also be titled "Blinded by love": "But of love Mr. Spillikins never thought. He had viewed it so eagerly and so often from a distance that when it stood here modestly at his very elbow he did not recognize its presence. His mind had been fashioned, as it were, to connect love with something stunning and sensational, with Easter hats and harem skirts and the luxurious consciousness of the unattainable."

[4-44] Given the lengthy review of the "preponderance" test as fashioned in *Faryna v. Chorny*, [1952] 2 D.L.R. 354, 4 W.W.R. 171 (B.C.C.A.) in Chapter 2, it will not be necessary to spend a great deal of time on this issue presently. For present purposes, a bias is evident when the witness fails to judge faithfully the information perceived and to reach the proper conclusion by reason of bias. In this light, reference is made again to the following comments, consigned in *Bairaktaris and 9047-7993 Québec inc. c. Bouras and Naim*, [2002] J.Q. no 4148 (Sup. Ct.), at para. 32(b):

> [32] [...] It is a matter in which so many human characteristics, both the strong and the weak, must be taken into consideration. The general integrity and intelligence of the witness, his power to observe, his capacity to remember and his accuracy in statement are important. <u>It is also important to determine whether he is honestly endeavouring to tell the truth,</u>

whether he is sincere and frank or
whether he is biased, reticent and
evasive. All these questions and others
may be answered from the observation of
the witness's general conduct and
demeanour in determining the question of
credibility [Footnote 4 refers to the
following authority: *White v. The King*,
[1947] S.C.R. 268, at page 272]
[Emphasis added]

ii) The concern as to non-conscious bias

[4-45] The first point to be made is that in many cases, the
bias which may be found to present is unconscious, as made
plain in the passage which follows, penned by Lord Shaw of
Dunfermline in Clarke v. Edinburgh and District Tramways
Company Limited, [1919] S.C. (H.L.). 35, at page 37: "...[a]
witness without any conscious bias towards a conclusion may
have in their demeanour, in their manner, in their hesitation, in
the nuance of their expression, in even the turns of the eyelid,
left an impression [upon the trier of fact]..."

iii) The concern as to patent bias

[4-46] Little time need be spent on this issue. As noted earlier
when discussing credibility, under the rubric "The interest or
stake a witness may have in the case's outcome", recall the
seminal guidance provided by Justice O'Hallaran at para. 10
of *Faryna v. Chorny*, [1952] 2 D.L.R. 354, (1951) 4 W.W.R.
(N.S.) 171 (B.C.C.A.):

> [10] The credibility of interested
> witnesses, particularly in cases of conflict
> of evidence, cannot be gauged solely by
> the test of whether the personal
> demeanour of the particular witness
> carried conviction of the truth. The test
> must reasonably subject his story to an

examination of its consistency with the probabilities that surround the currently existing conditions. [Emphasis added]

[4-47] Of note, this passage was was expressly approved by the Ontario Court of Appeal in *Phillips v. Ford Motor Co. of Canada* (1971) 2 O.R. 637 at page 645, as noted at para. 71 of *Vilamar S.A. v. Sparling*, [1987] R.J.Q. 2186, [1987] Q.J. No. 2708 (Sup. Ct.).

[4-48] In effect, it is common place for a trier of fact to assign little weight to testimony in which bias is evident, for example that of a loved one,[51] or by reason of interest or due to a myriad of other influences such as class, religion or other elements of 'solidarity' which displace the burden produced by the oath to be frank and fair.

iv) The involvement of intoxicants producing unreliable testimony

[4-49] This element as well may be disposed of briefly. It is common place for a Court to fail to assign weight to testimony by reason of unreliability when the person who made the observations was intoxicated or under the debilitating effects of medication, for obvious reasons.

---

[51]   On occasion, trial judges will have to discern that the protestations of a poor memory serve to disguise a reluctance to assist a party, chiefly by reason of a lack of sympathy. Of course, in some cases, a bias present on an earlier occasion will have worn off in time: "Time had worn away her bitterness against her son, and she was able to think with serenity. She put the vile side of him out of her mind, and dwelt only on recollections of his occasional acts of kindness to her." See Pudding'head Wilson, Ch. VII, p. 52.

Chapter 5
Judging Evidence of Demeanour

> By means of a number of seemingly insignificant
> details, such as the manner of being, of taking a
> seat, of looking out, Maigret recognized him as
> one of those unusual individuals who, though
> guilty of no wrongful act, cannot help but betray
> anxiety when confronted by the police.
> [Emphasis supplied]
>
> Le pendu de Saint-Pholien, p. 136.

1) Introduction

[5-1] At the outset, it is suggested that in the resolution of most
factual controversies, the issue of the relative merits of
demeanour evidence is bound to dominate the work of judges.
Indeed, the trier of fact is invited, as a matter of course it
seems, to decide whether to accept or to reject testimony in
large part by reason of the importance assigned to such
subjective factors as the tone of voice, the presence of an
ironic smile, the fact of swallowing prior to responding, or a
nervous twitch of the eyebrows, to name but a few examples.
From the perspective of the judicial officer and for the reasons
to be advanced in this chapter, it must be asserted that the
acceptance or rejection of testimony on such grounds is
fraught with danger. Consequently, great pains should be
taken in assessing such evidence in order that the search for
the truth is confined to objective criteria including such matters
as prior inconsistent statements, contradictory assertions in
examination-in-chief and during cross-examination, illogical
propositions, etc., as discussed in the earlier analysis of
evidence of credibility and of reliability, if for no other reason
that the unsuccessful party is often at a great disadvantage in
seeking appellate relief in that much of such evidence is
incapable of being recorded.

[5-2] In this chapter, the goal pursued is to illustrate the extent to which the Court is able to support or reject the credit of any witness on the grounds of demeanour by means of references to the animating case law, together with copious references to books and other elements of general culture. In considering the guidance presented, counsel would find it advantageous to recall the wise words of Chief Justice Gerald T.G. Seniuk of the Saskatchewan Provincial Court in "Reasons and the Bounds of Rationality" 4 C.R. (5th) 11-23 at page 18, footnote 18: "Suppose, for example, that a judge asserted that she believed one witness because of his 'demeanour'. What, though, does 'demeanour' mean, and what was it about this witness's demeanour that led the trial judge to believe him?"

2) The evaluation of demeanour in particular

1) A general introduction to the concerns surrounding demeanour evidence

[5-3] The best source for guidance at the initial stages of the discussion of demeanour evidence is thought to be the Supreme Court of Canada. At the outset, it must be noted that the Supreme Court of Canada has acknowledged that subjective factors may play a decisive role in the evaluation of credibility, and that the demeanour of a witness may lead to the rejection of that person's evidence. For example, in R. v. Lifchus (1997), 9 C.R. (5th) 1, 118 C.C.C. (3d) 1, 150 D.L.R. (4th) 733, 216 N.R. 215, 118 Man. R. (2d) 218, at page 11, para. 29 [C.R.], Cory J. held:

> ...there may be something about a person's demeanour in the witness box which will lead a juror to conclude that the witness is not credible. It may be that the juror is unable to point to the precise aspect of the witness's demeanour which was found to be suspicious, and as a result cannot articulate either to himself or others exactly why the witness should not

be believed. A juror should not be made
to feel that the overall, perhaps intangible,
effect of a witness's demeanour cannot be
taken   into   consideration   in   the
assessment of credibility.

[5-4] With respect, the difficulty is that a witness may be
disbelieved, simply because s/he made a poor impression due
to the choice of clothes, the mannerisms or the attitude
displayed, and yet the testimony was logical, coherent and
consistent.[52]   Ought we not to insist that there must be
something that we can point to that permits us to say, with
confidence, "that person lied!"

[5-5] In this respect, note the guidance put forward by Justice
Beetz in *La Corporation municipale des Cantons Unis de
Stoneham et Tewkesbury v. Ouellet*, [1979] 2 S.C.R. 172,
wherein our highest Court held, as consigned at page 195:

In a civil proceeding, where the rule is that
of a preponderance of the evidence and
the balance of probabilities, when a party
testifies and is not believed it is possible

---

[52]   A notable example of the troublesome clues that are
provided by demeanour evidence is found in Long Dark Road
Bill King And Murder In Jasper, Texas, by Ricardo C. Ainslie,
[University of Texas Press, 2004, Austin, Tx].   The author
returns constantly to the theme that Bill King, guilty of
dragging a black man to his death behind a truck, simply did
not appear by his demeanour to be capable of participating in
a lynching and yet he was to die by lethal injection for so
horrendous a crime. See pages 2 and 5 for example. Indeed,
page 8 records how the author is ambivalent as to the
offender's guilt such is the force of King's personality, which
he describes as "intense, persuasive, and profoundly
engaging".   In other words, may triers of fact be led to the
incorrect conclusion based on such unscientific clues as found
in an individual's qualities of personal engagement?

for the trial judge to regard his assertions and denials and his denials as admissions, taking into account contradictions, hesitations, the time the witness takes to answer, his expression, circumstantial evidence and the evidence as a whole. [Emphasis added]

[5-6] Further instruction from the Supreme Court of Canada in *Laurentide Motels v. Beauport (City)*, [1989] 1 S.C.R. 705, [1989] S.C.J. No. 30 (Q.L.), 94 N.R. 1, 23 Q.A.C. 1, 45 M.P.L.R. 1 at p. 799 S.C.R., para. 245. L'Heureux-Dubé remarks that triers of fact are at liberty to consider "the movements, glances, hesitations, trembling, blushing, surprise or bravado" of witnesses. [Emphasis added] The advantage in attempting to base decisions on some of these factors is that they provide an objective measure of evaluating information. For example, a witness who takes an undue period of time to answer the simplest questions may be judged to be merely attempting to recall a story that has been fabricated. The witness who demonstrates bravado in answering difficult questions may rightly be discounted on the grounds that one cannot be confident that the witness would admit to any failings. Lastly, note that a witness appeared to have looked over to another person prior to answering. This type of 'glance' for help is capable of objective evaluation. Refer to para. 244. The other factors, however, are quite subjective and difficult to evaluate.

[5-7] Hence, the question must be posed: are judges and triers of fact at liberty to merely reject testimony based on a 'feeling' or impression grounded merely on demeanour? In this respect, note the comments of the Court of Appeal for Ontario in *R. v. Strong*, [2001] O.J. No. 1362. As recorded at para. 9, "Second, the trial judge offered no reason for his rejection of the appellant's evidence. He simply said 'I do not believe him'. In such a case, some explanation for that conclusory statement was required." The Court went on to note that the evidence in question was not inherently incredible and it was

entirely consistent with what one would expect from a person trying to recall what to him would have been routine events 30 years ago. And, more to the point, "None of the usual indicia of unreliability were referred to by the trial judge (eg. prior inconsistent statements, evasiveness,[53] lies)."

[5-8] By way of contrast, it is notable that in other cases the trier of fact may not have been impressed with glaring contradictions and inconsistencies, and may decide issues on the basis of a favourable demeanour as made plain in *R. v. Francois* (1993), 64 O.A.C. 140, [1993] O.J. No. 1419, 14 O.R. (3d) 191, 82 C.C.C. (3d) 441, 21 C.R. (4th) 350, affirmed [1994] 2 S.C.R. 827, 116 D.L.R. (4th) 69, 169 N.R. 241, 73 O.A.C. 161, 91 C.C.C. (3d) 289, 31 C.R. (4th) 201.

[5-9] As recorded at para. 4, "In a very impressive cross-examination counsel for the accused made a number of points serving to paint the complainant's evidence as implausible. The two most prominent issues concerned the number of times she had been raped and prior sworn statements which

---

[53]   No review of the question of evasion by a witness is complete without reference to Chapter 6 of Stephen Leacock's, <u>Arcadian Adventures With the Idle Rich</u>, "The Rival Churches of St. Asaph and St. Osoph":

"For what time shall I order dinner?" she asked. "You and Philippa used to have it at half-past seven, did you not? Don't you think that rather too late?" "A trifle perhaps," said the rector uneasily. He didn't care to explain to Juliana that it was impossible to get home any earlier […] everybody was giving just now. "But don't trouble about dinner. I may be working very late. If I need anything to eat I shall get a biscuit and some tea at the Guild Rooms, or--" He didn't finish the sentence, but in his mind he added, "or else a really first-class dinner at the Mausoleum Club, or at the Newberrys' or the Rasselyer-Browns'-- anywhere except here."

would refute that she had ever been raped." Further, in paragraph 6, we read, "In cross-examination she was confronted with an affidavit she had sworn in 1986, saying that she had never been sexually abused. The affidavit had been filed in wardship proceedings concerning her. A second affidavit was put to her which she had sworn in 1989, in proceedings claiming support from a putative father of her son, stating that she was a virgin prior to 1985. She freely admitted that these were important statements in the proceedings in which they were filed and that they were untrue."

[5-10] Moreover, as noted at para. 6, "... she said that she believed them to be true because she had blocked the incidents involving the appellant out of her memory. This memory returned to her in a flashback in 1990 at a time when she was being interviewed by the police in connection with further wardship proceedings. This evidence in cross-examination was a clear contradiction of her testimony in chief that she did not complain until 1990 because of her fear of the appellant." Para. 7 recorded these comments, "There were additional less significant inconsistencies in her evidence and, overall, it would not have been surprising if the jury were left with a reasonable doubt concerning the guilt of the accused."

[5-11] Nevertheless, the jury found the accused guilty. In this respect, Carthy J.A. remarked at para. 13:

> [13] I struggle as well with the testimony of a mental block and flashback, raised for the first time in response to the presentation of previously sworn irreconcilable statements. This change of testimony is as much as a cross-examiner can hope for and, if this were a trial by transcript, would raise a reasonable doubt in most readers' minds. On the other hand, the complainant stood before the jury and, presumably, gave her

explanation in a straightforward and credible manner. The members of the jury were in a position to arrive at an intuitive judgment that her final evidence of mental block and flashback was the truth. I cannot see the complainant, hear the voice as it offers explanations, or observe the body language that we all use to separate truth from fiction in face-to-face encounters.

[5-12] It will also be instructive to consider the comments of Sopinka J. in *R. v. Burke*, [1996] S.C.J. No. 27, [1996] 1 S.C.R. 474, 194 N.R. 247, 139 Nfld. & P.E.I.R. 147, 105 C.C.C. (3d) 205, 46 C.R. (4th) 195. At para. 11-13, we read:

In 1989, fourteen years after the first investigation had closed, E. came forward with startling new revelations concerning the apparently brutal treatment he had received at the hands of the Christian Brothers. As a result of E.'s claims, the investigation was eventually re-opened and E. was called to testify before a commission of inquiry (the Hughes Commission). During the course of this inquiry, it became apparent that at least some of E.'s claims regarding the Christian Brothers, particularly those concerning Mr. Burke, were gross exaggerations to say the least. Indeed, at least some of the allegations made by E. were eventually proved to have been completely false.

Prior to his appearance before the Commission of Inquiry, E. appeared on the widely viewed "Oprah Winfrey" television program. While being interviewed on that program, E. gave detailed descriptions of the forms of abuse that he had suffered at the hands of the Christian Brothers. Perhaps the most shocking of these allegations was E.'s claim that the Christian Brothers had repeatedly engaged in sexual intercourse with the children who were entrusted in their care. Needless to say, the public outrage resulting from E.'s claim was overwhelming.

When E. finally appeared before the Commission of Inquiry, it became clear that his claims of sexual intercourse between the orphans and Christian Brothers were untrue. E. eventually admitted that the events he had described on "Oprah Winfrey" had simply never occurred. In explaining why he had invented the allegations in question, E. claimed to have been "tired" at the time the interview was conducted. <u>The trial judge wisely refused to accept this feeble explanation</u>. [Emphasis supplied]

[5-13] Secondly, it will be of assistance to refer once again to the classic instruction on the subject of the evaluation of credibility, as articulated by O'Halloran J.A., speaking on behalf of the British Columbia Court of Appeal, in *Faryna v. Chorny*, [1952] 2 D.L.R. 354, 4 W.W.R. 171, at page 356 [D.L.R.]. The Court cautions against the too ready resort to demeanour as the foundation for factual conclusions.

But the validity of evidence does not depend in the final analysis on the circumstance that it remains uncontradicted, or the circumstance that the Judge may have remarked favourably or unfavourably on the evidence or the demeanour of a witness; these things are elements in testing the evidence but they are subject to whether the evidence is consistent with the probabilities affecting the case as a whole and shown to be in existence at the time...

If a trial Judge's finding of credibility is to depend solely on which person he thinks made the better appearance of sincerity in the witness box,[54] we are left with a purely arbitrary finding and justice would then depend upon the best actors in the witness box. On reflection it becomes almost axiomatic that the appearance of telling the truth is but one of the elements that enter into the credibility of the evidence of a witness. Opportunities for knowledge, powers of observation, judgment and memory, ability to describe clearly what he has seen and heard, as well as other factors, combine to produce what is called credibility ... A witness by his manner may create a very unfavourable impression of his truthfulness upon the trial Judge, and yet the surrounding circumstances in the case may point decisively to the conclusion that he is actually telling the truth. I am not referring to the

---

[54] What may be said of the appearance of the witness in terms of the selection of clothes? For example, in his autobiography, Sur la ligne de feu [Stanké: Montréal, 1988] former Chief Justice Jules Deschênes cites the example of a witness who sported not one Iron Cross, but two, during the war crimes inquiry. See page 452.

comparatively infrequent cases in which a witness is caught in a clumsy lie.[55]

[5-14] In addition, note the following observations recorded at page 357 [D.L.R.] of *Faryna v. Chorny*:

> The credibility of interested witnesses, particularly in cases of conflict of evidence, cannot be gauged solely by the test of whether the personal demeanour of the particular witness carried conviction of the truth. The test must reasonably subject his story to an examination of its consistency with the probabilities that surround the currently existing conditions. In short, the real test of the truth of the story of a witness in such a case must be its harmony with the preponderance of the probabilities which a practical and informed person would readily recognize as reasonable in that place and in those conditions. Only thus can a Court satisfactorily appraise the testimony of quick-minded, experienced and confident witnesses, and of those shrewd persons adept in the half-lie and of long and successful experience[56] in combining

---

[55] At bottom, the issue that counsel must address is best expressed in Simenon's novel Le locataire, Tout Simenon, Volume 19, Paris: Presses de la City, 1992, at page 55: "He was not lying and yet he had the impression that he was lying!" This conundrum is further illustrated by the sentence on the next page: "The most extraordinary thing is that it was true and that he ended up doubting it himself." If the individual in question cannot discern truth from dissembling, how may a trier of fact?

[56] I turn to pages 61-62 of Reed Browning's excellent biography of Cy Young, A Baseball Life, [University of

skilful exaggeration with partial suppression of the truth.

[5-15] Noteworthy as well are the following remarks, taken from *Brethour v. Law Society of British Columbia*, [1951] 2 D.L.R. 138, 1 W.W.R. 34 (B.C. C.A.), as penned by O'Halloran J.A., at page 141 [D.L.R.]:

> The credibility of interested witnesses, particularly in cases of conflict of evidence, must reasonably be subjected to an examination of the consistency of their stories with the probabilities that surround the currently existing conditions. In short, the real test of the truth of a story of a witness in such a case must be its harmony with the preponderance of the probabilities which a practical and informed person would readily recognize as reasonable in that place and under those conditions. A Court of Appeal must be satisfied that the finding of credibility in the tribunal of first instance is based, not on one element only to the exclusion of others, but is based on all the elements by which it can be tested in the particular case.

[5-16] Note as well the pains taken by Hill, J. in *R. v. N.K.D.*, [1997] O.J. No. 3877 (Gen. Div.). His Honour made plain, at para. 27, that "[a]s the trier-of-fact, I endeavoured to pay close attention to the principal witnesses during their testimony. In

---

Massachusetts Press: Amherst, Mass, 2000] to illustrate the difficulties attendant upon the re-telling of accounts over time, particularly of one's own actions. "The elderly Cy Young liked to revisit his past; these tales remind us that he was neither the first nor the last yarn-spinner to believe that good stories invite embellishment."

the end result, however, my observation of the demeanour of the witnesses was unhelpful in determining the issue of guilt or innocence."

[5-17] It might be explained that Justice Hill was at a loss to evaluate fully the subjective demeanour of the witnesses given the objective fact that he did not know these persons. Stated otherwise, how do we fully assess the demeanour of strangers in that we cannot hope to seize upon non-verbal cues such as a momentary blush unless we know that these cues are associated with certain emotions or thought process? An example is offered from Arcadian Adventures With the Idle Rich, by Stephen Leacock, drawn from "A Little Dinner with Mr. Lucullus Fyshe":

> What passed between Mr. Boulder and the Duke that evening is not known. That they must have proved congenial company to one another there is no doubt. In fact, it would seem that, dissimilar as they were in many ways, they found a common bond of interest in sport. And it is quite likely that Mr. Boulder may have mentioned that he had a hunting-lodge - what the Duke would call a shooting-box - Wisconsin woods, and that it was made of logs, rough cedar logs not squared, and that the timber wolves and others which surrounded it were of a ferocity without parallel.
>
> Those who know the Duke best could measure the effect of that upon his temperament. [Emphasis added]

[5-18] Having considered the shortcomings of the demeanour evidence, the Court opined that "[i]n evaluating the testimony of a complainant, a number of factors are worthy of consideration including the internal consistency of her

evidence, the logic and common sense of the testimony in terms of the circumstances described, the consistency of the complainant's evidence against the standard of prior statements made by her and against the defence evidence and the exhibits filed." Refer to para. 30. Noteworthy as well are these helpful observations, found at para. 33: "It is generally recognized that some differences or discrepancies in a witness' testimony, in particular when compared to prior statements of that witness out of court, may well be indicative of a truthful witness -- one who has not provided a scripted and rehearsed account, but rather one which suffers only from certain human frailties, for example, the product of a dulled memory, confusion from the stress of being a witness or other cause too insufficient to significantly affect the witness' credibility and reliability."

[5-19] By way of summary at this point, four observations may be of assistance:

1) The demeanour of a witness is an available feature in the appreciation of credibility, based on the two judgments of the Supreme Court of Canada in *R. v. Lifchus, La Corporation municipale des Cantons Unis de Stoneham et Tewkesbury v. Ouellet* and *Laurentide Motels v. Beauport (City)*;

2) A witness may present a 'positive' demeanour, including a good tone of voice and appropriate body language, that succeeds in overcoming any concerns the trier of fact may have with respect to the content of the testimony, as made plain in *R. v. Francois*;

3) A witness may be disbelieved based on the content of the testimony, as contrasted with earlier statements, notwithstanding any favourable

impression while testifying, as may be gleaned from *R. v. Burke*; and,

4) The evaluation of demeanour may be far less reliable a gauge for the veracity of testimony than is the examination of the logic and coherence of an account, chiefly on the basis of *Faryna v. Chorny*.

[5-20] In addition, it must be added that in our modern society, many individuals who testify are fluent in neither English nor French, and the Court must always be vigilant to ensure that no adverse demeanour finding is predicated upon a poor impression either as a result of resorting to an interpreter, or by failing to resort to one and having spoken in a fashion that was not as impressive as might be expected for one at least conversant in our official languages. William Zinsser's very enjoyable tome, <u>Spring Training The Unique American Story of Baseball's Annual Season of Renewal</u>, [Harper & Row: New York, 1989] includes these comments on what former Manager Jim Leyland of the Pittsburgh Pirates called "the language barrier". "I took it for granted that the Latin players on teams I managed here in the States knew what I was talking about. Some of them didn't." See page 65. The additional danger is that the advocate who has not spent sufficient time with the client may have jumped to the same conclusion.[57]

2) An examination of a precise and telling instance of demeanour evidence

---

[57] In considering the question of demeanour and difficulties with the language, refer to <u>Sosa An Autobiography</u>, by Sammy Sosa (with Marcos Breton) [Warner Books: New York, 2000]. The book reminds us of the difficulties faced by individuals who must move to a different country, in which the culture and language are different and that one should not be surprised to find that many difficulties are encountered. See page 110 in particular.

[5-21] Mindful of the instruction advanced by the Courts discussed herein, it will be of assistance to recall the guidance offered by Edgar Allan Poe in his classic story, The Tell-Tale Heart, penned in 1843. No better example of a witness literally disintegrating before the trier of fact is known, having earlier shown nothing of his guilt and having presented, *au contraire*, a confident and calm manner. Hence, this example serves to make plain that notwithstanding the general guidance to the effect that demeanour may not be too helpful in most cases, not unlike the situation of the drunken ballplayer whose bed was on fire, on occasion demeanour evidence is decisive in denying all credit to the testimony being advanced.

[5-22] In The Tell-Tale Heart, the offender believes himself safe from any prosecution for the murder he has committed, confident that the disposal of the body of his victim under the floorboards was carried out secretly. However, "As the bell sounded the hour, there came a knocking at the street door. I went down to open it with a light heart, -- for what had I now to fear? There entered three men, who introduced themselves, with perfect suavity, as officers of the police. A shriek had been heard by a neighbour during the night; suspicion of foul play had been aroused; information had been lodged at the police office, and they (the officers) had been deputed to search the premises." Refer to para. 14.

[5-23] As we read, the offender "smiled for what had he to fear?" Indeed, the murderer

> ... bade the gentlemen welcome. The shriek, I said, was my own in a dream. The old man, I mentioned, was absent in the country. I took my visitors all over the house. I bade them search -- search well. I led them, at length, to his chamber. I showed them his treasures, secure, undisturbed. In the enthusiasm of my confidence, I brought chairs into the room,

and desired them here to rest from their
fatigues, while I myself, in the wild
audacity of my perfect triumph, placed my
own seat upon the very spot beneath
which reposed the corpse of the victim."

[5-24] Refer to para. 15. Poe went to write, at para. 16:

The officers were satisfied. My *manner*[58]
had convinced them. I was singularly at
ease.[59] They sat and while I answered
cheerily, they chatted of familiar things.
But, ere long, <u>I felt myself getting pale</u> and
wished them gone. My head ached, and I
fancied a ringing in my ears; but still they
sat, and still chatted. The ringing became
more distinct: I talked more freely to get
rid of the feeling: but it continued and
gained definitiveness... [Emphasis
supplied]

[5-25] Eventually, as the villain continues to hear the heart's
beating, louder and more insistent in its constancy and effect,
his actions betray his mind's secret. The police officers
witness him speak "more quickly, more vehemently". They
saw him arise and argue "about trifles, in a high key and with

---

[58] In italics in text.

[59] On the question of seeming poise in judging demeanour,
consider <u>Arcadian Adventures With the Idle Rich</u>, by Stephen
Leacock, at Chapter 5, "The Love Story of Mr. Peter
Spillikins": "For she could see from the poise of his head how
awfully clever he was; and from the way he stood with his
hands in his side pockets she could see how manly and brave
he must be; and of course there was firmness and strength
written all over him. In short, she saw as she looked such a
Peter Spillikins as truly never existed, or could exist - or at
least such a Peter Spillikins as no one else in the world had
ever suspected before."

violent gesticulations". He then began to pace "the floor to and fro with heavy strides, as if excited to fury by the observations of the men". He then foamed ... raved ... swore!" Eventually, he swung the chair upon which he had been sitting, and grated it upon the boards. Ultimately, he confesses by words what his actions clearly have shown: "I admit the deed! -- tear up the planks! -- here, here! -- it is the beating of his hideous heart!" Refer to para. 17.

3) An examination of less obvious badges of "telling" demeanour evidence:

a) Introduction

[5-26] The function of the Court in the evaluation of demeanour evidence is to assess whether there is a typical manner of responding to questions that one expects of a credible and reliable witness and to the extent that the mannerisms of the witness whose evidence is challenged departs from this 'silhouette', which is suggested is suggestive of credit, to scrutinize it with care and, if found wanting, to refuse to accept it. The example of President Clinton touching his nose repeatedly during his "discovery process" comes to mind as does the scene from Ocean's Eleven wherein Brad Pitt coaches Matt Damon on how he should behave when answering questions, including where to look, whether to move his hands, etc.

[5-27] A digression may be apt at this point in the discussion. In reviewing the examples of potential badges of credit or discredit below, note that none is as revealing as Pinocchio's nose. The Court (and the advocate) may simply not count upon this form of involuntary lie-detector and must be mindful however that lay triers of fact may somehow believe that it is within the advocate's province to demonstrate the near-equivalent result after the impeachment by cross-examination, save perhaps in an metaphorical sense as in the case of *R. v. Burns*, [1993] A.J. No. 998, 144 A.R. 282 (Prov. Ct.), at para.

2: "This matter began as a small lie... But like Pinocchio's nose the lie grew and grew..."[60]

b) Demeanour evidence: what of the tone of voice of the witness?

[5-28] Earlier, in the introduction to the subject of demeanour evidence, reference was made to the question of the relative weight to be assigned in the evaluation of testimony to such subjective factors as the tone of voice, the presence of an ironic smile, to swallowing prior to responding, or to a nervous twitch of the eyebrows, to name but a few examples. In such cases, the question was posed: Is not the acceptance or rejection of testimony on such grounds fraught with danger? Attention is now drawn to the first of these problems: the tone of voice of a witness. May the judge or jury or other trier of fact in cases such as administrative tribunals evaluate fairly the credit to be assigned to the testimony of a witness based on that person's tone of voice?

[5-29] In this regard, recall the words of Justice Carthy respecting body language and the tone of voice in *R. v.*

---

[60]   On occasion, Jeppito' puppet may be offered to support the credit of a witness. For example, Wood J. advanced these remarks at para. 2 of *R. v. B. (S.)*, [1991] O.J. No. 244 (Prov. Div.) in the course of an examination to determine whether a child could be called as a witness: "... though she did not understand the nature of an oath, she was certainly aware of her duty to tell the truth and of the importance of her promise to do so. In response to my questioning on the consequences of telling a lie, she responded that she would get a long nose. I am satisfied that the fate of the untruthful Pinocchio was much more vivid and real to this five year old than either the concept of divine retribution or legal consequence." See also the illustration of the public's understanding of the "long liar's nose" in *Future Shop Ltd. v. A. & B. Sound Ltd.*, [1994] B.C.J. No. 851, [1994] 8 W.W.R. 376, 93 B.C.L.R. (2d) 40, 55 C.P.R. (3d) 182 (S.C.), at para. 23.

Francois (1993), 64 O.A.C. 140, [1993] O.J. No. 1419, 14 O.R. (3d) 191, 82 C.C.C. (3d) 441, 21 C.R. (4th) 350, affirmed [1994] 2 S.C.R. 827, 116 D.L.R. (4th) 69, 169 N.R. 241, 73 O.A.C. 161, 91 C.C.C. (3d) 289, 31 C.R. (4th) 201at para. 13:

> [13] I struggle as well with the testimony of a mental block and flashback, raised for the first time in response to the presentation of previously sworn irreconcilable statements. This change of testimony is as much as a cross-examiner can hope for and, if this were a trial by transcript, would raise a reasonable doubt in most readers' minds. On the other hand, the complainant stood before the jury and, presumably, <u>gave her explanation in a straightforward and credible manner</u>. The members of the jury were in a position to arrive at an intuitive judgment that her final evidence of mental block and flashback was the truth. <u>I cannot see the complainant, hear the voice as it offers explanations, or observe the body language that we all use to separate truth from fiction in face-to-face encounters</u>. [Emphasis supplied]

[5-30] What assistance is found in the world of fiction? A first instance is found in the works of Georges Simenon. "His tone of voice was less firm, proof that James was lying deliberately." Are we to follow Simenon's lead in this respect? Are we to attach credence to this apparent badge of dishonesty, the unsure or hesitant tone of voice? It appears that Commissaire Maigret did.[61] But what of the real world, the world of trials, of courtrooms, and of the almost infinite varieties and conditions of witnesses? In fairness, it may be

---

[61]   See <u>La guinguette à deux sous</u>, (<u>The Guinguette by the Seine</u>), Tout Simenon 17, at page 161.

argued with vigour that an honest witness may well be nervous and find it difficult at first to speak with any degree of confidence. This concern is typically the reason why counsel often seek to undertake questioning of a favourable witness with a series of "soft" questions to provide the witness with an opportunity to establish a measure of ease and confidence in testifying. Thus, an honest and reliable witness may not speak with a strong voice and yet present strong evidence.

[5-31] In addition, to what extent is such a badge of reliability a cultural construct, tributary as much to stereotypical views of strong men and a poor if not wholly flawed standard upon which to base findings of fact? In *Faryna v. Chorny*, [1952] 2 D.L.R. 354, 4 W.W.R. 171 (B.C.C.A.), courts are urged not to base findings of fact upon the view of which person "made the better appearance of sincerity in the witness box," as opposed to which person enjoyed the better is not the best "Opportunities for knowledge, powers of observation, judgment and memory, ability to describe clearly what he has seen and heard, as well as other factors, combine to produce what is called credibility." Refer to page 356 D.L.R.

[5-32] Nevertheless, the judgment in *R. v. Francois* (1993), 64 O.A.C. 140, [1993] O.J. No. 1419, 14 O.R. (3d) 191, 82 C.C.C. (3d) 441, 21 C.R. (4th) 350, affirmed [1994] 2 S.C.R. 827, 116 D.L.R. (4th) 69, 169 N.R. 241, 73 O.A.C. 161, 91 C.C.C. (3d) 289, 31 C.R. (4th) 201, by its reference to hearing the voice of the witness as she offered her explanations for the patent inconsistencies in her accounts, is authority for the proposition that the tone of voice of the witness is a badge of credit, to the extent that demeanour may be taken into account, and may be assessed in the evaluation of the merits of the testimony a witness has advanced.

[5-33] Finally, it may be necessary once in a while for Courts to remind themselves that some witnesses can simply not be made to speak without cursing; they are being honest when they speak in that fashion and would be less than candid if they acted otherwise. In this respect, it may be useful to recall

the views of the venerable sports writer Roger Kahn in his poetic book <u>Memories of Summer When Baseball Was An Art, And Writing About It a Game</u> [Hyperion: New York, 1997]. In attempting to describe the antics of Mickey Mantle at pages 214-231, he nevertheless opined in a balanced manner at pages 224 "Once you got past all that bristling and obscenity, in many ways he was a nice sort: A snarling, sullen hero, true, but within that frame there lived a decent fellow, waiting to break out."

c) Demeanour evidence: what if the witness swallowed while answering questions?

[5-34] The problem may be stated as follows: May we evaluate the credit to be assigned to the testimony of a witness based on that person's having swallowed prior to answering? It is a further example of a "two-edged" badge of poor demeanour in a witness that may arise and obviously a challenge may be raised by reason of a pronounced habit of swallowing prior to answering a question. For instance, in <u>L'affaire Saint-Fiacre</u>,[62] a lawyer who is described as having to swallow before having the composure to continue with his answers.

[5-35] In such a situation, it appears obvious that the Court will have to evaluate if the person testifying is a reliable witness, one "fitting the silhouette" of a trustworthy person, and ought to be able to answer without these "tell-tale" indications of nervousness or fear of having to advance unhelpful information. Indeed, it may be suggested by counsel that the fact of swallowing is simply a time gaining device,[63] not unlike

---

[62]   (<u>The Saint-Fiacre Affair</u>), Tout Simenon 17, page 339.

[63]   In attempting to evaluate such cues for lack of credibility and reliability, note that in Edgar Allan Poe's "The Facts in the Case of M. Valdemar", we read at the fourth last paragraph: "...There was an instant return of the hectic circles

the artifice of having the lawyer repeat the question in order to gain time to craft an answer. Hence, even if it suggested that the fact of swallowing is merely a nervous tic, it may be instructive for counsel to point out, on the record, that this is taking place only during cross-examination or only when the answers sought should be obvious if they are true... Indeed, it may be necessary for the Court to do so at some point, but without depriving counsel of the opportunity to exploit this element, a rather difficult tightrope to walk it seems...

d) Demeanour evidence: what if the witness hesitates prior to answering questions?

[5-36] Prior to addressing the concerns raised by this question directly, it will be of assistance to consider certain passages drawn from literature. Thus,

> "Gauthier has found sufficient sums?" A moment of hesitation, quite brief. "No, Commissioner... Let me explain it to you...".
>
> L'affaire Saint-Fiacre, (The Saint-Fiacre Affair), Tout Simenon 17, at page 319.
>
> She did her best to maintain an unaffected air, looked at her interlocutor in the eyes. But, in such cases, one may easily be misled by how natural this attitude is; the innocent who believes herself under suspicion is at times more troubled than the guilty party.

---

on the cheeks: the tongue quivered, or rather rolled violently in the mouth (although the jaws and lips remained rigid as before)."

Le passager du Polarlys [The Mystery of the 'Polarlys'], Tout Simenon 17, page 676.

[5-37] On the assumption that there is a distinction between the nervous witness and the apparently calm witness who hesitates in answering, what is the basis for the Court's evaluation of credibility? How long is too long to answer? In this regard, it must be noted that in the course of hearing the case, the Court may be well advised in appropriate (and rare) cases to time the responses of witnesses, either by producing a watch or by returning to the tape, in order to buttress a subsequent judgment that the testimony lacked spontaneity and was not credible.

[5-38] In this respect, one example of a hesitant witness who thereby betrays his lack of candour is found in Chez les Flamands (The Flemish Shop), Tout Simenon 17, page 411: "Tell me straightaway why did you make up this story of a woman you had seen on the docks". "Me?" He was trying to gain time to think, was feigning to be eating with gusto. It will be of assistance to note that Simenon expressed the view that "When someone answers 'me?' in this fashion, nine times out of ten he is attempting to buy some time." See Le fou de Bergerac (The Madman of Bergerac), Tout Simenon 17, page 508.

[5-38] What then of the apparently calm and hesitant witness who reacts in a forceful, if not too strong a fashion. Are the words found in L'affaire Saint-Fiacre, (The Saint-Fiacre Affair), Tout Simenon 17, at page 322 apposite? "He became a new man. He had been pushed to his limit. And, like all weak individuals, like all docile ones, he became unduly fierce."

[5-39] As well, it may be that proper credit should be given to those whose response are not marked by hesitation, or nervousness, such as the quick-witted response offered by Roger Couchet in L'Ombre chinoise, (The Shadow in the Courtyard), Tout Simenon 17, page 207. However, a

cautious, balanced approach might be wise in that it is rare, as noted, that an individual in a court room has not had time to prepare his or response. In fact, the Crown prosecutor in *R. v. Peavoy* (1997), 9 C.R. (5th) 83, 34 O.R. (3d) 620, 101 O.A.C. 304, 117 C.C.C. (3d) 226 (C.A.), was the subject of criticism for suggesting that the accused may have "shaped a story without fear of being contradicted by any Crown witness" in light of the disclosure brief. See pages 88-89, paras. 10-14 [C.R.].

[5-40] All in all, the hesitation may be the result of an honest attempt to search one's memory, consonant with the duty to speak the truth, as in <u>Le fou de Bergerac</u> (<u>The Madman of Bergerac</u>), Tout Simenon 17, page 472-473: "Confused, the doctor searched his memory." And, of course, a direct and apparently appropriate answer may well be entitled to great weight. For example, in <u>The Prince and the Pauper</u>, at Ch. XV, page 123, Mark Twain wrote: "The sheriff, however, saw nothing consequential in the inquiry; he answered, with simple directness..."

e) Demeanour evidence: what if the witness answers quite quickly?

[5-41] Having just now considered the precise issue of the fact of swallowing, as an example of a time gaining artifice, and the general issue of hesitation prior to answering, it may be of assistance to discuss briefly the opposite situation. In other words, what credit should the Court assign to prompt answers seemingly delivered without the time thought required to craft untruths? As a general rule, such alacrity should be assigned favourable credit. Of course, not every quick reply is worthy of credit. In this vein, consider the potential judgment you might craft of Mr. Snodgrass, Dickens' wonderfully evasive character. When it was suggested that he might have been somewhat under the influence by reason of alcohol, Snodgrass replied immediately: "It wasn't the wine ... It was

the salmon that led to his impairment of fine motor skills."[64] Recall as well the prompt response of the baseball player who was once hauled from a burning hotel room by an irate hotel manager who accused him of starting the fire by careless smoking in bed. The player's answer, which appears to have been unhesitating, was "That bed was on fire when I got into it."[65] Although apparently prompt, and thus less open to the criticism that it was the product of invention, it was so obviously bereft of inherent credit and reliability that even the most unskilled and ill-prepared advocate would succeed in discrediting the witness.

f) Demeanour evidence: what if the witness answers quite slowly?

[5-42] As noted earlier, at times it is suggested that a witness who takes a long time to answer is attempting to deceive the Court. Justice L'Heureux-Dubé had remarked in *Laurentide Motels v. Beauport (City)*, [1989] 1 S.C.R. 705, [1989] S.C.J. No. 30 (Q.L.), 94 N.R. 1, 23 Q.A.C. 1, 45 M.P.L.R. 1 at p. 799 S.C.R., at para. 245 that triers of fact are at liberty to consider the hesitations of witnesses, as did Justice Beetz in the prior judgment styled *La Corporation municipale des Cantons Unis de Stoneham et Tewkesbury v. Ouellet*, [1979] 2 S.C.R. 172, at page 195 in these words: "[…] it is possible for the trial judge [to take] into account contradictions, hesitations, the time the witness takes to answer, his expression, circumstantial evidence and the evidence as a whole [..]"

[5-43] Thus, the trier of fact may consider that any unexplained undue length of time in responding betrays fabrication in any given case. The choices open to the trier

---

[64]   Refer to Pickwick Papers, Garden City, N.Y.: Mean & Co., 1944, at page 87.

[65]   Quoted by former baseball commissioner Bowie Kuhn in his autobiography, Hardball - The Education of a Baseball Commissioner, [N.Y.: Times Books, 1987], at page 3.

of fact appear to be the following: on the one hand, a witness may be quite frank, yet very slow and deliberate in answering questions, or lying and resorting to the stratagem of dilatory responses in order to gain time to lie, on the other. Admittedly, the resolution of this vexing question is quite problematic. Although the issue does not purport to permit a simple answer, the world of fiction may assist. In <u>To Kill A Mockingbird</u>, we read that "Atticus sometimes said that one way to tell whether a witness was lying or telling the truth was to listen rather than watch: I applied his test - Tom denied it three times in one breath with no hint of whining in his voice, and I found myself believing him in spite of his protesting too much."[66] In other words, he did not hesitate to respond, and this was taken as a badge of reliability.

g) Demeanour evidence: what if the witness smiles?

[5-44] In this instance, what is debated is the problem of how the Court may evaluate the credit to be assigned to the testimony of a witness based on that person's smile. For example, the Mona Lisa's enigmatic smile has confounded generations of viewers. What was the model thinking? In the same vein, what may counsel submit in respect of a so-called "ironic smile"?[67] May judges (and juries) look to such a factor in assessing credit and reliability? Once again, it may be said that such an action is a badge of bad faith, of an attempt to deceive that is betrayed unwittingly by a nervous action. In addition, it may also be argued that without a profound knowledge of the witness in question, how may it be argued with any degree of confidence that the witness is not simply nervous?

---

[66] See page 204. [J.P. Lippincott Co.: Philadelphia, 1960].

[67] See <u>L'Ombre chinoise</u>, (<u>The Shadow in the Courtyard</u>), Tout Simenon 17, page 207.

[5-45] Recall the instruction of the Supreme Court of Canada in *Laurentide Motels v. Beauport (City)*, [1989] 1 S.C.R. 705, [1989] S.C.J. No. 30 (Q.L.), 94 N.R. 1, 23 Q.A.C. 1, 45 M.P.L.R. 1 at p. 799 S.C.R., at para. 245, wherein L'Heureux-Dubé remarked that triers of fact are at liberty to consider "the movements, glances, hesitations, trembling, blushing, surprise or bravado" of witnesses." Thus, if the trier of fact may consider blushing, surely s/he may consider smiles that are somewhat more of a voluntary action than is a blush.[68] Not unlike the suspicious mother in La danseuse du Gai-Moulin who "...would watch for any expressions on the face of her son"[69] in order to gauge the veracity of his words, judges and juries in their attempt to evaluate not only the words of witnesses, but their demeanour, may look to such actions as smiles, but warily one would suggest.

[5-46] A further example is drawn from Arcadian Adventures With the Idle Rich, by the celebrated Canadian economist and humourist, Dr. Stephen Leacock, more precisely from Chapter 3, "The Arrested Philanthropy of Mr. Tomlinson" and illustrates how difficult it is to distinguish a sneer from a smile:

---

[68] A good example is drawn from Le locataire, Tout Simenon, Volume 19, Paris: Presses de la City, 1992, at page 38: "'Elie avait le sang aux joues." [Translation: "Elie's cheeks had reddened."] Note as well page 102, Ch. XIV of Mark Twain's The Prince and the Pauper: "A sharp pressure upon Tom's arm stopped his foolish tongue and sent a blush to his face; but no countenance there betrayed any sign that this strange speech had been remarked or given concern."

[69] (At the Gai-Moulin), Tout Simenon 17, page 30. At page 48 of the same novel, one reads that a person being questioned appeared sincere in the surprise he manifested at a question. Can it be said that any such observation is grounded in anything but a subjective evaluation devoid of being subjected to any form of objective review?

And a few hours from that, while the town was still ringing with news of his downfall, the Wizard with his wife and son walked down from their thousand-dollar suite into the corridor, their hands burdened with their satchels. A waiter, with something between a sneer and an obsequious smile upon his face, reached out for the valises, wondering if it was still worth while […]

[5-47] While we are on the subject of a person's look. Consider a further example taken from Chapter 1, "A Little Dinner with Mr. Lucullus Fyshe". It provides a useful example of what I the author fittingly described as "the dumb pathos look".

There are broad steps leading up to the club, so broad and so agreeably covered with matting that the physical exertion of lifting oneself from one's motor to the door of the club is reduced to the smallest compass. The richer members are not ashamed to take the steps one at a time, first one foot and then the other; and at tight money periods, when there is a black cloud hanging over the Stock Exchange, you may see each and every one of the members of the Mausoleum Club dragging himself up the steps after this fashion, his restless eyes filled with the dumb pathos of a man wondering where he can put his hand on half a million dollars. [Emphasis added]

[5-48] In terms of any possible analysis, may we as judges know that the witness who presents with such a look is seeking a half million dollars, had a fight with his or her partner, is sad that pitcher Eric Gagné did not make it big with

158

the Red Sox, etc? What may be discerned from the looks of a witness is beyond science and is not an art. Finally, in the evaluation of credibility in respect of the facial expression, Whitey Ford's autobiography Slick, (written with Phil Pepe) [William Morrow and Company, Inc.: New York, 1987] may be of assistance as the Hall of Fame pitcher explains how Lew Burdette, who "had the reputation of throwing the best spitter in baseball" took him aside one day and stated "I'll show you how to throw it even though I don't throw it myself." See page 192. Ford added, "Lew said it with a straight face."

h) Demeanour evidence: is it not simply a question of nervousness versus deceit?

[5-49] The foregoing discussion might have originated with this theme but it was thought wiser to structure the presentation of the elements of the discussion in the manner selected to better make plain how so many of the so-called badges of demeanour amount to an evaluation of nervousness versus deceit. In this vein, consider the following examples drawn from the world of Commissaire Maigret.

> Maigret displayed a quite neutral expression, a look bereft of any thoughts. Is it not strange, that we all met again after so many years! ... added Van Damme, who did not appear to be able to suffer a period of silence.
>
> Le pendu de Saint-Pholien (Maigret and the Hundred Gibbets), Tout Simenon 16, page 136.
>
> By means of a number of seemingly insignificant details, such as the manner of being, of taking a seat, of looking out, Maigret recognized him as one of those unusual individuals who, though guilty of no wrongful act, cannot help but betray

anxiety when confronted by the police.
[Emphasis supplied]

Le pendu de Saint-Pholien (Maigret and
the   Hundred   Gibbets),
Tout Simenon 16, pages 143-144.

And Maigret examined the hands of the
civil servant, who blanched to the point
that the Commissioner thought for a
moment that he would faint. His lips were
trembling. He was unable to speak.

L'Ombre chinoise, (The Shadow in the
Courtyard),
Tout Simenon 17, page 205.

[5-50] Not unlike the example Simenon provides in the text above, what of the nervous, often garrulous, witness who fills any period of silence with additional comments or observations? Are they to be disbelieved in the judgments we pen because they do not follow the usual admonition to only answer the questions that are posed by counsel, a piece of advice made famous of late before Justice Oliphant? Will this result in unfairness to the garrulous witness who appears to be less than stolid due to the very fact of being in a court-room? In considering the answers to these questions, note simply the assistance found in the title of Mr. Alan D. Gold's comment, "The Average, Nervous, Inadequate, Inarticulate, In Short, Typical Accused's Defence", in 22 C.R. (4th) 253. Many witnesses, not just the accused, may be described in that fashion.[70]

---

[70]   At times, especially when counsel is suggesting that a witness made a quite poor impression while testifying and that the person's degree of inarticulateleness suggests a lack of credit, it may be useful to point out the quite signal instruction found in Mr. Gold's article. In fact, a judgment in appropriate

[5-51] What is important in such cases is for the Court to determine whether the witness is attempting to "pad the story", so to speak, by means of additional unsolicited comments or, instead, if the person is simply nervous and speaking, "afin de meubler le silence". [To fill in dead air] A further example is found at page 243 of Le charretier de la Providence, (The Crime at Lock 14), Tout Simenon 16. Simenon notes that the individual being questioned by Commissaire Maigret was, at the same time, incapable of containing herself and incapable of lying as well. Otherwise, it is added, she would have advanced a far more complex account of events.

[5-52] For yet a further example, note that in Pietr le Letton (The Case of Peter the Lett), Tout Simenon 16, page 429, we find an interesting description: "The Lett was trembling. It was patent. And, he was unusually nervous. His face, his entire body was agitated by multiple nervous tics". Consider also the inherent shortcomings of drawing conclusions respecting demeanour from factors such as the "... actions of his white hands betrayed his nervousness...". See La Nuit du Carrefour (The Crossroad Murders), Tout Simenon 16, page 476.

[5-53] Of course, one must answer the question: is the nervousness due to a guilty mind or by reason of the involvement of the authorities and the fear of being a victim of a mistaken belief in guilt held by the authorities?

---

cases may include reference to individuals who should be at ease when speaking, let us say a television or radio announcer, but who may well have a remarkable lack of precision on a bad day. One example is found in Tom Cheek's informative book, Road to Glory An Insider's Look at 16 Years of Blue Jays Baseball, (with Howard Berger) [Warwick Publishing Inc: Toronto, 1993]. As we read at page 60, one broadcast partner of Mr. Cheek once stated "... there's a ground ball to first ... he goes to second for one, back to first ... not in time! Well dad-gum-it, they didn't done it at first but they did at second."

[5-54] On the other hand, the Court must consider whether the individual who testifies in a relaxed, self-assured, fashion is not, in the words of Simenon, at page 157 of <u>Maigret and the Hundred Gibbets</u>, merely bluffing. Consider the comments in <u>Les 13 coupables</u>, Tout Simenon 17, at page 849, in which Simenon writes: "They are shown to be lying and they remain untroubled. They will go on to relate another story, with the same unawareness."

[5-55] In this respect, note the comments of the Court of Appeal in *R. v. Ahluwalia*, [2000] O.J. No. 4544, 149 C.C.C. (3d) 193 (C.A.), at para. 35:

> I find it hard to give any credence to a submission that the appellant established entrapment on the balance of probabilities based on a version of events which is directly contrary to his own evidence and places the entrapment some weeks before the appellant says there was any mention of drugs. The appellant's argument comes down to this: O'Connell J. erred in failing to find that the appellant had established entrapment on the balance of probabilities based on events which the appellant insisted never happened! <u>The futility of the submission is self-evident</u>. [Emphasis supplied]

i) Demeanour evidence: what of laughter in separating nervousness versus deceit?

[5-56] Once again, it will be of assistance to begin the discussion of this theme by means of certain references to the world of Georges Simenon and to Commissaire Maigret. In the first example, "Did you not think to speak to the authorities of Mr. Clément's visit? My goodness... To hide his concern, he tried to laugh," taken from <u>Monsieur Gallet, décédé</u> (<u>The Death of Monsieur Gallet</u>), Tout Simenon 16, page 40, it

appears obvious that the witness is pausing to think, having resort to the artifice of laughter. On other hand, note the following comments: "Blood's oath... You are saying that I would have... Ha ha! If that doesn't beat all... This is better than what you see at the cinema..." Refer to <u>Au Rendez-Vous des Terre-Neuvas</u> (<u>The Sailors' Rendez-vous</u>) Tout Simenon 16, page 681. One gains the definite impression, if not belief, that the laughter is meant to permit some invention to be devised.

[5-57] In this respect, as made plain by these two examples, it is not uncommon for triers of fact to be confronted with witnesses who react to stressful questions by laughing. Is this a hint that they are insincere or, to the contrary, is it the badge of the honest witness whose demeanour is upset by the stress of the situation?[71] Common sense and experience will suggest that honest individuals may react to difficult questions by smiling and, at times, by laughing. Thus, although laughter may well be a sign of lack of respect for the court and it may betray a lack of concern for the solemnity of the occasion, it is not always a signpost for lack of candour. As noted earlier, Trainor, J. advises jurors as follows: "Bear in mind that a courtroom is a strange place for most people..." Refer to *Vanderbyl v. I.C.B.C.*, [1993] 6 W.W.R. 725, 79 B.C.L.R. (2d) 156, [1993] B.C.J. No. 1007 (S.C.), at para. 20:

> In both civil and criminal proceedings when sitting with a jury it is the responsibility of the trial judge to instruct them on the course they should follow when dealing with the testimony of

---

[71] A further example of laughter being a nervous reaction to an unexpected event is drawn from <u>Le locataire</u>, Tout Simenon, Volume 19, Paris: Presses de la City, 1992, at page 23: « Ce qui arriva alors fut si inattendu qu'il faillit éclater d'un rire nerveux. » [Translation: « What then transpired was so unexpected that he might have burst out from nervous laughter. »]

witnesses. Those instructions apply, as well, to the task facing a judge sitting without a jury. I usually say something to a jury along the following lines:

> When you think about the evidence of a witness concern yourself about their opportunity to observe. What chance did they have to observe whatever it was about which they are testifying? What are their powers of observation? Generally what kind of an individual are they? Are they the kind of person that you can rely on to give you an accurate account? You have to make that decision on the basis of their general evidence and your impression of the individual as they gave you their evidence.
>
> ...
>
> In carrying out your task you should reflect upon the demeanour or appearance in the witness box of each of the witnesses. With each witness you will look at his interest or disinterest, integrity, knowledge of facts. Is he reliable? Is he careful? Gauge as well as you can the honesty and capacity of a witness. <u>Bear in mind that a courtroom is a strange place for most people</u>, and remember that the testimony of each of the witnesses must be regarded in the light of all of the circumstances, including what other

persons have said. [Emphasis supplied]

[5-58] In the ultimate analysis, are triers of fact able to "read faces"?[72] In attempting to frame a response, note that in Le locataire, Simenon wrote: « [Translation: Elie's smile was mechanical. It was a result of nerves. In reality ... he was watching Mrs. Baron's face and he had seen something pass over her features: a doubt, a suspicion, possibly even less than that, a reticence or a fugitive thought. »[73] Is it really possible to be able for anyone firstly to note all of these impressions from observing someone, even someone known to us and, if so, is it possible to make fine judgments as to what is going in the mind of someone else?

j) Demeanour evidence: What of the inarticulate individual?

[5-59] The inarticulate individual is a great challenge for the Court. As Mr. Gold points out in his above-noted article, a good number of accused persons, and witnesses for that matter, will not be articulate. In fact, many witnesses appear to be in the habit of communicating in half sentences, for fear of saying too much or, more simply, out of fear of resorting to the wrong word or expression. Not infrequently, people are in the habit of communicating in an elliptical fashion with their spouses, by way of limited example, and they may present themselves in a poor light in the witness stand as a result. At times, this is the case of individuals who commonly resort to profanity to pepper their words and who cannot express

---

[72] Note the following observations consigned at page 72 of the immortal Cry, The Beloved Country" by Alan Paton: "Her face was honest and open, and she did not drop her eyes again." [Scribner: New York, 1987].

[73] Tout Simenon, Volume 19, Paris: Presses de la City, 1992, at page 39. In the same vein, what do we make of the description at page 72 that the party was raising his eyebrows either by reason of discomfort or as a result of contemplation.

themselves clearly, out of habit, if they cannot curse at the same time.

[5-60] Literature illustrates these troubling situations. For example, "You three were in agreement to propose to me... It was not necessary to complete the sentence. All could be understand with half-words. Even silence could be understood; one could almost hear the other's thoughts." See Le pendu de Saint-Pholien (Maigret and the Hundred Gibbets), Tout Simenon 16, page 170. Consider also: "His countenance, however, spoke volumes respecting his thoughts... ", a quote taken from La danseuse du Gai-Moulin (At the Gai-Moulin), Tout Simenon 17, page 50.

[5-61] Again, care should be taken to assess the demeanour in a responsible fashion, being guided, to track the language of the above noted judgments, by considerations including the internal consistency of the evidence, the logic and common sense of the testimony in terms of the circumstances described, the consistency of the evidence against the standard of prior statements and against the contrary evidence and the exhibits filed.

[5-62] At bottom, in this and in each instance of demeanour evidence, is there not a fundamental flaw in attempting to ascertain the thoughts of individuals based on their countenance?[74] It is no doubt appropriate in many cases to evaluate a person's thoughts based on actions that appear instinctive or spontaneous, such as the recognition of a person when this is unexpected. For example, in La danseuse du Gai-Moulin (At the Gai-Moulin), Tout Simenon 17, at page 63, Simenon writes "Suddenly he turned around, saw Maigret, pointed him out while turning crimson." But the courtroom is rarely a place for spontaneous physical reactions given the time to reflect upon the questions to be put.

---

[74] In the tale, "The Fall of the House of Usher", Edgar Allan Poe records at para. 8 "A glance, however, at his countenance convinced me of his perfect sincerity.'

k) Demeanour evidence: What if the witness presents with a 'blank expression'?

"The poor are in the habit of curbing the expression of their lack of hope...".

Le pendu de Saint-Pholien (Maigret and the Hundred Gibbets), Tout Simenon 16, page 123.

She had the look of someone who is troubled but who wishes to present a natural appearance...

La tête d'un homme (A Battle of Nerves), Tout Simenon 16, page 782.

Quite an odd individual, half one thing and half another, neither young nor old, not handsome, not plain, perhaps devoid of any thoughts, perhaps chock full of secrets.

La guinguette à deux sous, (The Guinguette by the Seine), Tout Simenon 17, page 118.

[5-63] The question that the advocate must ask and the Court must answer is: What if these individuals are in the habit of curbing their sorrow, their dejection? Will this fact rebound to their disadvantage in a case in which they have been victimized? In a courtroom setting, the trier of fact "meets" the witness from the box and must judge that person based on the demeanour of the witness and the answers provided to the questions being put. Will a true portrait emerge, not just of the "warts and all" but of the life experience of the person, and of the subtle influences that have left an indelible imprint on that person's personality and manner of expression. In this

respect, consider *R. v. Shokohi-Manesh* (1991), 8 B.C.A.C. 263, 17 W.A.C. 263 (C.A.), wherein the Court of Appeal notes the opinion of a probation officer that the accused's ongoing pattern of criminal activity may have been consistent with the "second year syndrome" which many newcomers to Canada experience. It is characterized by loneliness, depression, confusion...". Refer to page 264, para. 6. If an individual who testifies is labouring under this difficulty, will the trier of fact know of it?

[5-64] On the other hand, the confident witness may be seen as too sure of him(her)self, as in <u>Le Relais d'Alsace</u> (<u>The Man from Everywhere</u>), Tout Simenon 16, at page 856: "He was young. His eyes expressed the thought: Whack! Try to top that answer!" In this vein, note that, Dr. H.E. Emson, the author of <u>The Doctor and the Law</u>, (3rd edition) [1995, Butterworths, Markham] remarks that doctors are accustomed to work in a highly structured micro-society which they dominate and implies that this sometimes serves to place them in a somewhat unfavourable light when testifying in the context of the adversarial system. See pages 69-70

[5-65] In addition, we must always be mindful that signal issues arise when a person remaining mute when faced with a damning accusation. See <u>Les 13 coupables</u>, Tout Simenon 17, at page 845, wherein the police drew unfavourable conclusions from the refusal of the person interviewed to answer questions. See also <u>Chez les Flamands</u> (<u>The Flemish Shop</u>), Tout Simenon 17, at page 405.

I) Demeanour evidence: What if the witness testified with facial expressions?

[5-66] Having just now considered counsel's options in the case of a witness who testifies with a 'blank expression', it will be of assistance to consider the converse scenario: that is to say what may the advocate submit in respect of the presence

of facial expressions? More to the point, if counsel wishes to point out to the trier of fact how certain facial reactions may have betrayed the true thoughts of a witness, reference may be had to The Prince and the Pauper, at Ch. III, page 12 wherein Mark Twain wrote: "… the young prince sprang to the gate with his face flushed, and his eyes flashing with indignation…" On the other hand, in cross-examining a police officer, you may wish to recall the words found at Ch. XV, page 123 of the same novel: "The sheriff, however, saw nothing consequential in the inquiry; he answered, with simple directness…" Note as well the following example to illustrate that the expression of a witness may demonstrate the truth or falsity of the words spoken. As we read in Prince, at Ch. XIX, page 159: "… the boy's face, and his answers, too, showed that the things she was talking of were not familiar to him."

[5-67] Further, a judge must ask: what does a stone gaze, or other facial expression, tell us about the truth of an account? It is possible to lie while looking straight into the eyes of the person sought to be deceived?   Consider this example, "'Grant me one thing'", he said, "Let your eyes rest upon mine, so that I may see if they be steady. There – now answer me." Refer to The Prince and the Pauper, Ch. XXVI, p. 210.

[5-68] One further example from the same book follows: "She stood still, during an impressive pause of several moments; then slowly lifted up her head and looked into Hendon's eyes with a stony and frightened gaze; the blood sank out of her face, drop by drop, till nothing remained but the gray pallor of death; then she said, in a voice as dead as the face, 'I know him not!' and turned, with a moan and a stifled sob, and tottered out of the room." See Ch. XXV, pp. 203-204.

[5-69] Twain provides one example of this sort of situation, which I may describe as that of an apparent "frank look". At p. 14, Ch. I, of Pudding'head Wilson, we read: "He was a homely, freckled, sandy-haired young fellow, with an intelligent blue eye that had frankness and comradeship in it and a covert twinkle of a pleasant sort." [Emphasis supplied] That

people can be mistaken, or of two minds, while attempting to read one's thoughts by the expression of the face, is demonstrated by the next reference: "Angelo thought he had a good eye; Luigi thought there was something veiled and sly about it." See Chap. XI, p. 70.

[5-70] Consider as well the assistance provided by Shakespeare. Thus, in attempting to counter opposing counsel's submissions that the demeanour of witnesses was not satisfactory, it may be of assistance to refer to <u>Macbeth</u>, at Act I, sc. iv, l. 12: "There's no art To find the mind's construction in the face...".[75] Of course, as is often the case with litigation wherein it is the function of counsel to "reverse the proposition", so to peak, this submission may be countered with a reference to Act I, sc. vi, l. 63: "Your face, my thane, is a book, where men May read strange matters."[76]

[5-71] Further assistance is found in Chapter 2 of <u>Arcadian Adventures With the Idle Rich</u>, by Stephen Leacock, "The Wizard of Finance" which I would title: "Judge the puzzled look: if you are able to, not being an insider". Although the passage is quite lengthy, I find it to be an outstanding example and expression of the shortcomings of demeanour evidence:

> And as the page boy found him and handed him on a salver a telegram to read, the eyes of the crowd about him

---

[75] Consider as well if the following reference is apposite: "False face must hide what the false heart doth know", found at Act I, sc. vii, l. 82 of <u>Macbeth</u>.

[76] On the question of the general lack of weight to be accorded to evidence of demeanour, see G. Renaud, "Evidence of Demeanour: Some Instruction Found in the Early Works of Georges Simenon" (1998), 21(4) <u>Prov. Judges J.</u> 523 and especially, <u>Demeanour Evidence On Trial: A Legal and Literary Criticism</u>, [Melbourne: Sandstone Academic Press, 2007.]

turned for a moment to look upon the figure of Tomlinson, the Wizard of Finance.

There he stood in his wide-awake hat and his long black coat, his shoulders slightly bent with his fifty-eight years. Anyone who had known him in the olden days on his bush farm [...] would have recognized him in a moment. There was still on his face that strange, puzzled look that it habitually wore, only now, of course, the financial papers were calling it "unfathomable." There was a certain way in which his eye roved to and fro inquiringly that might have looked like perplexity, were it not that the Financial Undertone had recognized it as the "searching look of a captain of industry." One might have thought that for all the goodness in it there was something simple in his face, were it not that the Commercial and Pictorial Review had called the face "inscrutable," and had proved it so with an illustration that left no doubt of the matter.

Indeed, the face of Tomlinson of Tomlinson's Creek, now Tomlinson the Wizard of Finance, was not commonly spoken of as a face by the paragraphers of the Saturday magazine sections, but was more usually referred to as a mask; and it would appear that Napoleon the First had had one also. The Saturday editors were never tired of describing the strange, impressive personality of Tomlinson, the great dominating character of the newest and highest finance. From the moment when the interim prospectus of the Erie Auriferous Consolidated had broken like a tidal wave over Stock Exchange circles, the picture of Tomlinson, the sleeping shareholder of uncomputed millions, had filled the imagination of every dreamer in a nation of poets.

[...]

"The face," so wrote the editor of the "Our Own Men" section of Ourselves Monthly, "is that of a typical American captain of finance, hard, yet with a certain softness, broad but with a certain length, ductile but not without its own firmness."

"The mouth," so wrote the editor of the "Success" column of Brains, "is strong but pliable, the jaw firm and yet movable, while there is something in the set of the ear that suggests the swift, eager mind of the born leader of men."

[...]

Some writers grew lyric about him. What visions, they asked, could one but read them, must lie behind the quiet, dreaming eyes of that inscrutable face?

They might have read them easily enough, had they but had the key. Anyone who looked upon Tomlinson as he stood there in the roar and clatter of the great rotunda of the Grand Palaver with the telegram in his hand, fumbling at the wrong end to open it, might have read the visions of the master-mind had he but known their nature. They were simple enough. For the visions in the mind of Tomlinson, Wizard of Finance, were for the most part those of a wind-swept hillside farm [...] And if the eyes of the man are dreamy and abstracted, it is because there lies over the vision of this vanished farm an infinite regret, greater in its compass than all the shares the Erie Auriferous Consolidated has ever thrown upon the market. [Emphasis added][77]

[5-72a] For those familiar with the book will know he knows nothing about finances, stocks, etc.!!! In fact, consider this further passage touching again on the relative lack of sound judgment which an assessment of the "look" of an individual permits in cases of what might be called a "put on appearance":

"I put it to him in a casual way," related, for example, Mr. Lucullus Fyshe, "casually, but quite frankly. I said, 'See here, this is just a bagatelle to you, no doubt, but to me it might be of some use. T. C. bonds,' I said, 'have risen twenty-two and a half in a week. You know as well as I do that they are only collateral trust, and that the stock underneath never could and never can earn a par dividend. Now,' I said, 'Mr. Tomlinson, tell me what all that means?' Would you believe it, the fellow looked me right in the face in that

---

[77]   Consider as well a further example from Chapter 3, "The Arrested Philanthropy of Mr. Tomlinson" touching upon the question of a flushed face: "At the sight of him the Wizard's face flushed for a moment, with a look of his old perplexity [...]" How might a detached neutral observer be able to know anything about this person's "old" state of mind"?

queer way he has and he said, 'I don't know!'" [Emphasis added]

"He said he didn't know!" repeated the listener, in a tone of amazement and respect. "By Jove! eh? he said he didn't know! The man's a wizard!" "And he looked as if he didn't!" went on Mr. Fyshe. "That's the deuce of it. That man when he wants to can put on a look, sir, that simply means nothing, absolutely nothing." [Emphasis added]

m) Demeanour evidence: What may we conclude from eye movements?

[5-72b] As noted earlier, in any discussion on the subject of credibility, the issue of the relative merits of demeanour evidence is bound to dominate. In deciding whether to accept or to reject testimony, reference was made to a number of so-called "badges" of honesty and of deceit, including the possible nervous twitch of the eyebrows. To be more precise, recall that in Laurentide Motels Ltd. v. Beauport (City), [1989] 1 S.C.R. 705, at p. 799 S.C.R., para. 245, L'Heureux-Dubé remarks that triers of fact are at liberty to consider "the movements, glances etc. In this respect, consider as well the comments of Lord Shaw of Dunfermline in Clarke v. Edinburgh and District Tramways Company Limited, [1919] S.C. (H.L.). 35, at page 37: "...[a] witness without any conscious bias towards a conclusion may have in their demeanour, in their manner, in their hesitation, in the nuance of their expression, in even the turns of the eyelid, left an impression [upon the trier of fact]..."

[5-73] Once again, some benefit is gained from studying the works of Georges Simenon." Indeed, what if the witness betrays no more than a nervous twitch, let us say of the

eyebrows.[78] May it be said of that person that s/he can fairly be castigated as being guilty of a tell-tale badge of dishonesty. Again, it may be advantageous to call the trier of fact's attention to when this occurs, but if it is possible to film the proceedings and avoid having the witness's attention drawn to the matter, this is the preferred course.[79] And, nevertheless, what weight may be assigned to a witness who is able (or not) to look the accuser in the eyes? As we read at page 69 of Le locataire, the police inspector looked at the suspect intently and she withstood his gaze without flinching.[80]

n) Demeanour evidence: The latest guidance from the Supreme Court of Canada

[5-74] Para. 49 of *R. v. R.E.M.*, [2008] 3 S.C.R. 3 makes passing reference to this question as follows:

> [49] While it is useful for a judge to attempt to articulate the reasons for believing a witness and disbelieving another in general or on a particular point, the fact remains that the exercise may not be purely intellectual and may involve factors that are difficult to verbalize. Furthermore, embellishing why a particular witnesss's evidence is rejected may involve the judge saying unflattering things about the witness; judges may wish

---

[78] See Le fou de Bergerac (The Madman of Bergerac), Tout Simenon 17, page 459 and Liberty Bar, Tout Simenon 17, pages 775 and 794.

[79] Note that in Le locataire, Tout Simenon, Volume 19, Paris: Presses de la City, 1992, at page 15, we are reminded that eyes may be constantly expressing laughter. « ... des yeux clairs qui riaient toujours ». On the other hand, as we read at page 45, a person's eyes may also express anger.

[80] Tout Simenon, Volume 19, Paris: Presses de la City, 1992, at page 69.

to spare the accused who takes the stand to deny the crime, for example, the indignity of not only rejecting his evidence and convicting him, but adding negative comments about his demeanour. In short, assessing credibility is a difficult and delicate matter that does not always lend itself to precise and complete verbalization. [Emphasis added]

3) Conclusion

[5-75] Recall that in The Prince and the Pauper, at Ch. XIX, page 159, Mark Twain wrote "... the boy's face, and his answers, too, showed that the things she was talking of were not familiar to him." It is suggested that this is the ideal situation for counsel who has called the witness or who relies upon the testimony in question. Indeed, whatever criticism demeanour evidence may be rightly accused of, an answer which is apparently corroborated by the look of the witness may well be accepted with little hesitation.

[5-76] At all events, as the examples taken from the world of Simenon illustrate, it is neither simple nor scientific to place too much emphasis on such intangible and subjective signs. In the final analysis, the appreciation of demeanour and of the credit and reliability to be assigned to testimony, as will be seen in the chapters that follow, is fraught with signal difficulties. In this context, it is important to recall the sage guidance of Georges Simenon in Le charretier de la Providence, (The Crime at Lock 14), Tout Simenon 16, at page 197: "...la réalité était invraisemblable". [Translation: The truth is implausible at times.]

Chapter 6
Concerns in judicial fact finding and the assistance gained from literature

1) Introduction

[6-1] By way of introductory comment, I do not wish to be understood to be suggesting that there is no assistance to be found in the existing professional literature on the task of adjudication as influenced by classic writings   To the contrary. I am suggesting that this book seeks to enhance our profession's ability to dispense justice by examining the scholarly writings, and other writings including popular literature, that are available from the perspective of a trial judge.   Indeed, I could not hope to improve upon the contributions of such excellent scholars as Professor Lucia A. Silecchia whose excellent and exhaustive contribution to the subject matter stimulated my original interest.[81]

[6-2] In effect, a number of authors have succeeded in integrating legal themes and structure into the very hearts of their novels, as pointed out by Professor Richard Weisberg in his introductory remarks to Volume VI(2) of the ALSA Forum 125-126 (1982), at page 125, with particular mention of Kafka, Camus and Dostoevski.

[6-3] Further, although this text has made reference thus far to classic literature, I do not wish to be understood to suggest that judges ought to concentrate solely on great literary works as a necessary apprenticeship to success as a member of the judiciary and thereby neglect the study of classic legal thought, far from it.   Indeed, one ought to enjoy the leisure of being able to devote some time each week to reviewing professional journals and texts in order to continue to add to

---

[81]   Refer to her article "Things Are Seldom What They Seem: Judges and Lawyers in the Tales of Mark Twain", (2002-2003) 35 <u>Conn. L. Rev</u>. 559-646

our knowledge of the Law in the broadest sense. By way of limited example, the first line of Professor Carol Weisbrod's article, "Family Governance: A Reading of Kafka's Letter to his Father", (1992-1993) 24 U. Tol. L. Rev. 689-723 quotes the immortal Jeremy Bentham: "The feebleness of infancy demands a continual protection."[82] I know of no better expression of the task that was entrusted to me when I presided over child protection hearings.

[6-4] In framing the parameters of the various themes to be addressed, I am mindful of the historical fact that judicial attitudes will be modified over the course of time, not least by the influence of the writings of novelists and playwrights, as has been the case repeatedly in the past.[83] Indeed, the attitudes of novelists themselves will be modified over the course of time, as made plain in the illuminating foreword to a Symposium entitled "Then, Now and Into the Future: A Century of Legal Conflict and Development", by Professor Lawrence P. Wilkins, (1994-1995) 28 Ind. L. Rev. 135-138, with particular reference to Mark Twain at pages 136-137.

[6-5] In this vein, I can do no better than to track the language of Mark Twain as consigned in a Tribute: "Loyalty to a petrified opinion never broke a chair or freed a human soul."[84]

[6-6] That being said, I wish to underscore that many writers and works are not relevant to this text which is devoted to fact finding. By way of limited example, there are passages which are found in Kafka's The Trial which are of assistance in cases

---

[82]   Quoting from Jeremy Bentham, Theory of Legislation (1840), at page 248.

[83]   Consider the brief reference to the development of judicial and legal attitudes toward private law found at pages 371-372 of a book review by Samuel Somenfield on Bernard Schwartz's The Law in America: A History (1974), found at pages 371-373, 24 Clev. St. L. Rev.

[84]   See Paul Roach's comments at page 305, (1992) 27 Land & Water L. Rev.

in which it is suggested by the prosecution that the material requested by the defence is so far-reaching in nature that to give effect to the request for production would result in aborting the trial in that little information about the activities of the defendant would fall outside of such an expanded notion of relevance. As we read at page 181 of "The Return of the Real Giving Consent to Abstraction", by Timothy J. Scott, (2001) 10 Griffith L. Rev. 179-191: "Innocence cannot, as Josef K. discovers, de declared – much less proved – in the absence of knowledge of the accusation; in the words of the arresting wardens, 'he admits that he doesn't know the Law and yet claims he's innocent.' Similarly, in drafting his defence, Josef K. notes that 'without knowing the nature of the charge and all its possible ramifications, his entire life, down to the smallest actions and events, would have to be called to mind, described, and examined from all sides'".[85]

[6-7] Finally, as a necessary caveat, I think it necessary to underscore that I profess no skill in literary criticism. Thus, I

---

[85]   [Footnotes omitted]   Consider as well the following passage taken from The Problem of Our Laws: "Our laws are not generally known; they are kept secret by the small group of nobles who rule us. We are convinced that these ancient laws are scrupulously administered; nevertheless it is an extremely painful thing to be ruled by laws that one does not know." Quoted at page 128 of "The Law of the State in Kafka's The Trial", by Martha S. Robinson, (1982) 6 ALSA Forum 127-148. It is not doubted that there are many who believe that any expression of what is claimed to be a legitimate wish to curtail inappropriate disclosure of a wealth of useless information in cases involving suspected terrorists is merely a sham or pretext. Consider the recent review of the entire question of suspected terrorists in the recently released [and heavily censored] The Eight O'Clock Ferry to the Windward Side Seeking Justice in Guantanamo Bay, by Clive Stafford Smith, New York: Nation Books, 2007.

agree with the following comment: "We do not pretend to be efficient in literary criticism..."[86] But this limitation ought not to hinder our purpose as fact finders in seeking out all of the resources which will enhance our skills in discharging our judicial tasks.

2) Discussion

a) The judge must acquire a general understanding of culture

[6-8] Although the contributions of Shakespeare to judging require no introduction, I will nevertheless make reference to Steven M. Oxenhandler's writings, specifically a quotation from Justice Felix Frankfurter by means of which he began his article, "The Lady Doth Protest Too Much Methinks: The Use of Figurative Language from Shakespeare's Hamlet in American Case Law", 23 Hamline L. Rev. 371-393, at page 371: "No one can be a truly competent lawyer unless he [or she] is a cultivated man [or woman] ... the best way to prepare for the law is to come to the study of law as a well-read person."[87]

---

[86]   A comment expressed by Professor Igor Grazin at page 339 of his article "Kafka's Myth of Law in the Context of the Legal Irrationality Inspired by the Russian Post-Communist Market Place", (1987) 8 Mich. YBI Legal Studies 335-364.

[87]   Although no reference is given, the quotation is found in a text entitled Trial and Error: An Oxford Anthology of Legal Stories, edited by Fred Shapiro and Jane Garry, Oxford, Oxford University Press, 1998.   Indeed, they refer to it as having been penned by Justice Frankfurter in a contribution entitled "Advice to a Young Man Interested in Going into Law". Refer to a book review of Trial and Error, by Sandra Petersson, [2001] VUW L. Rev. 53, at page 53 and to the review of Modern Eloquence, a ten set volume, at page 112 of (1902-1903) 1 Okla L.J. 112-113.

[6-9] Indeed, Professor Oxenhandler went on to remark at page 372: "... Besides relishing the beauty and lasting power of 'Shakespeare's] expression, lawyers, more than most people, depend heavily on words and language; they must be sensitive to nuance and meaning." The author then remarked: "Second, judges, like writers, are essentially 'wordsmiths'. ... [they] use the keyboard and paper as hammer and anvil to forge solutions to legal issues. Shakespeare used over 21,000 words, inventing 1,686 new words, including the word 'obscene'. Shakespeare's plays, therefore, serve as a fertile ground for judges to use when fashioning opinions." [Footnotes omitted]

[6-10] In addition, a further passage of note from page 372 reads: "Third, because the law is inherently about resolving disputes, Shakespeare's legal and non-legal themes provide insight into our own society, thereby aiding current-day judges in fashioning rules that people will understand and accept. The proper use of a Shakespeare quote illuminates a judicial opinion. Correct use of a Shakespeare quote serves not merely as description, ornament, or truism, it can form the essence of the case, permitting the legal principle to come alive within a particular set of facts."

b) Judicial comportment and demeanour

[6-11] "Gently to hear, kindly to judge"[88] sums up Shakespeare's advice as to the judicial demeanour which we judges must acquire. In my opinion, since there must perforce be a losing party or a rejected claim or testimony, it becomes imperative to have conducted oneself with the utmost degree of professionalism and equanimity so that the unsuccessful litigant will not be in a position to decry both the justice of the

---

[88] Refer to the prologue to King Henry the Fifth. You will recall that the Chorus reminds us all of the wisdom of the following words: '[...] your humble patience pray Gently to hear, kindly to judge, our play.'" See l. 32-33.

decision and the lack of just behaviour by the judicial officer. A judge neither dismisses a suggestion too hastily nor the worth of a witness too swiftly, lest a neutral third party be left with the belief that the case was prejudged or the arbiter prejudiced.

[6-12] Of course, I do not wish to be understood to suggest pusillanimity as a course of conduct or even bearing. But I do wish to be understood to suggest in the strongest terms that though judges do not bow before Kings in rendering judgment, they must be conscious of the fact that most litigants are of modest means and estate, especially in the criminal law sphere, and that for many the experience of appearing in a Court room is puzzling and often frightening if not intimidating. A sound example is found in Act 1, sc. 2 of <u>King Henry the Fifth</u>, at lines 7-32:

> King. Sure we thank you.
> My learned Lord, we pray you to proceed,
> And justly and religiously unfold,
> Why the Law Salique, that they have in France,
> Or should or should not bar us in our Claim:
> <u>And God forbid, my dear and faithful Lord,</u>
> <u>That you should fashion, wrest, or bow your reading,</u>
> <u>Or nicely charge your understanding Soule,</u>
> <u>With opening Titles miscreate, whose right</u>
> <u>Suits not in native colours with the truth</u>: [...]
> under this Conjuration, speak, my Lord:
> For we will hear, note, and believe in heart,
> That what you speak, is in your Conscience wash'd,
> As pure as sin with Baptism. [Emphasis added]

[6-13] Further assistance on the delineating the proper scope and nature of the judicial personality is found at page 681 of a book review penned by Judge Rousseau A. Burch of the Supreme Court of Kansas. As you consider these words, ponder the question how easily we judges may affect those who witness our judgments and the act of judging by reason of our facial expressions:

Let me illustrate the subject of judicial personality as a factor in the decision of causes: In making the play, The Merchant of Venice, live on the stage before the eyes of his audience, Henry Irving interpreted Shakespeare's words in such a way that Shylock appeared as having all the superb dignity of a representative of an ancient, noble, and long-oppressed race. In his insistence on the pound of flesh he seemed but an instrument of vengeance in the hands of the offended God of the Hebrew people. Against the appeal to mercy he stood pitiless, implacable, but majestic. When crushed by Portia's law, he seemed turned to stone, and he finally stalked from the stage with a sigh that made the scene one of tragic sadness. Edwin Booth would allow none of this. Reading the same text as Irving, he declared that Shakespeare had created a cruel wretch, filled with revengeful selfishness, incapable of pity and void of mercy, and Booth so portrayed the character.[89]

[6-14] In conclusion, judges ought not to demonstrate or betray any hint of surliness as this might lead a detached observer to conclude that the testimony or contention is ill received prior to the entire question having been presented, and deliberation upon it conducted. What is to be avoided is what we read of in King Henry the Fifth, Act 1, sc. 2, lines 200-205:

---

[89] See the review of The Nature of the Judicial Process, by Benjamin N. Cardozo, [New Haven, Yale University Press, 1921], in 31 Yale L.J. (1921-1922), at pages 677-681.

Canterbury: The poor Mechanic porters, crowding in
Their heavy burdens at his narrow gate:
<u>The sad-ey'd justice with his surly hum,</u>
Delivering o'er to Executors pale
The lazy yawning Drone [...] [Emphasis added]

c) Shakespeare on sentencing

[6-15] By way of introductory comment, I wish to explain that although sentencing does not appear at first blush to have much to do with fact finding, upon greater reflection it should become obvious that judges are called upon in every decision on punishment to judge the factual merits of an offender's rehabilitative potential and, more often than not, in evaluating the sincerity of any expressions of remorse. In fact, Shakespeare made certain valuable contributions in the field of sentencing in general, not least by the famous scene in <u>The Merchant of Venice</u> involving, or starring – to resort to a contemporary phrase – Portia and the 'quality of mercy'. Noteworthy is a passage in a recent book by Professor Julian V. Roberts, lately of Oxford University and formerly of the University of Ottawa, entitled <u>The Virtual Prison Community Custody and the Evolution of Imprisonment</u>, [Cambridge University Press: Cambridge, 2004], in which he points out that the words attributed to, Richard II, taken from Act V, sc. 1 may best be qualified as depicting a person suffering a form of 'house arrest'.[90] It might be the first such reference in modern English literature.[91]

---

[90] Refer to footnote 1, page 188: "Shakespeare's words illustrate the originally sharp distinction between custody and community [...] The deposed king's ruminations on prison and society are spoken while he reposes in a castle, not a dungeon; Richard was effectively under house arrest." The quoted words follow: "I have been studying how I may compare This prison where I live unto the world: And for because the world is populous And here is not a creature but myself, I cannot do it..." Refer to page 38 of <u>The Virtual</u>

d) Judging rehabilitative potential: The young do mature

[6-16] In terms of the Bard's instruction and guidance on the thorny issue of judging the potential for rehabilitation in the case of youthful adult offenders, I suggest that it might profit the members of the judiciary to consider the words found in King Henry the Fifth, Act 1, sc. 1, l. 25-35, to the effect that the shallowness of youth may give way to the wisdom of mature age and that often a significant event may be the trigger. Indeed,

> Archbishop of Canterbury: The King is full of grace
> and fair regard.
> Bishop of Ely: "And a true lover of the holy Church.
> Archbishop of Canterbury: The courses of his youth
> promis'd it not.
> The breath no sooner left his father's body
> But that his wildness, mortified in him,
> Seem'd to die too […]
> Never came reformation in a flood,
> With such a heady currance [and] and all at once […]
> [Emphasis added]

Prison and to the review I wrote of this text published in: (June 2005), 50(3) Criminal Law Quarterly 349-356.

[91]   On the question of sentencing, note Arcadian Adventures With the Idle Rich, by Stephen Leacock, the Chapter titled "A Little Dinner with Mr. Lucullus Fyshe" as to the potential impact of the tone of voice of a judge in sentencing:

> Gloom indeed hung over him. For, when one heard him talk of listed stocks and cumulative dividends, there was as deep a tone in his quiet voice as if he spoke of eternal punishment and the wages of sin.
> [Emphasis added]

[6-17] The subject is discussed at greater length in my text, The Sentencing Code of Canada: Principles and Objectives, [LexisNexis Inc., Markham, 2009], at chapter 5, section 3, pages 147-157. In this regard, I may be excused a further reference which I think apt to illustrate that offenders of all ages, but especially youthful ones, require a propitious home life if they are to avoid difficulties. Consider Act 1, sc. 2, lines 185-195 of King Henry the Fifth: "Canterbury. Therefore doth heaven divide The state of man in divers functions [...] The Act of Order to a peopled Kingdome. They have a King, and Officers of sorts, Where some like Magistrates correct at home: Others, like Merchants venture Trade abroad [...]" [Emphasis added] But, if the young offenders have no home, the correction of the Court will be of little moment.

e) Good may flower in the shadow of evil

[6-18] Stated otherwise, there is potential for reformation in all, if the optimum conditions may be found or associated and judges must be vigilant to assess facts in support of this situation. Consider in this vein the example consigned in Act 1, sc. 1 of King Henry the Fifth: "The Bishop of Ely: The strawberry grows underneath the nettle, And wholesome berries thrive and ripen best Neighbour'd by fruit of baser quality [...]"

f) Shakespeare on civil litigation

[6-19] At the outset, there are many reported judgments in which we find a phrase to the effect that judges "expect people to care ordinary precautions". I like to think that counsel quoted, or the members of the Bench were familiar with the words found in King Henry the Fifth, Act 1, sc. 2, lines 175-177 which provides a simple example of the belief that we expect people to take simple, ordinary precautions in safeguarding their valuables:

Exeter. It follows then, the Cat must stay at home,
Yet that is but a crush'd necessity,
Since we have locks to safeguard necessaries,
And pretty traps to catch the petty thieves.

g) Judging human nature

[6-20] The study of Shakespeare is also quite useful on the subject of judging human nature, though his writings illustrate the truism that there is no orthodoxy in how individuals perceive and interpret events. For example, consider the criticism of Shakespeare's opinion that "[…] men are merriest, when they are from home", words found in <u>King Henry the Fifth</u>. Refer to Act 1, sc. 2, line 273.

[6-21] I wish to add that on occasion, in the course of a written or oral judgment, it may be of assistance to decry the testimony of a witness by reason of the untoward protestations of innocence. Thus, one might cite with profit the "doth protest too much" comment contained in <u>The Tragedy of Hamlet, Prince of Denmark,</u> at Act III, sc. ii, 1. 235. This may serve to draw the focus of the inquiry away from the account to the manner of its presentation. For example, in <u>R. v. D. (G.C.),</u> [1988] O.J. No. 292 (C.A.), the trial judge appears to have assigned little weight to the defendant's testimony on the grounds that he "protested too much." Refer to para. 6, at p. 289. See also <u>Archibald v. Kuntz,</u> [1994] B.C.J. No. 199 (S.C.) (Q.L.), at para. 33: "But there is in this exhibition [of discomfort] almost an appearance that leads one to wonder whether or not it is just a bit too demonstrative. One is rather reminded of that line from Shakespeare about protesting too much."

[6-22] Further, I am hopeful that these writings have served to warn judicial officers that if someone doth protest too much, it might reflect poorly on the listener's evaluation of the account. In the *Mikado*, by Gilbert and Sullivan, the contrary occurs: there is too much boasting. Ko-Ko tells the Emperor how well he himself performed in executing the prisoner, adding "A tough fellow he was, too – a man of gigantic strength. His struggles were terrific. It was a remarkable scene". The trouble starts when he is asked to describe the scene in detail."[92]

---

[92]   See "The Criminal Credit as He Droppeth Him Down," Song No. 18, Act 2.

h) Judging criminal law: Circumstantial evidence

[6-23] Shakespeare is also valuable to those wishing to further their understanding of circumstantial evidence, in particular the reference in his play <u>Hamlet</u> to the itinerant players who re-enact the late King's suggested poisoning. The Bard concentrated the attention of his audience on the reaction of the putative murderers, Hamlet's uncle Claudius and his mother, Gertrude, to then invite us to consider whether their actions in response betrayed a consciousness of guilt.

i) The generation gap and classic literature

[6-24] A statement made in 1929 by one reviewer that "Some of the legal fraternity have read and still read Dickens and know his pages with intimate knowledge ...",[93] presents a contemporary challenge as it is quite doubtful that such a suggestion would be found valid today. Nor do I think it necessary that any one of us be capable of being described as "that *rara avis*, a lawyer who uses English with the happy facility of a Byron or a Shakespeare", to quote one reviewer,[94] in order to improve our ability to judge legal controversies and to communicate better our judgments. In sum, judges may improve every facet of their work by a considered review of the great titles in literature, notably the plays of William Shakespeare.[95]

---

[93]   Refer to page 365 of Arthur A. Alexander's book review of <u>Charles Dickens as a Legal Historian</u>, written by William S. Holdsworth (1928), (1928-1929) 17 <u>Geo. L.J</u>. 365-369.

[94]   Refer to page 108 of Sveinbjorn Johnson's book review of <u>Charles Dickens as a Legal Historian</u>, written by William S. Holdsworth (1928), (1930-1931) 25 <u>Ill L. Rev</u>. 106-108.
[95]   A Canadian jurist who excels in this vein is Justice Binnie of the Supreme Court of Canada. Indeed, His Lordship

j) Avoiding a narrow perspective on human nature

[6-25] One of the primary concerns in any fact finding enterprise surrounds the failure of the person judging to consider that his or her perspective may be either quite limited or uni-dimensional. The fear is that we might be guilty of a logical fallacy not unlike that associated with what is known as "Eurocentric thought", that is to say assuming that all those

---

quoted from Shakespeare's Julius Caesar to make plain how great a role advocates may play in the resolution of a trial:

> While it would be comforting to think that in a criminal trial facts speak for themselves, the reality is that "facts" emerge from evidence that is given shape by sometimes skilful advocacy into a coherent and compelling prosecution. The successful prosecutor downplays or disclaims the craftsmanship involved in shaping the story. Such modesty should be treated with scepticism. The rules of "prosecutorial" advocacy have not changed much since Shakespeare put a "just the facts" speech in the mouth of Mark Antony:
>
> > For I have neither wit, nor words, nor worth,
> > Action, nor utterance, nor the power of speech
> > To stir men's blood; I only speak right on.
> > I tell you that which you yourselves do know,
> > Show you sweet Caesar's wounds, poor poor dumb mouths,
> > And bid them speak for me.
>
> Julius Caesar, Act III, Scene ii.

See R. v. Rose, [1998] S.C.J. No. 81, [1998] 3 S.C.R. 262, 40 O.R. (3d) 576, 166 D.L.R. (4th) 385, 232 N.R. 83, 115 O.A.C. 201, 129 C.C.C. (3d) 449, 20 C.R. (5th) 246, at p. 462 C.C.C., para. 19. Mr. Justice LeBel has even made reference to the Kama Sutra in discussing the requirements of an affidavit. See para. 46 of R. v. Araujo, [2000] S.C.J. No. 65 (Q.L.).

189

who testify share a common heritage which is not Asian, African, Aboriginal, etc. In this vein, note that Nye's History of the United States contains a remarkable passage: it is said that Indians who saw Columbus' ships approaching exclaimed: 'At last we are discovered!'"

[6-26] It is suggested that an effort to engage in broad reading, including works not originally published in European languages may be useful in this perspective as they may expose us to a range of perspectives on a variety of elements of human behaviour. In this regard, Sir Walter Scott opined on the subject of literature for jurists. "A lawyer without history or literature is a mechanic, a mere working mason; if he [or she] possesses some knowledge of these, he may venture to call himself an architect". These words Scott penned for his character Paulus Pleydell, a lawyer found in Guy Mannering.[96]

[6-27] In the ultimate analysis, everyone is different as I have noted repeatedly. Some individuals take things literally, for example, as illustrated ably in the passage which follows, taken from Arcadian Adventures With the Idle Rich, by Stephen Leacock, found in the chapter entitled "A Little Dinner with Mr. Lucullus Fyshe":

> [...] he unexpectedly ran into the Viscount Belstairs [...] and Belstairs, who was in abundant spirits and who was returning to England [...] explained to the Duke that he had just borrowed fifty thousand pounds, on security that wouldn't be worth a halfpenny in England.

---

[96] Refer the foreword to a Symposium entitled "Then, Now and Into the Future: A Century of Legal Conflict and Development", by Professor Lawrence P. Wilkins, (1994-1995) 28 Ind. L. Rev. 135-138, at page 137, with particular reference to footnote 5.

And the Duke said with a sigh, "How the deuce do you do it. Belstairs?"

"Do what?"

"Borrow it," said the Duke. "How do you manage to get people to talk about it? Here I am wanting to borrow a hundred thousand, and I'm hanged if I can even find an opening."

At which the Viscount had said, "Pooh, pooh! you don't need any opening. Just borrow it straight out--ask for it across a dinner table, just as you'd ask for a match; they think nothing of it here."

"Across the dinner table?" repeated the Duke, who was a literal man.

"Certainly," said the Viscount. "Not too soon, you know—say after a second glass of wine. I assure you it's absolutely nothing."

[…] And the Duke, being as I say a literal man, decided that just as soon as Mr. Fyshe should give him a second glass of wine, that second glass should cost Mr. Fyshe a hundred thousand pounds sterling. [Emphasis added]

k) Assisting in looking at all sides of an issue

[6-28] In addition, it is submitted that literature will provide support for all sides of any possible issue. Indeed, what is fascinating about literature as a repository of legal reasoning with particular emphasis on fact finding is that support may be found for just about any conceivable view of a question or

issue. For example, if it is suggested that the prisoners of any prison are subjected to body, mind and soul destroying exactions by the very nature of modern facilities with their over-crowding and poor sanitary standards, it may also be argued that to some prisoners, jail is a "refuge from life's trivia", and books which may be cited in support include Graham Greene's <u>The Power and the Glory</u>, Aleksandr Solzhenitsyn's <u>The Cancer Ward</u>, <u>The First Circle</u>, and <u>One Day in the Life of Ivan Denisovich</u>, not to mention Robert Bolt's work, <u>A Man for All Seasons</u>.[97] Stated otherwise, literature is helpful in looking at all sides of an issue.

I) Literature to assist in making rational choices

[6-29] Any judge taking the time to research the references to Kafka's <u>The Trial</u> found in judicial opinions will conclude quite shortly after undertaking such research that Professor Scott Finet is correct in suggesting that "The use of references to <u>The Trial</u> demonstrates that judges realize that judicial decisions must be consistent with and integrate values shared among those directly affected by the decisions, as well as informed onlookers. First among those shared values is the central value of rational choice..." Refer to page 32 of "Frank

---

[97] Refer to Jolanta Juszkiewicz's review of <u>Romantic Outlaws, Beloved Prisons: The Unconscious Meanings of Crime and Punishment</u>, by Martha Grace Duncan, New York" New York University Press, 1996, at (1997), 61 <u>Fed. Probation</u> 79-80, at page 79. Refer as well to the superb example of political prisoners taking advantage of their confinement to study described in <u>Reflections in Prison Voices from the South African Liberation Struggle</u>, edited by Mac Maharaj, Boston: University of Massachusetts Press, 2001, which I reviewed in (October 2004) <u>Canadian Journal of Criminology and Criminal Justice</u> 46(5), at page 639.

Kafka's <u>Trial</u> as Symbol in Judicial Opinions", (1988) Vol. 12 <u>Legal Studies Forum</u> 23-32.[98]

m) Sympathy for the underdog

[6-30] Notwithstanding the foregoing comments, for my part, I agree fully with the observations of Professor Peter C. Myers who wrote, "It seems clear […] that the enormous and enduring popularity of Mark Twain's great novel [The Adventures of Huckleberry Finn] derives in large part from its appeal to a basic desire for justice, and in particular, to a moral sympathy for the underdog, for the humble and downtrodden, that finds so affecting a cause in Huck's and Jim's struggles against societal injustices." Refer to page 557 of "'Sivilization' and its Discontents: Nature and Law in <u>The Adventures of Huckleberry Finn</u>", (1998) 22 <u>Legal Stud</u>. 557-590. Hence, as fact finders, we must be vigilant and remind ourselves of the dangers of allowing appropriate sympathy for the situation of the underdog to cloud our judgment in respect of the bedrock question of the objective merits of the case at Bar.

n) Dickens not without his faults: Judging the whole, and not just an unrepresentative slice

[6-31] In the same vein, it has been suggested by W. Lewis Roberts, in the course of a book review of <u>Charles Dickens as</u>

---

[98] On the theme of rationality, it is of note that the exhaustive research of one author has led to the conclusion that it is not uncommon for judges to link references to Kafka with The Queen's pronouncement in Alice in Wonderland: "Sentence first – verdict afterwards", perhaps the least rational of all possible legal judgments. Refer to page 248 of Parker B. Potter's voluminous article, "Ordeal by Trial: Judicial References to the Nightmare World of Franz Kafka", (2004-2005) 3 <u>Pierce L. Rev</u>. 195-330.

a Legal Historian, written by William S. Holdsworth (1928), (1928-1929) 17 Ky. L.J. 182-184, that Dickens failed to present a balanced picture of the institutions he would assail.[99] Indeed, "He may go through a town selecting pictures of the slums and hovels of that town and have every picture accurate and still give a very false impression of that town as a whole." Refer to page 183. This concern, assuming it was valid in the case of Dickens, must serve to warn us to assess all sides of any question without partiality.

o) Literature assists in demonstrating the many facets of human relationships

[6-32] I invite interested readers to consider the pages of Kafka's brilliant text, The Trial, at Chapter Three, devoted to the incident involving K. and the young woman who is swept up, ostensibly to be carried off to the Examining Magistrate. I would suggest that the words and passages may fairly lead to a variety of interpretations touching upon the consent of the young woman to the physical actions of the male protagonist, and that one might conclude that she is being attacked while another might conclude that she welcomed the actions as advances. Indeed, two esteemed and respected authors, Justice Richard Posner and Professor Robin West have engaged in a lively debate in this respect. Consider pages 1439 to 1442 of Judge Posner's brilliant article, "The Ethical Significance of Free Choice: A Reply to Professor West", (1985-1986), 99 Harv. L. Rev. 1431-1456 and the earlier contribution by Professor West, "Authority, Autonomy, and Choice: The Role of Consent in the Moral and Political Visions of Franz Kafka and Richard Posner", (1985-1986), 99 Harv. L. Rev. 384-428, especially at pages 397-404.

---

[99] To the same general end is the criticism found in a review of Philip Collins' book, Dickens and Crime, written by Roy St. George Stubbs. Refer to (1962-1965) 1 Man. L. Sch. J. 211-214.

p) Literature to avoid a lifeless judgment

[6-33] It is to be understood clearly that I do not advocate that members of the judiciary refer to literature as a matter of course, far from it; what I do suggest is that there is often no better means of injecting a bit of interest to what might otherwise be a lifeless history of facts in a given judgment.[100]

q) Factual choices are possible in adjudication even in cases of evident paradox

[6-34] To briefly pursue this theme of the patent contradiction, let us consider it from the other pole, one often described as "adjudication of paradoxes" Once again, the writings of Franz Kafka are instructive as they also support the position that great caution must be exercised in any adjudicative task in that it is sometimes possible to perceive matters from opposite poles and yet be correct in both instances. As we read from The Trial: "The right perception of any matter and a misunderstanding of the same matter do not wholly exclude one another".[101]

---

[100]   Refer to page 95 of J.S. Kleinbard's book review of Charles Dickens as a Legal Historian, written by William S. Holdsworth (1928), (1928-1929) 3 Temp. L.Q. 95-96.

[101]   Refer to page 216 of the Schocken edition, New York: 1984, translated by Willa and Edwin Muir, edited by E.MM. Butler, quoted at page 173 of Frank Stringfellow's article, "Kafka's Trial: Between The Republic and Psychoanalysis", (1995) 7 Cardozo Stud. L. & Literature 173-205. Noteworthy as well is the following passage: "The question of the relation or, even, possible contradiction between morality and legal order resurfaces dramatically in what has been called the greatest American novel, Mark Twain's The Adventures of Huckleberry Finn." Refer to page 530 of "Politics and Literature: An Introduction", by Professors Catherine Zuckert and Micheal Zuckert, (1998) 22 Legal Stud. F. 529-534.

[6-35] On a lighter side, <u>Arcadian Adventures With the Idle Rich</u>, by Stephen Leacock, contains a valuable passage in the chapter styled: "A Little Dinner with Mr. Lucullus Fyshe" which teaches us that judging is highly subjective and may well depend on the age and background of the judge:

> Thus the members sit and talk in undertones that float to the ear through the haze of Havana smoke. You may hear the older men explaining that the country is going to absolute ruin, and the younger ones explaining that the country is forging ahead as it never did before; but chiefly they love to talk of great national questions, such as the protective tariff and the need of raising it, the sad decline of the morality of the working man, the spread of syndicalism and the lack of Christianity in the labour class, and the awful growth of selfishness among the mass of the people.

[6-36] Consider as well this further passage, from chapter 2, "The Wizard of Finance":

> "Well," said the wife of the Wizard as her husband finished looking through the reports, "how are things this morning? Are they any better?" "No," said Tomlinson, and he sighed as he said it; "this is the worst day yet. It's just been a shower of telegrams, and mostly all the same. I can't do the figuring of it like you can, but I reckon I must have made another hundred thousand dollars since yesterday." "You don't say so!" said mother, and they looked at one another gloomily.

r) Classic literature to foster the development of a value structure

[6-37] "One's ability to reason is only complete when it is informed by a firmly rooted value structure" is the advice advanced by Kevin H. Marino at page 113 of his comment, "Toward a More Responsible Profession: Some Remarks on Kafka's The Trial and the Self", (1983-1984) 14 Seton Hall L. Rev. 110-120. The author then quotes from the writings of John Stuart Mill as follows:

> But it is the privilege and proper condition of a human being, arrived at the maturity of his [or her] faculties, to use and interpret experience in his [or her] own way ... The human faculties of perception, judgment, discriminative feeling, mental activity, and even moral preference, are exercised only in making a choice. He [or she] who does anything because it is the custom makes no choice. He gains no practice either in discerning or desiring what is best. The mental and moral, like the muscular powers, are improved only by being used...[102]

[6-38] Hence, the passage which I have underlined should be taken to express the idea and the value that reading serves to enhance not only our minds, naturally enough, but our values. In the same vein, it is my view as noted throughout that fiction is a proper vehicle for a credible description of human behaviour. Noteworthy in this regard are the views of John Croft that fiction may be regarded as a subjective but more or less credible description of human behaviour and the novelist may be counted upon to portray well the social attitudes of the day. Refer to his review of Dickens and Crime, written by

---

[102]   Refer to On Liberty, (Norton ed. 1975), at page 55.

Philip Collins (1962), at pages 308-310 of (1962-1963) 3 Brit. J. of Criminology.

s) Literature to assess a person's 'blind spot'

[6-39] Many of the books, short stories and poems that might be considered by judges as a valuable adjunct to their work are not well known and it is my hope that I will have succeeded in pointing to certain jewels as sources of direct assistance in fact finding while incidentally providing enlightenment and entertainment. For example, Philip Roth penned a remarkable short story, "Eli, The Fanatic", which I have only found in Trial and Error: An Oxford Anthology of Legal Stories, edited by Fred R. Shapiro and Jane Garry, Oxford: Oxford University Press, 1998, starting at page 296. It is of contemporary advantage when considering the on-going debate on reasonable accommodations for cultural and religious practices and beliefs. A superb summary is found at page 131 of a book review of Trial and Error, by Steven D. Jamar, (1998-1999) 42 Howard L.J. 129-132. Shortly put, it concerns the request by citizens to employ legal means to convince a member of a visible religious group to dress in such a way as to become invisible. The lessons for a judge grappling with the application of cultural and religious imperatives in the course of a law suit are far reaching, but as well, great assistance is provided in respect to the assessment of testimony advanced by individuals who may be biased or who have a 'blind spot' so to speak when it comes to describing the actions of members of a group which they distrust or do not understand.[103]

---

[103] With respect to the application of the criminal law, note the recent publication of La défense culturelle: un moyen de défense non souhaitable en droit pénal canadien, by Marie-Pierre Robert, Cowansville, Éditions Yvon Blais, 2004, reviewed by the author in (Summer 2005), Vol. 28-1 Provincial Court Judges Journal, at page 53.

[6-40] Before moving on to the next rubric, it will be of assistance to note that one must take for granted that we judicial officers enjoy some measure of judgment which may be improved upon, as contrasted with the character penned by Stephen Leacock in <u>Arcadian Adventures With the Idle Rich</u>, at Chapter 5, "The Love Story of Mr. Peter Spillikins":

> Nor, to do him justice, did Mr. Spillikins confine his attitude to his view of women alone. He brought it to bear on everything. Every time he went to the opera he would come away enthusiastic, saying, "By Jove, isn't it simply splendid! Of course I haven't the ear to appreciate it--I'm not musical, you know--but even with the little that I know, it's great; it absolutely puts me to sleep." And of each new novel that he bought he said, "It's a perfectly wonderful book! Of course I haven't the head to understand it, so I didn't finish it, but it's simply thrilling." Similarly with painting, "It's one of the most marvellous pictures I ever saw," he would say. "Of course I've no eye for pictures, and I couldn't see anything in it, but it's wonderful!"

t) Sancho Panza and Oliver Wendell Holmes

[6-41] It has been noted in the past that efforts at promoting law and literature for lawyers, and for judges in the context of this book, have the regrettable potential to elevate the judgments of Sancho Panza in Don Quixote with those of Holmes or Brandeis.[104] I am mindful of these observations, but

---

[104] See the interesting review penned by Richard J. Kohlman of <u>The World of Law</u>, the two volume text edited by Ephraim London, at pages 38-40 of 1 <u>Santa Clara Lawyer</u> (1961).

it is suggested in the strongest terms that to draw illuminating images from the world of literature in which trials are depicted does not necessarily result in deprecating the judgments of the Courts. Wisdom may be acquired by studying the great opinions drawn by the most celebrated of jurists, but it is not self-evident that no wisdom is to be derived from judicious examples of literature, especially if well-known and easily understood such as Pinocchio's nose or Humpty Dumpty's fall? Nevertheless, law, literature, and life interact as made plain in the opening words of a book review of <u>Learned Hand on Patent Law</u>: "Law, literature, and life interact. Indeed they are intimately interrelated. [...] But perhaps because law and literature each reflect life from different angles, incumbents of the two disciplines generally employ markedly different styles of expression. A notable exception was Judge Learned Hand. To him the fact/fiction dichotomy between law and literature was no excuse for monotony but rather an opportunity for memorable and meaningful pronouncements." Refer to page 447 of Peter D. Rosenberg's review found at (1985) 67 <u>J. Pat. & Trademark Off. Soc'y</u> 447-448.

u) Certain visual images drawn from literature are very compelling and may be called in aid in judgment writing

[6-42] It is suggested that certain literary images are quite vivid and may be brought to the mind of the judge and jury, or other trier of fact, in quite simple terms. For example, Pinocchio as the universal symbol of lying comes to mind rather easily. Consider as well references to Tom Joad from Steinbeck's epic <u>The Grapes of Wrath</u> and to Robin Hood. Indeed, former President Clinton's defence team made numerous references to Inspector Javert when attempting to discredit the efforts of the Independent Counsel, Mr. Kenneth Starr.[105]

---

[105] Refer to "The Jackal Javert: What Javert Really Tells Us About the Rule of Law, Law Enforcement and Whether we

[6-43] In addition, it must be understood that literature may be valuable in reminding us as to the subjective nature of one's thought process; what is a terrible drought for a farmer may be endless days of sunshine for a sun lover. In this vein, note "A Little Dinner with Mr. Lucullus Fyshe", found in <u>Arcadian Adventures With the Idle Rich</u>, by Stephen Leacock, a passage which makes plain how difficult it is at times to understand another's inner thoughts and understanding of life:

> Herein lay the truth about the Duke of Dulham's visit and the error of Mr. Lucullus Fyshe. Mr. Fyshe was thinking that the Duke had come to lend money. In reality he had come to borrow it. In fact, the Duke was reckoning that by putting a second mortgage on Dulham Towers for twenty thousand sterling, and by selling his Scotch shooting and leasing his Irish grazing and sub-letting his Welsh coal rent he could raise altogether a hundred thousand pounds. This for a duke, is an enormous sum. If he once had it he would be able to pay off the first mortgage on Dulham Towers, buy in the rights of the present tenant of the Scotch shooting and the claim of the present mortgagee of the Irish grazing, and in fact be just where he started. This is ducal finance, which moves always in a circle.

[6-44] Lastly, members of the judiciary ought not to shy away from including, when appropriate in the legal context and in light of the cultural background of the parties, being concerned always to avoid narrow ethnocentric comments, to refer to well-known and well-understood images such as the Good Samaritan or the Prodigal

---

Need Him in Our Society?", by James A. Beckman, (2002), 11 <u>U.S. Air Force Acad. J. of Legal Studies</u> 83-97.

Son.[106] For example, I refer to page 288 of "Nineteenth Century Visions of a Twenty-First Century Bar: Were Dickens's <u>Great Expectation</u> for Lawyers Too Great?",[107] by Randy Lee: "Miss Havisham [...] would not tell a lie, but she also felt no compulsion to correct obvious misunderstandings influencing the behaviour of those with whom she dealt."

v)   Popular misunderstandings

[6-45] Of course, it will not be surprising for me to point out that many members of our community misunderstand the workings of the Courts and the nature and meaning of our judgments including our fact finding duties. In so doing, they may be applying the logic and sense of the Law that they have perceived as a result of exposure to literature and popular culture. As was noted by one commentator, "Twain was describing a process that we would do well to consult in our efforts to understand how the eighteenth-century 'right of the people to keep and bear Arms' has undergone a transformation similarly destructive of its original understanding and object. I refer – as did Twain – to <u>popular</u> understandings of constitutionalism, ideas at odds not only with the historical record but with the law as interpreted in our courts."[108]

---

[106]   Refer to "In Parables: Teaching Through Parables", by John J. Bonsignore, <u>Legal Studies Forum</u>, Vol. XII(2) (1988) 191-210, at page 194 in particular. Note as well the fascinating discussion of Kafka's parable involving the "door to the Law" at pages 321-325 of "'Before the Law': An Analysis of the Legal Profession", by Victor A. Fleming, 1 <u>U.A.L.R. L.J.</u> 321-331 (1978).

[107]   (2005-2006) 15 Widener L.J. 283-297.

[108]   Refer to page 540 of "The Persistence of Resistance: Civic Rights, Natural Rights, and Property Rights in the Historical Debate Over 'The Right of the People to Keep and Bear Arms'", by David Thomas Konig, (2004-205) 73 <u>Fordham L. Rev</u>. 539-547.

[6-46] Any efforts we undertake to address such misunderstandings must perforce be in the public interest. Further, it is suggested that the attention of our target audience, especially the lay party, is gained when reference is made to a figure which is well known and respected, and not least humorous, by reference to the quotation which follows, found in a farewell address: "[...] Mark Twain said, 'To be good is noble, but to teach others how to be good is nobler – and less trouble.'" Refer to the salutation of Justice John T. Grant, Nebraska Supreme Court, at page xviii of (1989-1990) 23 Creighton L. Rev.

x)Literature as providing lessons on judgment writing

[6-47] In addition to the foregoing elements of guidance on judgment writing in the area of fact finding, I suggest in the strongest terms that a study of literature will assist in a signal manner in avoiding errors of speech that might imperil the majesty of our judicial office and the respect our judgments should receive. By way of limited example, to quote injudiciously from The Merchant of Venice or The Adventures of Huckleberry Finn might result in visiting offence to certain individuals who are depicted in most unflattering terms by the authors of these works. In this respect, it will be of assistance to consider the guidance found in the lengthy passage which follows:

> As lawyers [and judges] know too well, talking can indeed be a (slightly) more civilized way of fighting. Speech is not only communication or the innocent naming of things. Speech is also action. To use fighting words, to coerce, threaten or deceive with words, also falls within the everyday use of language [...] To make matters worse, language represents embedded and unequal social relations, power structures and 'sociocultural grids

of communication' that distort, injure and oppress without our intending such violence, a point often made by contemporary feminists. Chambers writes:

> 'There are vocabularies, language games, and discursive practices that, above and beyond the intentions of the speakers, constrain, discipline, control, marginalize, oppress and dismiss us.'[109]

[6-48] Pursuing this line of thought, it will be advantageous as well to quote at length from the contribution of Professor Ian Ward:

> Words are power, of course. Nobody would deny this much. Words are power, moreover, because language excludes and creates linguistic hierarchies. Nowhere is such a privileged linguistic hierarchy more obvious than in the discourse of law. A popular example used by Law and Literature scholars here is Mark Twain's The Adventures of Huckleberry Finn. It is of course a theme which runs through Dickens' treatment of law. It is also an aspect of literature which has been noted by feminist critical lawyers...[110]

---

[109] Refer to page 363 of "Constitutional Interpretation: Between Past and Future", by A. Boshoff, (2001) 12 Stellenbosch L. Rev. 357-370. [Footnotes omitted]
[110] Refer to "From Literature to Ethics: The Strategies and Ambitions of Law and Literature", (1994) 145 Oxford J. Legal Stud. 389-400, at page 393.

y) Mark Twain's concern with fact distortion in trials

[6-49] As a general statement, Twain devoted a great deal of his work to the workings of the Courts and to trial scenes, obviously to entertain his readership, but also to promote justice and to denounce the purchasing of pardons, the celebration and lionizing of murderers, and, most importantly in light of the pedagogical goals of this book, the distortion of facts in jury addresses.[111]

z) Literature teaches us about bald and unconvincing narratives

[6-50] In penning the reasons for the rejection of evidence, judges are encouraged to track the "judgments" of Sir W.S.

---

[111] Refer to the brief but complete article by Alvin Waggoner, "Mark Twain – Legal Reformer" (1934-1935) 3 Kan. City L. Rev. 107-108 and in more detailed fashion in "A Calendar of Mark Twain's Celebrated Causes", (1934-1935) 13 Tenn L. Rev. 211-216. It is suggested that there are more than twenty trials or scenes that resemble court trials in Mark Twain's literature and that the courtroom and the circumstances leading to it served as dramatic vehicles for Twain's storytelling. Moreover, the trials provided Twain with the ideal setting to emphasize his major theme, that is to say, justice. These facts are presented by Kim M. Roam in "Mark Twain: Doctoring the Laws", (1983) 48 Mo. L. Rev. 681-718, at page 701. In the same vein, a very interesting review of the lawyers and the trial scenes penned by Dickens is found in Larry M. Weirtheim's "Dickens' Lesser Lawyers", (2001) 46 S.D. L. Rev. 695-711. My only quibble is the absence of a reference to the trial before Police Magistrate Fang at Chapter 11 of Oliver Twist. For his part, Mr. Allen Boyer has estimated that "Nearly three hundred books and articles have examined [Dickens'] relationship to the law." See "The Antiquarian and the Utilitarian: Charles Dickens vs James FitzJames Stephens", (1988-1989) 56 Tenn. L. Rev. 595-628, at page 596.

Gilbert, of Gilbert and Sullivan fame. Although he had an undistinguished career as a barrister,[112] he had an active and life-long career as a client of trial counsel. Biographies quoted suggest that the earned twenty-five pounds in his first two years of practice and that in four years, he averaged five, relatively impoverished, clients a year. Frank Bates remarked that Gilbert was "an extraordinarily unsuccessful barrister. See "A Reflection Upon Law and Literature" in (1980) 28 Chitty's L.J. 13-21, at p. 13.

[6-51] Gilbert has been described by the editor of the Canadian Law Times as "one of the most distinguished of the many men who practiced at the Bar before they wrote for the stage."[113] Prof. J.N. Turner wrote: "But he who reads Gilbert carefully will find an almost Kafkaesque mockery of both procedural and substantive law, much of which has relevance today."[114]

[6-52] In respect to the question of rejecting testimony that is devoid of substance, refer to a study of *The Mikado or the*

---

[112] See Pearson, Gilbert: His Life and Strife, at p. 19 (1957). Cited by Albert I. Borowitz in his article, "Gilbert and Sullivan on Corporate Law", (1973) 59 A.B.A.J. 1276-1281, at p. 1276. Weston P. Hatfield notes that Gilbert was "an outstanding economic failure at the Bar..." See "Sir William Schwenck Gilbert: Lawyer and Librettist", (1960) 46 A.B.A.J. 386-389, at p. 386.

[113] See "Sir W.S. Gilbert and the Law", (1911) 31 Can. L.T. 599-602, at p. 599. P. 601 records that he was a Justice of the Peace and frequently sat with the Middlesex magistrates.

[114] Refer to "Celebrated, Cultivated but Underrated? W.S. Gilbert as a Legal Satirist", in (1988) 9 Univ. of Tas. L. Rev. 117-131, at p. 117. As an aside, O. Henry's "Law and Order" contains a wonderful comment: "Law and order you say? Twenty years ago we had 'em here. We only had two or three laws, such as against murder before witnesses..." Quoted by Jack Watson, Q.C., now Watson J., in a book review at footnote 24 of (1993), 31 Alta L. Rev. 433.

Town of Titipu, his greatest libretto in terms of worldwide popularity,[115]   The dialogue that follows Song No. 19, Act. 2, contains the well-known comment, "Merely corroborative detail, intended to give artistic verisimilitude to an otherwise bald and unconvincing narrative." This passage is quoted by Darwin J. in <u>Lackersteen v. Jones et al.</u>, No. 596 of 1983 (Aust. S.C., N.T.), at para. 67, p. 63 (Q.L.). The Court added: "Now of course it is possible that a lying person may be sufficiently sophisticated to garnish the lie with a number of details which are designed to make it sound more convincing." In the result, the Court credited the detailed account partly on the basis that the witness was simply not sophisticated enough to have fabricated and recalled the information.

[6-53] To the same effect, note the remarks of Hollinrake J.A. in <u>R. v. D.K.R.</u> 104 B.C.A.C. 296, [1988] B.C.J. No. 651 (C.A.), at para. 3 (Q.L.), quoting from the trial judge's conclusions:

> The most notable features of the complainant's evidence are the details she provided and her consistency with respect to the essential elements of the crime. She provided small details about what the accused did before and after he assaulted her, such as wiping up his sperm with Kleenex and heating something in the microwave. She told about a time when she pushed his hand away and he elbowed her in the head, causing her to cry and to wake her mother up. She explained his habit of using vaseline to ease penetration. She relayed a

---

[115]   See <u>Operetta A Theatrical History</u> by Richard Traubner [Garden City, N.Y.: Doubleday & Company, Inc, 1983], at p. 169. See also p. 145 of <u>Sir Arthur Sullivan</u> by Percy M. Young [New York: W.W. Norton & Company, Inc., 1971] and <u>The Drake Guide to Gilbert and Sullivan</u> by Michael Hardwick [New York: Drake Publishers Inc., 1973], at p. 136.

conversation in the kitchen on the day of her mother's funeral when the accused whispered in her ear, 'Don't get me into trouble.' These types of details lent an air of verisimilitude to her testimony. But most importantly, this witness did not possess the guile or quickness of wit to create an atmosphere of credibility if it did not exist.[116]

[6-54] As well, see the apt observations of Master Hogan in Stewart v. Foster (1994) No. SC199 of 1992 (Sup. Ct. Aust, Cap. Terr.), a case involving a debt between family members: "It is also characteristic of this type of dispute that a great deal of time was spent on contesting peripheral matters which arose as 'corroborative detail, intended to give verisimilitude to an otherwise bald and unconvincing narrative'".[117]

[6-55] On the question of verisimilitude, note the dialogue that follows Song No. 23, Act 2, wherein the Emperor wishes an explanation for the false report that NankiPoo had been executed. Ko-Ko's 'logical explanation'[118] is that "When your Majesty says, 'Let a thing be done', it's as good as done – practically, it is done because your Majesty's will is law. Your Majesty says, 'Kill a gentleman', and a gentleman is told off to

---

[116]   See also R. v. J.J. Beamish Const. Co. Ltd. [1968] 1 O.R. 5 (C.A.), at p. 26 (Q.L.) and para. 13 of Milton v. Florence, [1993] B.C.J. No. 1773 (S.C., Master).

[117]   See also R. v. Smith (1989) 95 A.R. 304 (C.A.), at p. 29 (Q.L.), aff'd (1990), 111 N.R. 144, 109 A.R. 160 (S.C.C.). In addition, refer to Mr. Justice Anderson's judgment, Vasdani v. Sehmi, [1993] O.J. No. 44 (Gen. Div.), at para. 54 (Q.L.), Bragg v. Bailey and Others, [1995] N.L.O.R. No. 6 (H.C.J.), at para. 105 (Q.L.), Kission v. Comm. Of Income Tax [1988] J.C.J. NO. 27 (J.C.P.C.), at p. 8 (Q.L.) and para. 26 (Q.L.) of Fed. Comm. of Taxation v. Newton (1957) 96 C.L.R. 577 (High Ct.).

[118]   See p. 241 of The Gilbert & Sullivan Companion by Leslie Ayre [New York: Dodd, Mead & Company, 1972].

be killed. Consequently that gentleman is as good as dead – practically, he is dead – and if he is dead, why not say so?"

aa) Literature to assess if an account is plausible

[6-56] In cases of possession of recently stolen goods, the trier of fact must ask itself whether the account could reasonably be true. In this vein, note the Preface to The Prince and the Pauper: "It may be history, it may be only legend, a tradition. It may have happened, it may not have happened: but it could have happened.'" See p. ix. Is this not the best expression of the rule?

[6-57] In this respect, allowance must be made for human nature. Hence, in the opening paragraph of Finn, it is observed that "That book [Sawyer] was made by Mark Twain, and he told the truth mainly. There was things which he stretched, but mainly he told the truth. That is nothing. I never seen anybody but lied, one time or another, without it was Aunt Polly, or the widow…" It must be noted that on occasion, Huck would "resk the truth". For example, at Ch. XXIII, p. 174, of Finn.

bb) One must be careful with the references that are selected

[6-58] Having proclaimed the merits of literature in fact finding throughout this book, it is important to ensure that citations or references are accurate. As a first example, care must be taken not to credit Shakespeare for the "Oh what a tangled web we weave when first we practice to deceive" attack on credibility. The author is Sir Walter Scott and it is found in Marmion, Canto 6, stanza 17. See Canada Post Corp. and Canadian Union of postal workers (Seal Grievance), [1997] C.L.A.D. No. 158, [1997] C.P.A.S. No. 14, at para. 9.

[6-59] Note is made as well of a reference in an article entitled "A Reflection on Clerkships Past: A Tribute to the Honourable T. Emmet Clarie", by Henry S. Cohn and Thomas Smith, (Summer 1993), 25 Conn. L. Rev. 1027, at page 1045. The

two authors cite a book by Eugene D. Goodman, <u>All the Justice I Could Afford</u> (1983), at pages 63-65, in which it is said that Javert had exclaimed: "the law is the law, good, bad or indifferent." In fact, I cannot find any reference to that phrase in the novel, though it is uttered in the 1935 movie version by Charles Laughton.

cc) Literature as a source of moral exemplars

[6-60] Reference is made to a fine piece of academic writing by Professor Martha Minow, "Interpreting Rights: An Essay for Robert Cover", (1987) 96 <u>Yale L.J.</u> 1860, especially at pages 1893-1911. In effect, the author raises fascinating points arising from her experiences in reading works of fiction with judges and whether literary texts might be useful as a form of moral exemplars about the nature of domestic violence. Refer as well to "Rhetoric of Silence: Some Reflections on Law, Literature, and Social Violence" by James A. Epstein, (1990) 43 <u>Vand. L. Rev.</u> 1701-1706.

dd) The irony that many great writers studied Law and despised the subject and the profession

[6-61] In closing, it must be noted that a number of commentators have underscored the irony that so many great figures of literature, whose body of work I point to as greatly assisting in the essential fact finding leading to the resolution of trials, studied Law and despised both the subject matter and the profession. For example, Samuel Wolff and Kenneth Rivkin wrote at page 410 of their joint essay "The Legal Education of Franz Kafka", (1997-1998) 22 Colum.-VLA J.L. & Arts 407-412, that Goethe and Flaubert shared Kafka's dislike of the legal profession,[119] although Fielding did not, having served as a

---

[119] Note as well that Mark Twain was not very keen on the law, having studied it for all of two weeks, though his father and brother were lawyers. Possibly the lack of financial reward they experienced soured him on the profession's other attractions. See the brief but insightful comment "Some Legal Notions of

magistrate who "did much toward criminal reform in London …".[120] In addition, Thackeray also contributed to both the legal profession and to the literary world.

3) Conclusion

[6-62] It will be useful at this late juncture to note the concerns and criticisms of certain scholars as to the potential benefits of a study of literature for lawyers, and thus for judges. Hence,

> The notion for which [Professor James Boyd] White is most criticized is his <u>conviction that interaction with texts, particularly literary ones, will somehow inevitably lead to justice and morality</u> since 'the object of rhetoric is justice: the constitution of a social world.' Critics point out that such an approach is naïve, almost rationalizing, since merely forcing lawyers to acquire literary acumen will not necessarily bring about a more morally conscious character…[121] [Emphasis added]

[6-63] With the greatest of respect for those who think such efforts wasted or this philosophy one marked by the absence of an attainable object, I offer no apology. Indeed, I find myself in complete agreement with the following observation: "The inter-disciplinary study of law and literature has grown rapidly in recent years but has not produced much of special interest for

---

Mark Twain" at page 285 of (1915), 80 <u>Cent. L.J.</u> 275-278, by noted Twain scholar Alvin Waggoner.
[120]   Refer to page 356 of Mangum Weeks' book review of <u>Charles Dickens as a Legal Historian</u>, written by William S. Holdsworth, (1928-1929) 7 <u>N.C.L. Rev.</u> 356-360.
[121]   Refer to Daniela K. Pacher's article, "Aesthetics vs Ideology: The Motives Behind 'Law and Literature'", (1989-1990) 14 <u>Colum.-VLA J.L. & Arts</u> 587-614, at page 596.

labour and employment lawyers."[122]   In my view, this suggestion holds true for the judiciary as well in that very little attention has been drawn to the possible contributions of literature to the task of adjudication. The goal of this text and of this chapter especially has been to remedy this situation, in part at the very least.

[6-64] In the final analysis, I am of the firm view that to a certain extent, not to be exaggerated in terms of its significance but not to be undervalued as well, any resort to literature which succeeds in making our judgments better understood and, one hopes, better received is to be encouraged. As Mark Twain opined, by way of his character Hank Morgan in A Connecticut Yankee in King Arthur's Court, "To be vested with enormous authority is a fine thing; but to have the on-looking world consent to it is a finer".[123]

---

[122]   See page 309 of Anthony W. Kraus' article, "Assessing Mr. Samsa's Employee Rights: Kafka and the Art of the Human Resource Nightmare", (1999-2000) 15 Lab. Law. 309-319.

[123]   Refer to page 1568 of "The Equitable Distribution of Injustice: Raising Twain", by Aviam Soifer, (1999-2000) 32 Conn. L. Rev. 1565-1576.

Chapter 7
"Good counsel's" role in judging:
The duty of imagination and effort

> Ralph Kiner: [Has won the home-run title the last three years] "I think I deserve a raise. I am the star of the team. Without me, the team would be quite weaker."

> General Manager: "We have finished last with you as our star for three years in a row, we can finish last without you!"

1) Introduction

[7-1]　I can think of no better means of introducing the subject of counsel's signal role in the ultimate dénouement of the trial, the presentation by the Court of a fair and full judgment as to the credit and reliability of testimony than the following passage, taken from Act 1, sc. 1 of The Tragedy of Romeo and Juliet, by William Shakespeare. Indeed, Montague proclaims: "Black and portentous must this humour prove <u>Unless good counsel may the cause remove</u>." [Emphasis added]　In effect, the Court depends on good counsel to demonstrate energy, industry and imagination in seeking to counter the testimony and the submissions of the opposing side(s) with a view to facilitating the Court's opportunity to "remove the incorrect or faulty cause" of action, claim or prosecution, as the case may be.

[7-2] In so doing, it may well be that the best course for counsel to follow is to always seek to "reverse the proposition" being advanced by the other party or parties.　I recognize that this text is written for judges and is focused on judging but it is thought imperative to dedicate this last chapter to the important function of the advocates in assisting the Court's ultimate fact finding.

[7-3] Accordingly, attention is now drawn to best means of assisting the Court to test all testimony and all submissions, by means of the formulation or framing of a winning contrary contention, that is to say by inviting the Court to reverse the proposition it has been requested to accept as being sound. Perhaps the best explanation I can offer is by of an illustration, leaving aside the anecdote noted earlier touching upon Ralph Kiner. Recall that in the classic movie, *Adam's Rib*, the District Attorney played by Spencer Tracy prosecutes a woman accused of assaulting her straying spouse. The twist is that the defendant is represented by Tracy's wife, played by Katharine Hepburn, who attempts to recast the law. Indeed, as Cynthia Lucia comments astutely in the Introduction to her excellent book, <u>Framing Female Lawyers Women On Trial In Film</u>, [University of Texas Press: Austin, Texas, 2005], in what I consider an excellent example of reversing the proposition:

> ... Although [Hepburn's character] challenges the jury and the film audience to question basic assumptions about justice and gender – <u>asking the jury to imagine the accused woman as a man defending his home and the husband as an unfaithful wife</u> whose actions threaten family stability – ... An unwritten law stands back of a man who fights to defend his home. Apply this same law to this maltreated wife and neglected woman... [Emphasis supplied]

[7-4] If you will excuse this repetition proposed for emphasis, "reversing the proposition" occurs when counsel frames an argument in such a way as to stand on its head, or flip, the factual proposition being debated, thereby assisting the Court in its ultimate fact finding. Another well-known example arises at the conclusion of *A Time To Kill*, based on John Grisham first novel, in which the defence counsel invites the all jury to consider not the actual factual situation of a black man whose

black daughter was raped by two white men, but rather a factual background involving a blonde white girl who is violated by two black men.[124]

[7-5] A further quite simple example is found in Michael Harris' The Prodigal Husband The Tragedy of Helmuth and Hanna Buxbaum [McClelland and Stewart: Toronto, 1994], at page 289. When Mr. E.L. Greenspan, Q.C. sought bail on behalf of his client and buttressed his submission by advancing, among other things, an inventory of the religious pictures that adorned his client's home and "… a superficially impressive list of business associates and close family members who signed affidavits assuring the Court that Mr. Buxbaum was a devout Baptist, a model father, an outstanding businessman, and a law-abiding citizen…", the Crown countered with a request to cross-examine the affiants, to flip them so to peak with evidence suggesting a signal double life was being led by the defendant unbeknownst to them, leading the Court to state "… I suppose any scoundrel could find somebody to take an affidavit that would set forth some redeeming qualities about him." Refer to pages 288-289.[125]

[7-6] The Trial A History From Socrates To O.J. Simpson by U.S. educated attorney and English barrister Sadakat Kadri

---

[124] On the subject of reversing the proposition, note that page 405 of the "The Place of Law and Literature" (1986) 39 Vand. L. Rev. 391-417 by William H. Page includes a reference to a witness sobbing, "They forced me to say the opposite of what I was thinking."

[125] A book written in Canada would not be complete without a hockey reference. In Red Storey's biography, aptly titled Red's Story, (written with Brodie Snyder) [MacMillan Canada: Toronto, 1994], the former Argonaut Grey-Cup winner speaks of an incident while officiating a N.H.L. game involving Toronto. As we read at page 60, he admitted to having made a mistake while officiating, to then turn the table on the owner, Conn Smythe, who had been loudly critical to ask whether any of his players had made any mistakes themselves during the game in question.

includes a fascinating account of the trial of François de Saint-Méard before a revolutionary tribunal in Paris' Abbaye jail in August 1792. Accused of having edited a royalist newspaper, and having seen his trial interrupted by the summary judgment of others who were immediately executed, he was asked by the Court "You have told us many times what you were *not*, but what is it that you *are*?" "Saint-Méard desperately replied that he was a patriot and explained that far from plotting against the Revolution, he had considered it too timid. The claim, addressed to men who were diligently murdering in the Revolution's name was an audacious one." But he was successful. Thus, one might think that reversing the proposing is at times a risk worth taking. See p. xiii, [Random House, New York, 2005]. Finally, the classic example is found in Shakespeare's Macbeth, at 23-l. 24-40:

Porter: … and drink, sir, is a great provoker of three things.

Macduff: What three things does drink especially provoke?

Porter: Marry, sir, nose-painting, sleep and urine. Lechery, sir, it provokes and unprovokes; it provokes the desire, but it takes away the performance. Therefore, much drink may be said to be an equivocator with lechery: it makes him, and it mars him; it sets him on, and it takes him off; it persuades him, and disheartens him; makes him stand to, and not stand to…

[7-7] In essence, therefore, when one advocate argues that having consumed alcohol to excess, the other side's client was more likely to seek out sexual congress, and is met with the response that not only has it not been shown that this occurred, but it is equally likely that having consumed alcohol to excess, the client sought to sleep it off, the Court may be better situated to reach a sound conclusion as to where the

truth, if any, is to be discovered.[126]   In few words, no proposition is sound if it may be reversed as easily.[127]

[7-8] In the final analysis, it is suggested in the strongest terms, as will be illustrated by the many examples that follow, that this technique is quite effective in detecting any flaws in the reasoning engaged in by the opposing counsel and in ensuring that the ultimate winning argument is free of logical errors or mistakes of judgment.

---

[126]   After all, alcohol affects us all differently: "That which hath made them drunk hath made me bold" *Macbeth* (2-2-1).

[127]   Note that A.H. Ormerod's article, "The SS Collar" (1971) 17 <u>Catholic Lawyer</u> 289-299 touches upon the origin of the collar worn by Sir Thomas more in the famous Holbein portrait. Of interest, the brief article seeks to answer a number of questions but the advocate should note the passage found at p. 298, "To the question 'Why is he wearing the collar?' the proper answer may well be, 'Why should he not be wearing it?'" A superb example of reversing the proposition is found in the novel <u>Mary Barton</u>, by Elizabeth Gaskell. As we read at p. 108, " 'Ay Ay, the ladies (sweet souls) will come in shoals to hear a trial for murder, and watch the judge put on his black cap.' And then go home and groan over the Spanish ladies who take delight in bull-fights – 'such unfeminine creatures!'". Finally, at pp. 308-309 of "Essay and Play: Law's estrangement from Drama", by Jeremy M. Miller (1990), 18 <u>Western State U. L. Rev</u>. 265-311, the author noted that Gallahad's tale may be read as the account of a loser who died in the mountains on a foolish quest or as a hero who accomplished his goal."

2) Discussion

1) Reversing the proposition: An example of how to 'flip back" an important witness who has provided contradictory information in the pre-trial period.

[7-9] One may refer to this situation as the "John McGraw" problem. McGraw was the long-time and celebrated manager of the New York Giants, a member of the Baseball Hall of Fame and one of the most cantankerous and feisty characters one could imagine, as described ably by noted historian Charles C. Alexander of Ohio University in his acclaimed book, John McGraw, Penguin Books, 1989, New York, N.Y. In one celebrated instance of violence, he punched an umpire in the course of a post-game conversation, reportedly on the grounds that the official had besmirched McGraw's good character. Seemingly proud of his staunch defence of his good name, he was incensed at the subsequent fine and suspension levied against him and informed a journalist that he was the victim in this affair and had been treated most unfairly by the league president. Indeed, the journalist claimed that McGraw had been shown the story prior to it being filed and approved of the contents.

[7-10] Of course, as might be expected, once the story was published, further controversy arose. As quoted in Red Smith's column of June 15, 1980, in the New York Times, when called before the National Board of directors, McGraw had submitted a signed statement denying that he had made the remarks attributed to him. This presented a significant difficulty for the writer in question

[7-11] Of interest, McGraw confided to some other journalists subsequently that the Giants' attorney had the statement prepared and both the attorney and the owner of the team "kept at him until he signed it."

[7-12] Thus, when confronted with a statement that contains vital information contradicting previous information, counsel

might find it advisable to avoid a direct attack on the damaging information itself, which only serves to further draw unhelpful attention, and to seek to ascertain the background to the drawing of the damaging document itself, or focus the impeachment on the words of the statement. In other words, attack the message, not the messenger. From the Court's perspective, however, this anecdote makes plain the obligation to assess all the information available including the background facts which may become decisive in the ultimate assessment of the affair.

[7-13] By way of summary, the Court might wish to:

a) concentrate its attention on the time and the efforts the witness spent with those who drafted the statement in order to assess whether the time was sufficient to permit a full debate; and

b) it might also be wise to focus on the language of the statement to show that it does not contain vocabulary within the ken of the declarant, or if otherwise, not normally resorted to in order to make plain that the declarant repeated what was given to him or her to sign.

[7-14] In addition, the circumstances of the presentation of the contradictory information might be germane. In this instance, as reported by biographer Alexander at page 199 of his superb text, when presenting McGraw's retraction, the owner of the club was quoted as having said that McGraw had "signed the statement under no coercion whatsoever." Why insist on such an assertion if not to address the very suspicious circumstances that obviously were present?

2) Reversing the proposition: Can we ever be certain?

[7-15] In his excellent book, <u>Days in Court</u>, [Carswell: Toronto, 1958], R. Roy McMurtry Q.C. points to a remarkable example of brevity in cross-examination. Indeed, in a case of medical negligence, the plaintiff's evidence was quite formidable and the defendant's counsel chose to ask but one question of only one of the expert physicians called by the injured party. "Is it not true, Doctor, that medicine being such an uncertain science, no doctor can be really positive in his prognosis in any given case?" No matter what the answer, the damage that could be done to the defence case was quite limited. On the one hand, if the witness testified that medicine has achieved an exalted status in terms of knowledge, the civil jury would be no doubt sceptical; if the answer were that doubtless there is much truth in the assertion, the error of the defendant would appear far less significant. For the trier of fact, of course, this reversing of the proposition is not necessarily all that useful…

3) Reversing the proposition: Contradicting a witness without a foundation

[7-16] In "A Time to Kill", the forensic psychiatrist is asked how many times he has testified on behalf of the prosecution and the answer is then met by the question "Was it not rather this [higher number]?" That is a perfect example of the <u>R. v. Lyttle</u> (2004), 180 C.C.C. (3d) 476 (S.C.C.) type of admissible challenge based on nothing more than instinct.[128] If the witness answer demonstrates a perfect knowledge of such information, the jury will be invited to speculate later what

---

[128] An excellent review of the subject was penned by Andrea E.E. Tuck-Jackson, now a member of the Ontario Court of Justice. See "Lyttle – What Foundation Must Defence Counsel Have Before Cross-Examining A Witness", 4th Annual Six Minute Criminal Defence Lawyer, The Law Society of Upper Canada, Continuing Legal Education, Toronto.

pride the witness surely takes in these endeavours that s/he, in effect, puts a notch on his belt each time. If the doctor does not know, or will dissemble and suggest that the information is not known, then counsel may suggest a different answer confident that the Court or jury will see that as a good example of pains-taking trial preparation and research. Indeed, the witness may be led to believe that counsel has conducted impressive research and may not wish to be too liberal in testifying for fear of being shown to be incorrect.

[7-17] In Russ Conway's acclaimed book, Game Misconduct: Alan Eagleson and the Corruption of Hockey [MacFarlane Walter & Ross: Toronto 1995], we are offered a striking example at page 59 of a non-responsive answer touching upon the applicability of disability insurance. In effect, an official answers "I can't specifically say yes or no ... I've got a gut feeling it came after [the event in question]". In fact, counsel ought never to be confronted by such a situation in that no important question of an official, be it a police officer or emergency room physician, should be framed without counsel having done the leg work to ensure that the correct information is available to assist the Court in evaluating the importance of such a contradiction. Of course, if no information is available to impeach, it may be necessary for counsel to improvise and to bluff. For example, in "A Few Good Men", when Tom Cruise invites the Air Force crew members to sit in the courtroom in plain view of Jack Nicholson, although they have no relevant information, unbeknownst to Nicholson. In effect, it is a modified and modern version of the "blank piece of paper" trick, predicted on the belief that the witness believes information is available sufficient to reverse the proposition.

4) Reversing the proposition: The answer was unresponsive because the question was unintelligible

[7-18] The problem may be stated as follows: Counsel must avoid framing questions in such a way that the witness may not be able to provide assistance and be described as evasive, or unhelpful in testifying. In other words, if the client states

something that is clearly nonsensical, flip the responsibility to opposing counsel for framing an unintelligible question.

[7-19] A celebrated instance of an examination in which the questioner is remembered for the question framed, as opposed to the response obtained, is found in the record of the Senate Subcommittee on Antitrust and Monopoly investigative committee in 1958 investigating Major League Baseball's attempt to preserve its anti-trust exemption. As recorded for posterity (and popular reading) in Red Smith's column in the New York Times of January 18, 1981, Casey Stengel, the sexagenarian manager of the New York Yankees famous for mangling the Queen's English, was asked the following question:

> I had a conference with one of the attorneys representing not only baseball but all of the sports ... I wonder if you would accept his definition. He said they didn't want to be subjected to the *ipse dixit* of the Federal Government because they would throw a lot of damage suits on the *ad damnum* clause. He said, in the first place, the Toolson case was *sui generis*, it was *de minimis non cural lex*.

[7-20] As might be expected, the response of the witness was not helpful: "Well, you are going to get me there for about two hours."[129]

[7-21] The great jurist Benjamin Cardozo also makes the point, speaking to judges, "... opinion will need persuasive

---

[129]   Of interest, when Mickey Mantle was called next, he was asked whether he had any observations with reference to the issue being debated and responded as follows: "My views are just about the same as Casey's". In other words, he adopted all that was said even though it made little sense and was thoroughly unintelligible.

force, or the impressive virtue of sincerity and fire, or the mnemonic power of alliteration and antithesis, or the terseness and tang of the proverb, and the maxim. Neglect the help of these allies, and [the opinion] may never win its way." Refer to page 338 of <u>Selected Writings of Benjamin Nathan Cardozo</u> (Margaret E. Hall ed., 1947), the article titled "Law and Literature".[130]

[7-22] On the question of the appropriate vocabulary in advocacy, recall Carl Sandburg's poem "The Lawyers Know Too Much"

> ...
> In the heels of the haggling lawyers, Bob,
> Too many slippery ifs and buts and howevers,
> Too much hereinbefore provided whereas,
> Too many doors to go in and out of.

[7-23] In addition, I refer to "Of Writing by Lawyers" by G.V.V. Nicholls, published in (1949) 28 <u>Can. Bar Rev</u>. 1208-1228 which includes these observations: "... the ideal for the lawyer in his ordinary writing should be to sound as little as a lawyer as he can..." See page 1211. Consider this advice in light of the comment attributed to a lawyer contemporary of Sir William Blackstone "... any lawyer who writes so clearly as to be intelligible (to anyone) is an enemy of his profession." Refer to Vere Radir Norton, "Lawyers and Literature" (1932), 18 <u>A.B.A.J</u>. 301-306, at page 302.

---

[130] We lawyers are grateful to Judge Cardozo for reminding us that "... the search ... for the just word, the happy phrase, that will give expression to the thought..." Refer to page 225 of "The Growth of the Law", in <u>Selected Writings of Benjamin Nathan Cardozo</u> (Margaret E. Hall ed., 1947).

5) Reversing the proposition: Objective versus subjective facts

[7-24] In framing a sound judgment as to whether counsel succeeded in gaining the advantage over a witness by means of this technique, it is important for the Court to evaluate whether counsel delineated the objective information from the subjective impressions or beliefs. For example, a temperature of 30 degrees Celsius is an objective fact. For some, however, perceived on a subjective basis, it is too stifling to achieve anything and it is simply impossible to concentrate or to accomplish any task. On the contrary, for others, it is the highlight of the year! Thus, counsel who accept without challenge statements such as "It was just blistering" or "it was perfect weather for the beach" do not assist the Bench. The advocate must ascertain what "subjective" yardstick the witness is resorting to in framing the opinion that is being advanced and that must be challenged.

[7-25] In this respect, consider the height of an individual. The objective standard is best evaluated by reference to those "vertical measuring tapes" that are ubiquitous in store entrances. What counsel must find out is whether the belief by the witness that a 5'10" assailant is tall is an accurate estimate based on that individual's much shorter stature or illustrates a lack of understanding of what is involved in attempting to measure height (or to estimate height). In such cases, counsel might wish to have a number of foils stand up in the courtroom and request of the witness to judge whether they are tall or short, but not the height. In light of the answers, the defence would then call an investigator to state the heights of those involved to demonstrate how broad or how narrow is the height embraced by the expressions at play.

6) Reversing the proposition: Is the witness a positive sort or a pessimist?

[7-26] A further example of the merits of counsel adopting the practice of reversing the proposition as a matter of course in

litigation is found at page 45 of Tommy Lasorda's hugely entertaining autobiography The Artful Dodger, written with David Fisher [Arbor House: New York, 1985]. "A ballplayer discovers whether he is an optimist or a pessimist when he is involved in a deal between two clubs: The optimist is thrilled that his new team wanted him; the pessimist is depressed that his old team did not want him. If he is traded for other players, the optimist can't believe his old team actually got *those* players for him; the pessimist can't believe his old team got *only* those players for him. If it is a cash deal, the optimist believes he was bought; the pessimist believes he was sold." [Emphasis in original]

[7-27] In the same light, the Court must ascertain whether the perspective of the witness results in colouring that person's view of the world. For some, a speed of 130 kilometres an hour will surely lead to an accident and fatalities, their pessimist soul and outlook on the world dictates such a result; for others, this is surely a minimum speed to get anywhere safely given one's mastery of the wheel. In each case, it is the function of the Court to identify the objective factual elements that are being "twisted" by subjective aspects of a person's individual judgment.

7) Reversing the proposition: Arguing by analogy

[7-28] Returning to Tommy Lasorda's hugely entertaining autobiography The Artful Dodger, written with David Fisher [Arbor House: New York, 1985], page 90 provides an apt example of arguing by analogy. During the course of a baseball game in the Dominican Republic, Manager Lasorda punctuated a particularly powerful objection a ruling by an umpire by removing a good deal of his uniform, leaving him naked to the waist. Arrested for indecent exposure (it seems), Lasorda reasoned as follows in his public explanation that took the form of a radio debate:

> "... Do you have boxing matches in this country?" He said they did. "And do they

box with their shirts on or off?" Off, he admitted. "And let me ask you, do you have beaches in this country?" "Beautiful beaches", he said. "And when a man is walking on the beach, does he have his shirt on or off?" "Off", he admitted. "Okay", I concluded, "if people can go in the boxing ring with their shirts off and they're not insulting anybody, and they can walk on the beach without insulting anybody, who am I insulting when I take my shirt off."

[7-29] Of course, the response if you reverse the proposition is that people expect semi-clad persons to be found on the beach and in the boxing ring.

8) Reversing the proposition: Introducing multiple foils

[7-30] As discussed under the rubric of "Reversing the proposition: Objective versus subjective facts", the Court must evaluate to what extent counsel has successfully challenged certain opinions that are advanced by witnesses in certain circumstances by introducing certain foils. The most obvious is in the case of voice identification. Nothing is more effective in the case of a doubtful voice identification, and only in such cases, to have a number of recordings made by different persons who speak in a manner not unlike the subject voice and to invite the witness to select the correct voice. In the same fashion, if a person claims to be able to spot a 1993 Ford Tempo from a collection on 1992's and 1993's, then it may be advantageous to have a video made of a number of foils traveling together with the subject car and to invite the witness to pick out the correct vehicle.

9) Reversing the proposition: Credibility and malapropisms

[7-31] Joe Garagiola's hugely entertaining book, It's Anybody's Ballgame, [Contemporary Books: Chicago, Ill: 1988] includes an anecdote that might be useful in cases of a witness who appears to have said one thing, but intended to say the opposite. As we read at page 58, a player stated "My goals this season are to hit .300, score 100 runs, and stay injury prone." In such cases, it is always useful to have an example of this type situation to point to when trying to explain in the course of a judgment that the witness meant the opposite of what was said.

10) Reversing the proposition: One reveller gets arrested, a thousand get a police escort

[7-32] A classic illustration of the logic of the Courts and the justice system is that instrumental values inform a great deal of the exercise of judicial discretion. Hence, since the police can easily arrest one reveller celebrating the Dunsmore Cup results from Australia, they do so; since they cannot arrest a thousand students celebrating the Stanley Cup results from Montreal, they choose to ensure that the celebrants enjoy a path through the streets. In Seaver A Biography, by Gene Schoor [Contemporary Books: Chicago, Illinois, 1986] we are informed of the manner in which the fans celebrated the Mets' clinching of the division title in 1969, by pouring out onto the field by the thousands and tearing out home plate, the pitcher's mound, etc. See page 131. Indeed, we read later that pandemonium broke out in 1973 when a further pennant was won. Refer to page 211.[131] A further reference of value is taken from page 4 of Thomas Boswell evocative Why Time Begins On Opening Day, [Penguin Books: New York, 1984].

---

[131] See the period account of the 1871 riot in Chicago found in Pennant Races Baseball at Its Best, by Dave Anderson [Doubleday: New York, 1994], at page 34.

"You're safer spending the night in San Quentin than walking the streets of a town that just won a pennant."[132]

11) Reversing the proposing: To what were you paying attention?

[7-33] When counsel attempt to impeach the credit of witnesses by pressing for even greater and more exacting details, the Court must pay great attention to the details being elicited that might be corroborated or denied by someone else who was also present and who is excluded from being informed of the details of the testimony. This is often a good tactic to impeach a Carter defence respecting how much alcohol was consumed on the evening in question. For example, if the persons were at a wedding reception, and an inquiry is made of the witness how well s/he recalls what took place. On the one hand, if the recall of the "action" is quite detailed, the Court may question how the witness took in all of this information and still managed to observe closely the number of drinks consumed at the table. Consider at well the situation if a group was at a sports bar, and the witness is asked to can provide details of the game to show that either that or the drinking pattern was being observed closely. If the replies are to the effect that the drinking was quite noticeable, the Court must evaluate why this was of such interest, as opposed to the game, if there was little by way of drinking.

12) Reversing the proposition:
The impaired sing song

[7-34] What follows is of assistance to a trial Court in attempting to judge whether an investigating officer did indeed observe all that ends up in the note book. Typically, counsel

---

[132] See the description of the "positive" riot at the Polo Grounds after Bobby Thompson's historic home run at page 188 of Rickey & Robinson The Men Who Broke Baseball's Color Barrier, by Harvey Frommer [Macmillan Publishing Co., Inc.: New York, 1982].

would be well advised to obtain as many examples of that individual's notebook entries for similar investigations, preferably without making disclosure requests which might tip off this tactic, so to speak. The ideal method is to obtain these documents from other counsel. Prior to cross-examining the officer, counsel will draw a comparative chart of how often the same indicators are present, that is to say how often the notebook entries record "flushed face", "bloodshot eyes", "strong smell of an alcoholic beverage", "fumbling for the licence", "unresponsive to simple questions". Better yet, counsel may draw a list of how often the entries flowed in the same order and if the resulting package mirrors the information consigned against the defendant, the Court might be well positioned to conclude as to the lack of professionalism of the investigator.

13) Reverse the proposition:
Never admitting a mistake

[7-35] A further example of reversing the proposition is also found in Tommy Lasorda's hugely entertaining autobiography The Artful Dodger, written with David Fisher [Arbor House: New York, 1985]. As we read at page 163, a leather-lunged fan was screaming at Lasorda that he was an idiot for playing a particular pitcher as an outfielder after a nine year undistinguished career as a hurler. When the pitcher hit a rocket for a home run, the fan simply turned the matter on its head and bellowed that Lasorda was an idiot not to have played him sooner as an outfielder and to have left him in the bullpen for so long. For the judgment writer, this is merely another example of one facet of human nature: the witness who will never admit making a mistake.

14) Reversing the proposition: We are not all the same - our experiences differ

[7-36] In his haunting recitation of life in Philadelphia, Mississippi, two decades after three white civil rights workers were murdered, woven around the attempts by college football

programs to sign the greatest high school player of all time, or so it seemed at the time, The Courting of Marcus Dupree, [Doubleday & Company, Inc.: Garden City, New York, 1983], celebrated writer Willie Morris recounts how a college coach had picked up a potential recruit at the airport and was driving him along a pastoral stretch of highway when the young man asked "What's that?" and the coach responded that it was a cow. The player's response was that he had never seen one before and found the sight amazing." See page 124. Thus, in judging our fellows, we must be mindful that what might be obvious to us may be unheard of for others.

15) Reversing the proposition: Misunderstandings of what we subjectively perceive

[7-37] I owe it to the two co-authors of Home Games Two Baseball Wives Speak Out, Bobbie Bouton and Nancy Marshall [St. Martin's/Marek: New York, 1983] for quoting the following passage, which is always apposite when considering the human capacity to understand as much as to confuse wholly human interrelationships involving complex dynamics such as sex. As we read at pages 8-9, "We recently heard a lawyer say that there is no such thing as perjury: it's just that sometimes people recollect things differently. These recollections are our truth. But we also know Virginia Woolf was right when she wrote, in A Room of One's Own: '... when a subject is highly controversial, and any question about sex is that - one cannot hope to tell the truth. One can only show how one came to hold whatever opinion one does hold. One can only give one's audience the chance of drawing their own conclusions as they observe the limitations, the prejudices, the idiosyncrasies of the speaker.'"

16) Reversing the proposition: Attacking written proof or "Where Is It Written"?

[7-38] "Where is it written?" may be Yentl's way of verifying the accuracy or veracity of information but as made plain by the "Dewey Wins!" headline, one has to be careful that the information that finds itself reduced to print is accurate. One

sporting example is drawn from p. 238 of Reed Browning's excellent biography of Cy Young, A Baseball Life, [University of Massachusetts Press: Amherst, Mass, 2000]. As we read at footnote 48, a book on the life of John McGraw includes mention of his win in the 1895 Cup even though this is not accurate. Stated otherwise, the advocate's task may be to reverse the proposition by making plain that was is written is not accurate and the Court's function is to guarded lest inaccurate information be taken at face value.

[7-39] A further example is drawn from the book, Winston Churchill An Intimate Portrait, by Violet Bonham Carter [Konecky & Konecky: New York, 1965]. Reference is made to a remarkable example of an individual seeking to take one position, or to be understood to have always been of one view, when the record demonstrates amply that the opposite is true. As we read at page 317, Churchill complained to his father that a certain official was being quoted as saying that "... he was against the Dardanelles and had been all along..." notwithstanding the fact that this Sea Lord had agreed in writing to every prior element of that military endeavour and the general enterprise as a whole.

17) Reversing the proposition: Look at it from the child's perspective

[7-40] It is important for the fact finder to always consider a situation from the perspective of the witness and this is never truer than in the case of a child witness. The best example I can point to is found in Thomas Boswell evocative Why Time Begins On Opening Day, [Penguin Books: New York, 1984]. Major league umpire Lou DiMuro observed "The first five years I was in the majors, my four sons never got to see me ... I'd try to catch a plane home for a few hours, then hop back out to the next tow. The kids at school asked my oldest boy what I did for a living. He was real proud. He told 'em: 'My daddy works at the airport.'"

18) Reversing the proposition: The witness no longer believes what she once did

[7-41] The Court must always be alert to the very real possibility that witness will no longer be motivated by whatever favourable inclinations were at play when they first were interviewed, especially if significant periods of time have elapsed. By way of limited example, former Premier Lucien Bouchard once exclaimed to Her Excellency Adrienne Clarkson, then the agent-general for Ontario to France, "Had I ever seen Vancouver before I would never have been able to be committed to taking Quebec out of Confederation." See page 107 of Lawrence Martin's controversial biography, The Antagonist Lucien Bouchard and the Politics of Delusion, [Viking: Toronto 1997].[133] One does not doubt that Mr. Bouchard was sincere when he said it, and one does not doubt that he was equally sincere when other imperatives moved him to think otherwise subsequently. In the same vein, a witness who was prepared to testify, notwithstanding the limited scope for this type of evidence, that the music teacher you represent in a sexual violence case is a paragon of virtue, s/he may later have second thoughts and counsel must be vigilant to ensure that no last second thoughts are now being entertained.

19) Reversing the proposition: Immaturity is not unknown in older individuals

[7-42] In trying to decide whether counsel succeeded in obtaining at least a grudging concession from a police officer that perhaps, once upon a time, she had decided that what might appear to be an offence was no more than an example of fun, albeit stupid fun or jocularity, it might be worthwhile to recall certain examples that are often found in the

---

[133] If nothing else, The Antagonist demonstrates clearly what painstaking and diligent research may uncover of potential controversies and contradictions as recorded and reported in the public record.

biographies of famous politicians and sporting figures to make plain that "boys will be boys" at all ages. For example, Volume 1 of Lawrence Martin's brilliant biography of former Prime Minister Jean Chrétien, The Will to Win, [Lester Publishing: Toronto, 1995], includes a description at page 155 of a mischievous politician who was to meet Mr. Chrétien and who, unable to find a parking spot, mischievously rammed vehicles back and forth as if playing bumper car on a carnival midway until sufficient room had been created.

20) Reversing the proposition:
Avoiding cultural 'flips'

[7-43] On occasion, it may be necessary for counsel to prepare a witness by attempting to identify and to isolate and then neutralize any cultural elements that might impede or impair the witness' ability to be as convincing as possible on the stand. In other words, to avoid the type of "reversing" that the other side(s) may engage in. For example, in Austin Clarke's highly acclaimed and celebrated novel, The Polished Hoe, [Thomas Allen Publishers: Toronto, 2002], we read at page 177 that a character has been "... educated to believe that anything from Over-and-Away is ... superior to anything we have...".[134] Many individuals are prepared to defer to suggestions made by others that if they say that an object was dark, and another person has said greyish, and that person claims certain objective qualities, let us say place of origin or educational achievement, and then they will modify their

---

[134] To the same effect is the quote attributed to Michele Landsberg, "Nous avions été élevés dans l'idée que rien de ce qui était canadien n'avait d'intérêt." [Translation: We had been raised in the belief that nothing that was Canadian was worthy of our interest]. See Ed Broadbent La conquête obstinée du pouvoir, by Judy Steed, [Les Éditions de l'homme: Montréal, 1988], at page 65.

opinion and defer to the other's view of the matter.[135] Obviously, the trier of fact must be careful to only assess the answers at their core, as opposed to their obvious or evident sense.

21) Reversing the proposition: Decisions based on facts as opposed to beliefs

[7-44] John Madden's delightful book [written with Dave Anderson], One Knee Equals Two Feet (And Everything Else You Need To Know About Football) [New York: Villard Books, 1986] includes a revealing account at page 72 of an executive not wishing to examine information or to consider arguments that might indicate a flaw in the reasoning that led to the original tentative decision. In effect, John Madden questions whether a particular running back should be drafted as highly as was intended in light of his success in college on artificial turf given that the team in question played on a natural surface. To every hesitation and concern raised by Madden, the executive would merely respond by his profound belief in a given factual situation. In effect, "I do not wish to look at numbers or statistics or information, I merely want to do what I want to do (or advance the opinion I wish to advance) even though I cannot defend the conclusion I have reached save for a gut feeling, an instinctive belief. This situation will be encountered often in the world of litigation and the Court must be mindful of this possibility and counsel gas a duty to assist in marshalling a great deal of information lest the intuitive beliefs win the day.

[7-45] The converse situation is discussed at length in Mind Game How The Boston Red Sox Got Smart And Finally Won A World Series, edited by Steve Goldman et al., [Workman Publishing: New York, 2005], where the principal author and his collaborators point out, time and time again, how certain decisions, how the Book if you wish, is quite simply dead

---

[135] One is reminded of the quite sexist interplay that dominates The Taming of the Shrew.

wrong if the numbers are allowed to dominate the discussion. In fact, if one leaves aside received wisdom, and if the raw statistical data are considered coolly and in a detached and objective fashion, we see that successful teams eschew bunts by non-pitchers for example, notwithstanding he many examples of successful coaches and managers touting the bunt. In the same fashion, many doctors will cling to certain bedrock beliefs taught to them early on in their careers and these beliefs are clung to notwithstanding the paucity of supporting evidence if not in the face of abundant contradictory information. In one instance, Dr. Charles Smith testified that children do not die of minor household falls otherwise we would be seeing them in our autopsy rooms. Note the logical fallacy. Since other health professionals are better informed and know perfectly well that many children suffer fatal injuries in such fashion, autopsies are not sought, creating the lack of numbers that the pathologists seizes upon to justify his conclusion which rests upon nothing more than "impressionistic" or "anecdotal" evidence.

22) Reversing the proposition: The actions of a person may not reflect their thoughts

[7-46] In his superlative biography Hitter The Life And Turmoils of Ted Williams, [Harcourt Brace & Co.: New York, 1993], Ed Linn recounts an incident in which Ted's bat flew into the crowd at Fenway Park and hit a fan, who was employed by a high-ranking team official. As we read at page 297, "Completely disgusted with himself for taking the pitch [and striking out], Ted turned toward the dugout and angrily flung his bat away. Unfortunately, the bat caught for a moment on the sticky substance he used on it to give himself a firmer grip. Instead of skidding across the dirt, the bat spiralled into the air, sailed into the box seats seventy-five feet away, and hit a sixty-year-old woman." The team official was quoted as saying, "It was an impetuous act, but no one is sorrier than Ted is... It was unfortunate, but we certainly know Williams didn't do it intentionally."

[7-47] A number of questions must be flow-charted by a Court called upon to adjudicate as to what the player's intention was in such circumstances. The questions might include the following:

> a) Does the consequence, the grave one of the bat striking an elderly woman, influence our view of the action? Stated otherwise, should the jury only be shown the first part of any video recording lest the consequences influence the evaluation of what the actor did?;
> b) Does the employer-employee relationship between the injured party and the team official influence unduly, or at all, the view taken of the factual elements?
> c) Does the employer-employee relationship between the player and the club influence the view taken of the incident? In other words, if a bench warmer had acted so, would it matter?

[7-48] There are a great number of other questions that have to be considered as well. For example, Ted Williams reacted by breaking out into tears when he saw the woman injured. Does this reaction matter?[136]

23) Reversing the proposition: For some, an obvious answer need not be expressed directly

[7-49] In the book <u>Season of Glory The Amazing Saga of the 1961 New York Yankees</u>, Ralph Houk and Robert W. Creamer [G. P. Putnam's Sons: New York, 1988] relate the question asked of Roger Maris by a reporter "Do you fool around on the road?" to which Maris responded directly "I'm a married man."

---

[136] See also page 112 of Donald Honig's, <u>Baseball Between the Lines, Baseball in the '40s and '50s As Told By The Men Who Played It</u>, [Coward, McMann & Geoghegan: New York, 1976].

The reporter was not dissuaded by the answer, retorting, "I'm a married man myself but I fool around on the road." See page 230. The point to be drawn from this example is that the objective truth of the first answer, "I'm a married man" did not necessarily convey a negative answer to a person who was a philanderer. To those triers of facts, a negative reply or a denial was required lest the answer would be seen as evasive. This question and answer are offered as an illustration of the need for a witness to be instructed to respond in the briefest yet the most direct fashion.

24) Reversing the proposition: What of apparent contradictions?

[7-50] The world of sports may also be a useful venue to select examples of seemingly healthy individuals who are considered disabled, in order to assist the claims of certain injured parties in civil litigation including claims before various workers' compensation boards. Perhaps the best-known example is Mickey Mantle, who was considered unfit for military service by American authorities though he appeared to be the foremost example of American sporting achievement in his early years. As we read in the informative book The Last Hero The Life of Mickey Mantle, by David Faulkner, [Simon & Schuster: New York, 1995], at pages 83-85, it is often impossible for an outsider and one not possessed of medical qualifications to appreciate the pain and or limitations another person is experiencing.

25) Reversing the proposition: Cross-examination on prior record

[7-51] If there is any truism in the world of criminal litigation, it is that people believe that they do not have a criminal record based on any of the following facts, chosen from what seems to be a well-nigh infinite list, and accordingly deny that they have a relevant criminal past when asked about, such answer being objectively false:

a) it happened more than 5, 3, 2 years ago;
b) it happened in another province;
c) it happened before I was 21;
d) I did not get a fine;
e) I only got a fine;
f) There has been a general amnesty since;
g) I have gotten into the States since then...

[7-52] A simple example is found at page 148 of the well researched tome, <u>Balls & Strikes The Money Game in Professional Baseball</u>, by Kenneth M. Jennings, [Praeger: New York, 1990.] The author points out, mistakenly, that the general public and an arbitrator consider that Ferguson Jenkins did not commit a serious offence in that he was found guilty but given no sentence arising out of his prosecution in Canada. In fact, the great Hall of Famer from Chatam, Ontario, received an absolute discharge, which is a form of sentence. All of which to say counsel are well advised to not insist too greatly on any supposed lack of candour by a witness who might profess not to have a record, but counsel would be well advised to thoroughly explain the meaning of such entries as might have been disclosed and to provide stern guidance on the need for candour, lest the type of situation discussed herein arises

26) Reversing the proposition: The use of interpreters

[7-53] On occasion, advocates will wish to suggest that an individual has not been candid in failing to answer directly in the language of the interview certain questions, whether as a witness at the scene or during court proceedings. This is a very controversial area. On balance, if the judge or jury is capable of understanding the language of the interview and the individual's language in response, it may not be necessary to add much in submissions. Stated otherwise, a

Francophone judge will know whether a Francophone was capable of doing better in English than what was shown, but will not be able to know whether the witness's grasp of a different language was strong or not.

[7-54] I wish to underscore that in our modern society, many individuals who testify are fluent in neither English nor French and counsel must always be vigilant to ensure that no adverse demeanour finding is predicated upon a poor impression either as a result of resorting to an interpreter or by failing to resort to one and having spoken in a fashion that was not as impressive as might be expected for one at least conversant in our official languages. William Zinsser's very enjoyable tome, Spring Training The Unique American Story of Baseball's Annual Season of Renewal, [Harper & Row: New York, 1989] includes these comments on what former Manager Jim Leyland of the Pittsburgh Pirates called "the language barrier". "I took it for granted that the Latin players on teams I managed here in the States knew what I was talking about. Some of them didn't." See page 65. The additional danger is that the advocate who has not spent sufficient time with the client may have jumped to the same conclusion.[137]

[7-55] In addition, as pointed to perceptively in her delightful book Glory Jays Canada's World Series Champions, Rosie DiManno [Sagamore Publishing: Toronto, 1993], at page 162 in discussing Juan Guzman, "The City of Toronto was learning something about Guzman a well. He was not as bland, as diffident, as might originally have been thought. That perception was due largely to an unwillingness to discourse

---

[137]   In considering the question of demeanour and difficulties with the language, refer to Sosa An Autobiography, by Sammy Sosa (with Marcos Breton) [Warner Books: New York, 2000]. The book reminds us of the difficulties faced by individuals who must move to a different country, in which the culture and language are different and that one should not be surprised to find that many difficulties are encountered. See p. 110 in particular.

extensively in English, a language he knew well enough but felt self-conscious about in using..."   There are many valid reasons why someone wishes to testify with the assistance of an interpreter but the fact remains that it often permits the witness more time within which to craft an appropriate response.

27) Reversing the proposition: Do not accept at face value the words spoken

[7-56] At times, baseball books provide useful illustrations of certain circumspect answers that might assist the witness unless opposing counsel is vigilant in challenging the true meaning of the words, an important consideration for the trier of facts. A good example is found in Bill Lee's iconoclastically funny biography The Wrong Stuff, written with Dick Lally [The Viking Press: New York, 1984], at page 21. In discussing his use of marijuana while a University student, the "Spaceman" noted that he was asked if he had experimented with other than pot. His answer was in the negative. To Lee's view of the world, "I never experimented with pot. I just took it."[138]

[7-57] In other words, if a witness answers a question, "Did you experiment with weed by answering no, that witness may believe that s/he has answered truthfully in that there was no experimentation. Not unlike answering a question, "Were you ever alone with Monica..." by saying "No" by reason of the fact that one is not alone if with someone else.

[7-58] A further example is found in the aptly titled biography, Nobody's Perfect, [The Dial Press: New York, 1975], wherein former 31-game winning pitcher Denny McLain wrote, with

---

[138]   Mr. Lee was of the view that one of his former team mates, arrested with a great deal of marijuana, should advance the defence the stash was for personal use as the defendant expects to live to see his one hundred and twelfth birthday, and the stash would only have lasted until his eighty-second year. See page 105 of The Wrong Stuff.

Dave Diles, about an encounter with investigators seeking information about his gambling habits. As we read at page 23, Mr. McLain opined, "Now, I really don't think I lied to those gentlemen. It's just that I did not tell the complete truth. I figured they really didn't have anything on me and probably were after bigger fish, so why should I implicate myself any more than I had to?" Of interest to counsel, Mr. McLain added, "Anyway, I wasn't represented by an attorney at the meeting..." Hence, counsel must be vigilant to guard against these superficially correct but fundamentally flawed response.[139]

28) Reversing the proposition: "Old Enough to Know Better" implies that some are not

[7-59] In Harvey Frommer's classic examination of the 1919 Black Sox scandal, Shoeless Joe And Ragtime Baseball [Taylor Publishing Company: Dallas, 1992], page 145 quotes Hall of Famer Eddie Collins as follows: "They were old enough to know the difference between right and wrong." In the result, the Court must judge whether the individual in question is not sufficiently old enough to be held accountable as if able to make these mature distinctions and ought not to be held to so exacting a measure of conduct.[140]

---

[139]   I refer to an anecdote told by a very respected jurist, Justice James A. Fontana, the learned author of a series of books on search warrants published by Butterworths who relates the testimony of a former client who answered the Crown's question in the course of an impaired trial, "How much did you have to drink?" by responding "As I told the police officer, no more than three." Thus, the careful and circumspect answer is a lie by omission in that the witness did not respond candidly with the information sought.

[140]   One assumes that the father of Lou Piniella, the manager of the Tampa Bay Devil Rays, was "old enough to know better". As explained in his biography Sweet Lou (written with Maury Allen) [G.P. Putnam's Sons: New York, 1986], Mr. Piniella Sr. elected not to "bail out" his son from the

29) Reversing the proposition: Mothers (and all other relatives) are not very objective witnesses

[7-60] Relatives are often called in litigation to support an alibi, or to act as a surety and the advocate should be mindful that this offers a fertile ground for "flipping" or "reversing" tactics. For example, if the father of the defendant is a proposed surety in case involving high levels of drug trafficking, it may be opportune for the prosecutor to draw out at length how surprising is all of this alleged misconduct. Human nature being what it is, honest law-abiding individuals will naturally attempt to distance themselves from any taint of illegal activity. Hence, the father may well be heard to say, "… it came as a total shock to suspect any such involvement". Armed with this admission, prosecuting counsel will attempt to demonstrate that the proposed surety must not have been entertaining a close relationship to the defendant if nothing was known of the drug consumption, or the poor associations, or the unexplained funds with which to purchase luxury items.

[7-61] On the flip side, if the father were to testify that he well knew of the unlawful behaviour or changed lifestyle, or had grave suspicions, and did not act upon such information, it may be comparatively easier for the Crown to suggest that this relative is poorly situated to contend that he is now able to exercise adequate supervision or that the defendant will suffer this form of supervision, must less accept it in a positive spirit.

[7-62] The same technique applies for an alibi situation. Any relative, for example, is susceptible of being flustered when asked the question, "You would not want your [check one: husband, wife, close personal friend, etc.] to be [check one: jailed, lose employment, be found to be a child abuser, lose driving privileges, etc.], so naturally you would say anything to help and protect …" Once the standard question is asked and

---

local police jail cells one night after his son was caught drinking under-age. As his father is quoted as saying at page 41, "let him stay there. Maybe he'll learn something. I'll pick him up in the morning."

answered with the ubiquitous "I will not [check one: lie, perjure myself, risk jail], the next series of questions must make plain how much both the witness and the defendant have to lose. Thus, counsel will go through the financial, emotional, and other contributions of the person whose liberty is at stake prior to attempting to impeach the alibi evidence itself. If the witness is very helpful in answering these personal questions but reticent to answer the "alibi" questions, this will be enhanced in submissions. If the witness is reticent to answer the personal information, but demonstrates no hesitation respecting the alibi questions, the submissions will highlight how pat was the scenario.[141]

[7-63] Mary Barton, by Elizabeth Gaskell, includes an interesting passage on alibi. As quoted in "On Reading Mary Barton with Friedrich Engels" (1976), 29 Rutgers L. Rev. 298-316, by Earl. F. Murphy, at p. 313, as taken from the book at p. 320:

> "At the climax of the trial Mrs. Gaskell has a worker tell a lawyer exactly what the profession is worth. The prosecutor has just sneered at Will Wilson for the alibi he has furnished Jem. The lawyer wants to know how much money Will Wilson has been paid for coming from The Docks "or some less creditable place." Mrs. Gaskell endows Will Wilson with "bright, clear eyes, flaming with indignation." The lawyer cannot stand the integrity of the

---

[141] In this respect, note that in Larry Moffi's This Side of Cooperstown an Oral History of Major League Baseball in the 1950's [University of Iowa Press: Iowa City, 1995], the author relates at page 75 how my favourite "Boys of Summer" Carl Erskine commented "The only [fan] that doesn't think that Roger Clemens isn't worth $1,500 a pitch is his mother. His mother thinks it's wonderful ... and that'd be true with any mother."

honest worker and his "look fell at last before that stern, unflinching gaze." Will asks counsel: "Will you tell the judge and jury how much money you've been paid for your impudence towards one who has told God's blessed truth, and who would scorn to tell a lie, or blackguard any one, for the biggest fee as ever lawyer got for doing dirty work? Will you tell, sir?"

30) Reversing the proposition: Turning Queen's evidence not limited to those motivated by noble intentions

[7-64] In "The Mystery of Marie Roget", by Edgar Allan Poe, we obtain some guidance on the credit to be granted to accomplices who have, to borrow the traditional expression, "turned Queen's evidence" or become "grasses". As set out at para. 10, "... In the proclamation setting forth this reward, a full pardon was promised to any accomplice who should come forward in evidence against his fellow..." Simply put, the motivation for implicating others is the same as for throwing out other survivors from a lifeboat...

31) Reversing the proposition: Innocent persons, not just guilty ones, may give a poorly detailed alibi (especially when not given sufficient time to think)

[7-65] Returning to "The Mystery of Marie Roget", by Edgar Allan Poe, it includes the following passage, at para. 19 which is illustrative of the quite logical possibility that a first attempt to explain one's whereabouts may be unsatisfactory as not having been undertaken seriously or with sufficient resolve: "... St. Eustache fell especially under suspicion; and he failed, at first, to give an intelligible account of his whereabouts during the [relevant time]. Subsequently, however, he submitted ... affidavits, accounting satisfactorily for every hour of the day in question."

32) Reversing the proposition: We do not all react the same way to tragedy – the Nurse Nelles principle

[7-66] Any discussion of his issue must begin with a review of the contribution by Austin M. Cooper Q.C. found in <u>Counsel For The Defence The Bernard Cohn Lectures in Criminal Law</u>, edited by E.L. Greenspan, Q.C., [Irwin Law: Toronto, 2005], "Susan Nelles: The Defence of Innocence", at pages 27-42 and Chapter 20 of the autobiography of the Hon. David Vanek, <u>Fulfilment Memoirs of a Criminal Court Judge</u>, The Osgoode Society for Canadian Legal History: Toronto, 1999]. In effect, this individual may have become a strong suspect because she did not cry demonstrably or grieve outwardly.

[7-67] Further, note the guidance found in "The Mystery of Marie Roget", by Edgar Allan Poe. This tale suggests clearly that one may be suspicious of a too controlled reception of striking information.   As we read at para. 22: "... M. St. Eustache [the victim's fiancé...] deposes that he did not hear of the discovery of the body of his intended until the next morning ... For an item of news like this, it strikes us it was very coolly received." The next paragraph, however, decries this original report and suggests that "... far from receiving the news coolly, [St. Eustache] was distracted with grief..."

33) Reversing the proposition: The relevance of the irrelevant

[7-68] The advocate might profit from assisting the Court by attempting to demonstrate whether the instruction found flowing from the pen of Edgar Allan Poe in "The Mystery of Marie Roget", at para. 61 might be the foundation block for a successful argument that irrelevant information was characterized as such only by reason of the fact that what we designate as relevant is tributary to a quite flawed form of reasoning. "... Not the least usual error in investigations such as this is the limiting of inquiry to the immediate, with total disregard of the collateral or circumstantial events. It is the

malpractice of the courts to confine evidence and discussion of the bounds of apparent relevancy. Yet experience has shown, and a true philosophy will always show, that a vast, perhaps the larger, portion of truth arises from the seemingly irrelevant."

34) Reversing the proposition: Losing sight by too close attention or losing sight of the forest by reason of the presence of the trees

[7-69] Note that in "The Murders in The Rue Morgue", Edgar Allan Poe gives some instruction on the dangers of over-analysis. As we read at para. 56: "Vidocq, for example, was a good guesser, and a persevering man. But, without educated thought, he erred continually by the very intensity of his investigations. He impaired his vision by holding the object too close. He might see, perhaps, one or two points with unusual clearness, but in so doing he, necessarily, lost sight of the matter as a whole." This same type of problem in analysis may have been engaged in by the authorities and should be examined closely by counsel.

35) Reversing the proposition: After the fact conduct

[7-70] In Edgar Allan Poe's "Von Kempelen and His Discovery", we can read the following at para. 10: "... coming upon him suddenly, [the police] found him, as they imagined, in the midst of his counterfeiting operations. His agitation is represented as so excessive that the officers had not the slightest doubt of his guilt." Of course, in most cases, this type of scenario may be reversed or flipped quite easily. People are invariably spooked by the presence of the police and sometimes, as demonstrated by the tragedy involving the London police, individuals run away from the authorities to hide some difficulty which is not the subject matter of the inquiry.

36) Reversing the proposition: "I killed him" or "They say I killed him"

[7-71] If you recall the dialogue found in the arrest scene "My Cousin Vinny", you will understand how critical it is to have every word of a potentially incriminating situation recorded and understood in context. Another well known scenario involves the detainee being overheard to say to someone on the phone, while attempting to impress an operator blocking the attempt to reach counsel, "They say I killed John!" If the person overhearing catches only the last three words, a prosecution is sure to ensue...

[7-72] In this respect as in so many others, baseball books are also of assistance in mounting a defence to such accusations if they can assist in underscoring that the witness misheard what was said. Of the many quite interesting accounts of former baseball players found in Larry Moffi's This Side of Cooperstown an Oral History of Major League Baseball in the 1950's [University of Iowa Press: Iowa City, 1995] the one that is the most gripping was related by Vic Power who indicated at page 99 that when he first came to America, his accent when speaking English was so pronounced that when he asked a waitress for a fork, she heard a request for fornication. This gives a more vivid emphasis on the need to explore whether the hearer of any supposed threat, admission, etc. heard the comment fully and fairly.

37) Reversing the proposition: Even the most upright may deceive

[7-73] Although one is naturally inclined to believe that certain figures are inherently worthy of belief, the advocate must be mindful of the fact that we are human, and may be possessed of the fabled "clay feet". In Edgar Allan Poe's "The Thousand-and-Second Tale of Scheherazade", we read the following at the last para. 57: "... she knew the king to be a man of scrupulous integrity, and quite unlikely to forfeit his word..." In

other words, it was still possible that he might do so. Consider as well the astonishment shown by the General Staff when, in the movie Gallipolli, the novice advocate wishes to question Lord Kitchener. When it was asked of him whether he thought it possible that a revered figure such as the Commander in chief might order barbarities, counsel answered, quite correctly in my view, "I don't know, I'll ask him!

38) Reversing the proposition: Truth is stranger than fiction

[7-74] If counsel wish to point out this obvious fact, one may quote from the insights advanced by Edgar Allan Poe at para. 9 of "Von Kempelen and His Discovery": "... it is clear that the truth may be stranger than fiction."

39) Reversing the proposition: My experiences are not narrow, it is just that yours are somewhat different

[7-75] One of the things I have to remind myself of constantly as a trial judge is that I have lived a sheltered life. Whatever experiences I have encountered, they are no doubt far less interesting than anybody else and the fact that I have never heard of certain actions, practices, etc., does not mean that they are not common or quite ordinary. Although I do not think that any Canadian may credit the account found at pages 237-238 of former Oklahoma Sooner and Dallas Cowboy coach Barry Switzer's biography Bootlegger's Boy (written with Bud Shrake) [William Morrow and Company, Inc: New York, 1990] it is not because the following account is neither inherently incredible nor unreliable, only that it falls outside of my life experiences and it is therefore incumbent on counsel to point out how much life there is out there that we are missing. "If I had a dollar for every round of ammunition that has been shot out the windows of athletic dorms at universities all over the country ever since there has been such a thing as an athletic dorm, I would be rich enough to buy myself a kingdom in the Alps. There is something about playing football and loving to go hunting that just kind of fit together and always

have. I won't try to explain it, but everybody knows it is true. The next thing you know, a guy is wanting to show his pals his new shotgun, so he goes to the window and blasts away." In this respect, recall the rookie with the Toronto Blue Jays who presented himself at Canadian Customs with a handgun and was aghast to discover that Canadians regulate the possession of such personal items, having never hears of such a thing...

[7-76] The point of the comment is that the trier of fact must be educate to understand and appreciate the other person's experiences as being worthy of acceptance and validation. In a sense, it is almost a question of judicial notice of uncommon matters and in considering the question of what the trier of fact may know as opposed to what certain individuals may know, one is reminded of the passage from "The Unparalleled Adventures of One Hans Pfaall", by Edgar Allan Poe, at para. 4 "... It appeared to be -yes! it was undoubtedly a species of balloons; but surely no such balloon had ever been seen in Rotterdam before. For who, let me ask, ever heard of a balloon manufactured entirely of dirty newspapers?" The fact, as I have stated, that the trier of fact has not does not end the enquiry but surely the advocate must assist in "educating" those called upon to decide.

[7-77] Consider as well an anecdote found in inspiring life story of one courageous player, Born to Play The Eric Davis Story, with Ralph Wiley, [Viking: New York, 1999]. Page 29 records that neighbours would feel themselves allowed, if not mandated, to discipline young Eric if he got into trouble as a youth. Again, the purpose of this illustration is merely to indicate how multi-faceted are relationships and that the trier of fact must be alerted to the myriad of methods in which people live and are raised.

Chapter 8
An example of note taking and judgment writing

1) Introduction

[8-1] In this brief chapter, attention is drawn firstly to the everyday 'nuts and bolts' problems associated with taking down the testimony of witnesses and secondly to the concerns arising from the need to draw comprehensive findings of facts. Stated otherwise, I offer some personal guidance on techniques of note taking and on a method I find useful to organize factual information and how best to draw that part of the judgment touching upon factual issues.

2) Discussion

a) Advice on note taking

[8-2] At the outset, I wish to point out that note taking is highly subjective and that the judicial styles range from the modern touch typist who records every single word flawlessly, best epitomized by the late and highly respected jurist, Justice Archie Campbell, whose mastery of the keyboard was such that I recall well being told by my fellow counsel in the War Crimes Section of the Department of Justice that whenever a question arose as to what a witness has said in the case of Finta,[142] Justice Campbell would search for the passage and be reading out the exact quote in the flash of an eye.

[8-3] At the other extreme are well respected jurists whose style consists of paucity in note taking as they concentrate all of their energies on listening intently to the testimony. In effect, such a style is consistent with what is taught at Faculties of Education: when your students are writing furiously, they are not listening attentively.

---

[142]   *R. v. Finta*, [1994] 1 R.C.S. 701, 88 C.C.C. (3d) 417.

[8-4] That being said, I suggest that whatever style is adopted, fact finders might well profit from the ready insertion into their notes of certain simple marginal comments that serve to highlight the immediate impressions made upon them by certain elements of testimony. Allow me to illustrate: a young child is testifying in a trial about alleged sexual misconduct by a neighbour and is asked by counsel for the accused about his or her knowledge and belief of certain fantastic beings such as Santa Claus and the Tooth Fairy. In my estimation, it is proper to include right then and there a marginal note in a different coloured pen to indicate how the witness reacted to this line of questioning. My habit is to write "29-A" to alert me that this part of my notes is devoted to the question of potential misconception of events by a young witness who may still be under the impression that the world includes witches and spirits and Kris Kringle. The reference of "29-A" is drawn from Mr. Justice David Watt's Manual of Criminal Jury Instructions, Thompson/Carswell: Toronto, 2005, at pages 211-212. The advantage is that when I receive submissions on a precise point, whether in the form of an objection raised subsequently which refers to such testimony or at the stage of submissions, I can find this passage quite readily.
Indeed, it is often wise to review one's notes at the breaks or lunch periods to insert these "guides to memory" in order that our notes are easily scanned to find the legal or factual issues that have been considered.

[8-5] Following along in the same vein, I suggest that marginal notes in a different coloured pen be added as son as time permits to refer to certain themes or "memory aids" such as "the shower incident", the "confrontation about money", or "the first meeting" to permit ease of location subsequently.

[8-6] Leaving aside the initial advantage that I suggest is available in drawing attention to these points in testimony, and recognizing that they are readily capable of 'capture' on the record, in the sense that these elements of evidence will be recorded on the transcript no matter how poor our note taking

was, I now wish to draw your attention to the importance of this technique in respect to matters that are lost if not recorded immediately. For example, if a witness glanced over at a friend or work mate prior to answering a question, this type of action will not be recorded by the Court reporter and must be noted in some fashion. The same is true of blushes, frowns, curls of the lips, *et cetera* and other badges of demeanour evidence.

[8-7] The final point is to note the advantage I find in recording immediately, by way of marginal note, my views as to the timing of the responses. It is true that this may also be verified subsequently by listening to the tape of the proceedings but it is wise to avoid such time consuming verifications by means of an immediate note.

[8-8] I am fond of writing "P" to indicate a pause I found to be noteworthy, if you excuse the redundancy. I write "LP" for long pauses and "LLP" when the pause is rather extraordinary and, on rare occasions, "OTTS" when the pause indicates that the witness is acknowledging having been caught in the type of clumsy lie described so ably by Justice O'Halloran. ["OTTS" means "order the tome stone", the witness's credibility just expired!]

[8-9] In the final analysis, it is always wise for judges to review their notes at the end of the day to recast them in thematic fashion and to underline those passages which will serve to support or infirm the weight to be assigned to the facts described by the various witnesses. It is rarely wise or useful to allow our impressions to be lost by reason of undue delay in consigning our opinions touching upon the value of the testimony.

b) Advice on judgment writing: The facts form themes

[8-10] It is suggested in the strongest terms that all factual questions should be grouped and considered as separate and

discrete "thematic" questions, the narrower the better, and that the most signal elements of factual controversy will have been identified by the cross-examination conducted by the parties. To illustrate the advantage of narrow thematic groupings, I will quote at length from a judgment of the Court of Appeal, *R. v. Prebtani*, 2008 ONCA 735.

[8-11] As we read at para. 8, Justice Rosenberg organised the trial materials in such a way as to facilitate the reader's understanding of what testimony the trial judge heard as contrasted with the fresh evidence submitted to the Court of Appeal, together with a recitation of trial counsel's explanations for the steps he took, the whole to permit a sound examination of the wisdom of the conclusions reached at trial. In assessing the merits of this technique in organising trial testimony and exhibits, emphasis must be placed on the importance not only of the grouping of information but on the need for bold and prominent headings to orient our review and analysis. In fact, I would suggest that in organising this material initially, Justice Rosenberg might have or probably could have added a number of internal "marquees" to better assist in following the various witnesses and that these "orientation guides" were deleted when the judgment was completed.

THE TRIAL EVIDENCE

[9] The allegations against the appellant relate to his wife, S.S. While evidence was led of a number of incidents, the Crown relied upon an incident in August 1999 as the basis for the charges of assault with a weapon and threatening death, and an incident in November 1999 for the assault charge.

The Background

[10] The appellant and the complainant met in late 1997 or early 1998 through friends at a mosque that they both attended. They married in June 1999. At

the time, the complainant was a pharmacist and the appellant was completing his studies to be a physician. The day following their marriage, the couple moved into a condominium apartment. Below, I have set out a summary of the events covered at the trial, together with the findings made by the trial judge, the allegation of incompetence, and the fresh evidence relating to that allegation.

The Furniture Question

The Trial Evidence

[11] The complainant testified that she was surprised to find that the condominium had no furniture. She claimed that the appellant told her that in Islam a bed, utensils or a dining table were not needed. As a result, she slept on an air mattress for 6 to 8 weeks before a bed arrived. The appellant gave no evidence about furniture in the apartment.

The Trial Judge's Reasons

[12] The trial judge referred to the complainant's evidence about the lack of furniture as part of her review of the complainant's testimony.

The Fresh Evidence

[13] In trial counsel's file was a receipt showing that a bed and double-sized luxury mattress had been purchased 16 days after the couple moved into the condominium, but was not paid for until 23 days after the marriage. The documents do not show when the bed was delivered. There was no fresh evidence from the appellant as to when the bed was delivered, nor why he waited over two weeks before ordering the bed.

[14] Trial counsel acknowledged that it was an oversight not to have confronted the complainant with the receipt. However, he did not consider it to be a serious oversight because he had led this evidence through the appellant. In fact, he had not done so.

Ownership of 55 Chapletown; The August Assault with Weapon and Threatening Incident; The Ripped Wedding Invitation

The Trial Evidence

[15] The complainant testified that sometime before they were married, the appellant told her that the house at 55 Chapletown, where he lived with his parents and sister, was his. He stated that he was paying the mortgage on the house, and that they would live there once they were married. However, she did not want to live with his parents and so they moved into the condominium. Shortly after the marriage, however, she began asking about the house at 55 Chapletown, and the appellant said that it was not his house, that it belonged to his father. She therefore asked her father, a lawyer, to do a property search. According to her, the property search disclosed that a few days before the marriage, the appellant had transferred ownership from his name to his father's name. She testified that the house had been in the appellant's name alone before the transfer.

[16] The complainant testified that she was afraid to discuss the matter with the appellant, for fear that he would throw things and grab her, but she decided she had to. In August 1999, she asked the appellant if there was anything he needed to tell her about the house. He said no, but she continued to press the matter and finally told him that she knew he had transferred the house. The appellant became very

angry, saying that she was just a woman and had no right to question him. He started to hit the wall. The appellant then grabbed the complainant, pushed her up against the wall, and tried to punch her. He ended up hitting the wall instead, making dents and holes. He then took a knife from the kitchen and held it up to her neck. He said to her: "You're ruining my life. You know S., I'm a doctor. I know every part of the human body. You know what I'm capable of doing to you." He said that he wanted to kill her and himself. He also said that she was "untraditional in Islamic for questioning him". She apologized and said she would be more Islamic. He then left the apartment. She testified in chief that she had bruises on her neck but did not show them to anyone. She called her parents and told them what had happened, but said she was alright and for them not to come over. There was no objection by trial counsel to the complainant testifying to the contents of her conversation with her father.

[17] That night, the appellant called her from his office at Toronto General Hospital and asked her to meet him at College Park. He said everything would be fine, that they needed to talk. However, when she arrived he grabbed her again, telling her that she was ruining his life. He said she was a bad woman and "unIslamic". Eventually, they went back to the condominium where she slept in the bed and he slept on the couch.

[18] The next day, after the appellant had gone to work, the complainant's father, brother and a friend of her brother, R.T., came to the apartment. They saw the damage, and her father said he could not leave her there. She decided to go with her father, and ended up staying at her parents' home for about a week.

[19] Trial counsel cross-examined the complainant on whether any of her co-workers noticed anything. She testified that on one occasion someone noticed some marks, and that one of her co-workers thought it was a hickey. The complainant laughed it off because she did not know what to do.

[20] The appellant had quite a different version of this incident. He testified in chief that upon arriving home late from work one day, the complainant began yelling at him, using foul language, complaining that he never took her anywhere, and did not buy her flowers like her father did for her mother. The appellant eventually left, and returned to his office at the Toronto General Hospital. He stayed there for a few hours before returning to the condominium. The complainant was asleep in the bedroom so he slept on the sofa. He went to work in the morning but when he returned that evening the complainant was gone and the apartment was in shambles. Various wedding gifts were on the floor and there were some holes in the wall. As well, the couple's wedding invitation had been ripped up. The appellant testified that he was in shock and tried to reach his parents. When he could not find them, he called his aunt. At some point, the complainant's father called him and used abusive language. The appellant assumed that the complainant must have been with her parents. The appellant denied using a knife or threatening to kill the complainant or harm himself.

[21] In cross-examination, the appellant was asked whether he had ever discussed the home at 55 Chapletown with the complainant. At first he denied it, but then admitted that the complainant did bring up the subject of his transferring title to his father before the marriage. He could not remember exactly when she brought it up except that it was in August or September. When she brought it up she was

screaming at him, using foul language, and throwing things. He denied that he was angry at her for having searched the title.

[22] In cross-examination, the appellant explained that 55 Chapletown was his father's home, and that his name had been on the deed to assist his father in getting a mortgage. However, when he was about to get married and the couple was not going to live at the house, there was no reason for his name to be on the property.

[23] The appellant was cross-examined on what he did when he came home and found the condominium in disarray. In particular, he was questioned about why he did not do anything to try to locate the complainant. He testified that he assumed that she had gone to her parents' home, which was confirmed when her father called the next day. The appellant said that he was in shock and terrified.

[24] R.T. testified for the Crown that he went to the condominium with the complainant's brother and father. The complainant was very upset and crying. There were clothes and picture frames scattered on the floor and some dents in the walls. In cross-examination, Thorne testified that the complainant said that the appellant had become very angry and threatened her. He did not see any bruises on the complainant.

[25] The complainant's father testified for the Crown that he went to the condominium after receiving a call from his daughter. She was in distress, saying that the appellant had threatened to kill her and had beaten her. When he arrived at the apartment he saw that the complainant was crying. She looked distraught and dishevelled. She told him that she had a problem with the appellant over money. The

appellant had accused her of hiding money, and she had confronted him about transferring the house to his father's name before they were married. The complainant showed him the holes in the wall that were caused when the appellant attempted to hit her. She told him that the appellant had threatened to kill her, and had put a knife to her throat. In direct examination, the father was asked whether he had called the police. He said that he had not because the complainant wanted the marriage to work. He was also concerned that a complaint to the police would seriously affect the appellant's profession. There was no objection to any of the father's testimony of what the complainant told him.

[26] In cross-examination, the complainant's father agreed that he had done a title search of the property at 55 Chapletown. The search showed that the property had been in the names of the appellant and his father. The property was then transferred into the appellant's father's name alone a few days before the wedding. He denied that he was the one who ripped up the wedding invitation. Defence counsel told the witness that there would be evidence that he tore up the invitation. The father confirmed in cross-examination that he had not called the police, even though he was told that the appellant had put a knife to his daughter's throat and threatened to kill her. He also testified in cross-examination that he did not attempt to persuade the complainant to return to the appellant; that it was her decision. He was then confronted with his testimony at the divorce proceedings in which he said that he did persuade her to go back to the matrimonial home.

[27] M.D., the appellant's aunt, testified for the defence. She testified about the appellant's telephone call to her when he returned home and found the condominium in disarray. She was allowed to testify

without objection from Crown counsel about the contents of the telephone call. She confirmed that the appellant told her that he had just arrived home to find things thrown on the floor and what looked like punch marks in the wall. He told her that it seemed like the apartment had been ransacked.

[28] Ms. D. also testified that the complainant's father telephoned her a few days later. He said that the complainant had returned to live with her parents, and that he wanted to talk about the relationship between the appellant and the complainant. He also made what seemed to be a threat: "you know how educated I am and you know I -- what I can do, what I'm capable of doing". Crown counsel did not cross-examine Ms. D.

The Trial Judge's Reasons

[29] The trial judge reviewed all of the evidence relating to the August incident, including the various versions of events as related by the complainant to her father and Mr. T. The trial judge said this about that evidence:

The evidence demonstrates that she told her father about the assaults and the threat, and she told Mr. Thorne about the threat. Further, she described these events in her counter petition months before going to the police. Therefore, there is no credible evidence of recent fabrication. I accept her evidence in its entirety.

[30] The trial judge referred to the evidence of the complainant and her father. She noted that the complainant's father testified that he discovered that the appellant "had transferred his interest in the house to his own father before the marriage".

[31] The trial judge rejected the appellant's version of these events. In particular, she noted that the appellant did not report the damage to the police or condominium security, and did not attempt to find out where the complainant was when he returned to the condominium and found it in disarray. She found that he did not report the damage because he had caused it. She found his version of the August events to be "completely incredible".

The Fresh Evidence

[32] The appellant's trial counsel did not confront the complainant with the deed showing that the house at 55 Chapletown had originally been held in the name of the appellant and his father. He explained that he did not do so because the appellant and his father never provided the deed to him. However, when he was shown his file, which contained a copy of the deed, counsel said that he believed that he could only show the complainant the original of the deed, not a copy.

[33] It will be recalled that trial counsel had put to the complainant's father that there would be evidence that he tore up the wedding invitation. In cross-examination, trial counsel acknowledged that he had expected Ms. D. to testify that the father had admitted to her in the telephone conversation a few days after the ransacking of the apartment that he had torn up the invitation. Counsel stated that he could not lead the witness, and so had been unable to obtain this evidence from her. He did not think to ask Ms. D. a follow-up question when she testified that the complainant's father said, "you know how educated I am and you know I -- what I can do, what I'm capable of doing", and ask him what he told her about what he was capable of doing. In hindsight, he agreed that it would have been a permissible question and might have drawn out the evidence he was seeking.

[34] Counsel testified that he had not obtained a statement from the witness prior to trial to use to refresh her memory. He was then shown what appears to be a statement from Ms. D., dated May 31, 2002, which refers to the telephone call from the complainant's father and includes reference to his admission that he ripped up the wedding invitation. It is unclear where this statement came from. Trial counsel was unable to say whether he had it during the trial.

[...]

[8-12] I am hopeful that the foregoing lengthy extracts from the judgment of Rosenberg J.A., and the further references to follow, will serve to demonstrate the advantages (if not the superior nature) of such a method as opposed to the common method of simply listing in order the testimony of each witness with a recitation of all of their evidence without a unifying link or theme. As noted, to further illustrate the value of the thematic approach to fact finding, I have listed further themes but without any mention of the discussion of facts, from *R. v. Prebtani*.

The First Security Guard Issue

The Trial Evidence

The Trial Judge's Reasons

The Fresh Evidence

The Black Dress and Memorial Service Incidents

The Future Shop Incident (The November Assault Incident)

The Trial Evidence

The Trial Judge's Reasons

The Edwards Garden Incident

The Second Security Guard Incident

The Port Perry Incident

The "Niece" Incident

The Divorce

The Complaints to the Police by the Appellant and the Complainant

Chapter 9
Some guidance on judging cross-examination

1) Introduction

[9-1] This chapter seeks to bring to the reader's attention a number of less well known and certain unorthodox views on the scope and extent of cross-examination in order to guide fact finders in the exercise of their discretionary power to limit cross-examination, especially in the case of vulnerable witnesses. In his vein, I note at the outset the excellent comment, "Ethics – The adversarial System and Business Practice", penned by the Hon. Justice Geoffrey Nettle who reminds us at page 73 that it has been suggested "[...] that cross-examination is, in the words of John Wigmore, 'the greatest legal engine ever invented for the discovery of truth' and that it is a most effective weapon to test dishonest witnesses and ferret out the truth [...]" [Footnotes omitted] See (2005), 10 <u>Deakin L. Rev</u>. 67-82.

[9-2] At all events, this chapter should assist fact finders in understanding the numerous elements that are at play when advocates seek to impeach testimony and should guide advocates in the framing of submissions to broaden (or restrict) the scope of such measures to contradict testimony.

2) Discussion

a) Cross-examining children

§1) The need for patience

[9-3] Having noted in passing the concerns arising from cross-examining vulnerable witness, it will be of assistance to begin the discussion by noting the wise counsel of Dr. Mirko Bagaric and the Hon. Justice Geoff Flatman who have commented at pages 5-6 of their article "Problems in Prosecuting Cases Involving Historical Child Sexual Abuse: The Victorian

Experience" (1997-2000), 4 <u>Deakin L. Rev</u>. 1-20 on the need for increased patience by judicial officers when children are being examined in such cases. As the learned authors note:

> The suspicion with which the evidence of children is viewed, however, remains. For example, in New South Wales the guilty verdict rate for child sex cases is about 33% compared to about 45% for other offences that proceed to trial. Despite the fact that the thrust of empirical evidence generally supports the soundness of the evidence of children, there is one particular danger with such evidence. A significant body of literature shows that younger children are more suggestible than older children and that children can be led to make false reports about significant matters. Despite this, little work has been undertaken to work out how best to circumvent this danger. Part of the answer here must obviously lie in limiting the use of leading questions, given that when children are questioned in an open-ended style the accuracy of the information they supply is the same as for adults. The temptation for asking leading questions to young children stems from the fact that they provide less spontaneous and pointed answers than adults. However in the interests of truth, it may be necessary to extend far greater patience when examining, or for that matter cross-examining, children. [Emphasis added – footnotes omitted]

§2) Rules for cross-examination evolve: Complainants in sexual violence prosecutions

[9-4] Whether they are evolving as a result of legislative intervention, or as a result of judicial innovation, the rules governing cross-examination are always in a relative state of flux. Note by way of limited example the brief observation advanced in 1983 by Professor Philip McNamara about the evolution of the manner in which a complainant in a sexual assault trial may be the subject of impeachment. Refer to his book review of Cases on Evidence in Australia, by E J Edwards, 3rd edition [Law Book Co, 1981] in (1982-83), 8 Adel. L. Rev. 225-226, at page 225.

[9-5] In this vein, note the trenchant comments as to the doubtful relevance of much of the evidence which is now the subject of curtailment in the passage which follows:

> 3) No Cross Examination Regarding Sexual History
>
> There is also a statutory prohibition on cross examination of sexual abuse victims regarding their sexual history, unless, broadly, it is in the interests of justice. The interesting feature of this 'protection' is that it was necessary in the first place. Evidence of sexual history is hardly likely to pass the threshold test of relevance for admissibility of evidence and is rarely a matter which goes fairly to credit. [Footnotes omitted]

[9-6] Refer to Dr. Mirko Bagaric and the Hon. Justice Geoff Flatman, "Problems in Prosecuting Cases Involving Historical Child Sexual Abuse: The Victorian Experience" (1997-2000), 4 Deakin L. Rev. 1-20, at page 13.

§3) Rules for cross-examination evolve: Expert witnesses in child welfare cases

[9-7] A sound discussion of the concerns raised by permitting full cross-examination of experts called upon to assist the Courts in cases of child welfare is found in the comment entitled "Separate Representation in Custody Cases", by Sibylle Kobienia, (1977-78), 6 <u>Adel. L. Rev</u>. 466-479. For present purposes, what is to emphasized is that counsel will succeed in gaining the fullest degree of latitude by the Court if they are mindful (and make plain this fact) of the specialized nature of such hearings and the fundamental interests and values that are of prime interest to the presiding judicial officers. Stated otherwise, to fail to moderate one's approach to account for the overarching goal of the Court will result in a disservice to the client as the Court will restrict even further any permissible scope for impeachment. In this regard, it is suggested at page 478 that cross-examination of the welfare worker may be required in order to test their objectivity, and to enable the judge to assess the soundness of the reasoning on which the welfare worker's conclusions are based. Surely counsel should be capable of framing a submission which permits this function while not attacking the scheme of the legislation and the other values that are given precedence.

[9-8] Refer as well to the useful discussion found in the comment entitled "The Adoption of Children Act 1968", by B.H. Crauford, in (1968-1970), 3 <u>U. Tas. L. Rev</u>. 115-119, especially at page 116.

b) Judges seek guidance to the exercise of their discretion

[9-9] In considering how much judges require the guidance of counsel in making fact findings, recall that in Gibbon's, <u>Decline and Fall of the Roman Empire</u> (Bury's edition), iv. 46, this passage appears: "In the space of ten centuries the infinite variety of laws and legal opinions had filled many thousand volumes which no fortune could purchase and no capacity

could digest. Books could not easily be found and the judges, poor in the midst of riches, were reduced to the exercise of their illiterate discretion."

c) Terror of cross-examination:

[9-10] Any evaluation of this subject must be sensitive to the generally held view that cross-examination involves, as a matter of necessity, exposure by a witness to a terrifying ordeal. As we read in the initial paragraph of an unsigned case comment entitled "Evidence The Unsworn Statement", "The right of an accused to make an unsworn statement from the dock, while not submitting himself to the terrors of cross-examination by eloquent and experienced counsel, has recently received the attention of the Supreme Court of South Australia on two occasions." See page 224 of (1960-1962), 1 <u>Adel. L. Rev.</u> 224-228.

d) Impressive though the oath may be, be wary!

[9-11] Counsel's function is to make plain to the trier of fact, especially in cases of jury trials, civil or criminal, that the mere fact that a witness takes an oath is of no moment. In this vein, note the following commentary touching upon what has been described as the first trial in Greek literature, which occurs in the Homeric <u>Hymn to Hermes</u>:

> The infant Hermes, on the night of his birth, steals the cattle of Apollo, who eventually tracks him down. Hermes in the meantime has climbed back into his crib and donned his swaddling clothes. He indignantly denies the deed and swears mighty oaths of innocence: 'I will swear the great oath on my father's

head. I vow that I myself am not the culprit ...'[143]

e) Oath and the duty to assist the Court

[9-12] Note that in the course of reviewing the text, <u>Criminal Law</u>, by Rollin M. Perkins [Brooklyn, N.Y.: The Foundation Press Inc., 1957], the esteemed Dr. Norval Morris remarked that the author had opined that an "[...] oath administered to the witness calls on him freely to disclose the truth in the first instance and not to put the court and the parties to the disadvantage, hindrance, and delay of ultimately extracting the truth by cross-examination, by extraneous investigation or other collateral means." This statement was in reference to whether a witness might be prosecuted for perjury if he or she disclosed the untruth prior to concluding the testimony. See the review at pages 101-102 of (1960-62), 1 <u>Adel. L. Rev.</u>, at page 101.

f) Inviting the witness to explain himself or herself

[9-13] As a general rule, a witness being cross-examined should be invited to provide an explanation of the contested or impugned action(s) which is not to be confused with an invitation to repeat damaging information given in chief. In other words, as noted by Archibald MacLeish when he stated he had to explain himself to a skeptical law club on how he had spent his career as a poet after graduating from Harvard,[144] a witness should be presented with a summary of the testimony advanced and invited to agree that this represents the essence of the claim.

---

[143] Refer to "Some Greek Trials" Order and Justice in Homer, Hesiod, Aeschylus and Plato", by Professor David Luban, (1987), 54 <u>Tenn. L. Rev.</u> 279-325, at page 280.
[144] Refer to "Apologia", pages 1505-1511, (June 1972), 85 <u>Harv. L. Rev.</u> at page 1505.

g) Some persons squeeze a word till it hurts

[9-14] Advocates must always be mindful that a trial judge or jury must be satisfied that a witness is not being true to their oath, as opposed to squeezing a word till it hurts, to track the language of Archibald MacLeish in "Apologia", found at page 1507 of (June 1972), 85 Harv. L. Rev. at pages 1505-1511. As explained by the author, "Poets [...] are literal-minded men who will squeeze a word till it hurts."

h) Different degrees of speech for different tasks

[9-15] It is also suggested that the selection of the words best suited for cross-examination is a radically different exercise than the language fit for opening or closing submissions. In the case of these steps in the trial, it is thought wise to follow the suggestion of the Rt. Hon. Lord MacMillan who opined: "There is no reason why legal argument [...] should not be expressed in good English. There is every reason why they should. The advocate who can impart a literary flavour to his address adds to its persuasiveness and attraction." See page 664 of "Law and Letters, in (1930), 16 A.B.A.J. 662-665.

i) Objections to cross-examination: Irrelevant evidence

[9-16] Note that in a book review of J.L. Glissan's text, Cross Examination Practice and Procedure An Australian Perspective [Legal Books, 1985], published in (1985-86), Vol. 10, Adel. L. Rev. at pages 512-513, Professor Philip McNamara observed at page 513:

> There are some propositions in the text with which some will disagree. For example, at pp 36 and 82, the advocate is cautioned not to object to a question unless the anticipated answer is "both inadmissible and clearly damaging". It is this reviewer's opinion that there can be

no justification for permitting the eliciting of irrelevant information and that all questions which might foreseeably elicit irrelevant information should be objected to. A failure to object will tend to lengthen the hearing, contrary to the public interest and to the private interests of one's client. Furthermore, in a practical sense, some irrelevant material has a tendency to compel or invite an answer, thus increasing the number of issues in a trial.

[9-17] With respect, although it is difficult to gainsay the submission that a failure to object in these circumstances might result in lengthening the proceedings and in promoting the tendency to seek to rebut information which is not probative, at the end of the day the careful advocate will be guided by two verities of the practice of litigation: firstly, the party tending to introduce irrelevant information tends to lose the interest of the trier of fact, especially if it is composed of lay persons, and thus runs the peril of not being able to count on the Court's undivided attention when material information is advanced and, secondly, the Court tends to view with a critical eye any lack of rigour in the introduction of testimony and soon concludes that the party calling irrelevant testimony lacks a sound and coherent theory.

[9-18] In addition, caution is suggested when objecting to any irrelevant information as a lay jury may conclude, often hastily and without foundation, that the other party is seeking to prevent it from entertaining information, no matter how remotely relevant.

j) Common law right to cross-examine: To demonstrate innocence

[9-19] Professor P. McNamara reminds us at page 293 of his article, "Cross-Examination of an Accused as to Collateral Crimes Relevant to Guilt Corak and Palmer v. R.," (1983-

1985), Vol. 9 <u>Adel. L. Rev.</u> 290-306 of the following: "A defendant has a common law right to cross-examine every defendant-witness as to matters sufficiently relevant to the innocence of the cross-examiner". Footnote 12 refers to <u>R. v. Hilton</u>, [1972] 1 Q.B. 421.

k) Cross-examination as a step to prove a relevant fact and proof of other allegations of misconduct:

[9-20] Further guidance from Professor McNamara is set out below:

> [...] The law accepts that the mere fact that a person has been charged with a crime is no evidence of that person's guilt of that crime, either directly or via credibility. An unconcluded charge, or a charge concluded in favour of the defendant, is regarded as a misfortune and is not probative. In other words, an unconcluded charge is not a proper objective of proof, either in the prosecution case in chief or in the cross-examination of the defendant [...] a mere charge is not a proper objective of proof, because it is not probative [...][145]

[9-21] The learned author went on to observe at page 296, footnote 19: "[...] Cross-examination as to a charge is authorised where it is merely a step in the attempt to prove a relevant fact. See eg <u>G (an infant) v Coltart</u> [1967] 1 QB 432, 439-440; <u>R v Ollis</u> [1900] 2 QB 758, 783.

---

[145] With reference to page 296 of his article, "Cross-Examination of an Accused as to Collateral Crimes Relevant to Guilt Corak and Palmer v. R.," (1983-1985), Vol. 9 <u>Adel. L. Rev</u>. 290-306. [Footnote omitted]

l) Bad character and cross-examination: Generally not permitted

[9-22] As we read at page 483 of Professor Andrew Ligertwood's review of Cases and Materials on Evidence, by J. D. Heydon [Butterworths, London, 1975): "The general rule excluding evidence of the accused's bad character applies equally in cross-examination unless legislation equivalent to s.1 of the Criminal Evidence Act, 1898 applies. These exceptions are based on exceptional probative value or ideas of adversary fairness (e.g., that the accused must always be able to discredit his accusers)." Refer to (1973-76), 5 Adel. L. Rev. 480-484.

m) Courts might accept the original opinion of a witness notwithstanding apparent success in cross-examination

[9-23] The case comment entitled "Separate Representation in Custody Cases", by Sibylle Kobienia, (1977-78), 6 Adel. L. Rev. 466-479 is of interest in pointing out the possibility that a witness might modify an opinion even before Court proceedings are fully engaged for fear of having to endure cross-examination, though no objective grounds exist to justify this *volte face*. Refer to page 478. For present purposes, what is to be understood from this passage is that witnesses have been known to "cave in" during the course of being challenged at trial and yet the Court will accept their original position, on the foundation that there was no justification shown to demonstrate a reason for the retraction, recantation or modification. Thus, prudent counsel offers some basis for the amended view of things.

n) Counsel have walked out of Royal Commissions over their right to cross-examine

[9-24] It must be stressed at the outset that it is not unheard of for counsel, both learned and perhaps not so, to have voiced vociferous objections over any perceived limit on their right to

contest testimony by means of a vigorous cross-examination. One of the best known examples is that of counsel for Rupert Max Stuart who "marched out" of a Royal Commission of Inquiry touching upon his client's conviction for murder, "claiming that he had been prevented by the Commission from cross-examining police witnesses in the way he desired, and in the way he said was necessary in Stuart's interests." Refer to the book review of K.S. Inglis' book, The Stuart Case, [Melbourne University Press, 1961] by Professor D.P. Derham, found in (1960-62), 1 Adel. L. Rev. 354-356, at page 355 in particular.

o) Complexities of cross-examination

[9-25] Pages 238-239 of Professor Vicki Waye's article, "Video Tape Recording of Custodial Interrogation" includes an interesting observation to the effect that "Generally, translation evidence [of a recording] should be given orally rather than tendered in documentary form. However, the departure from ordinary practice was justified in Butera's case because of the complex nature of the cross-examination of the translations." Refer to (1989-90), 12 Adel. L. Rev. 230-242. It is suggested that cross-examination of the experts who drew the translation is nevertheless required to provide a sound foundation for the reception of the expert opinion as to what the recording purports to have contained in the speaker's language.

p) Discernment is a requirement in cross-examination

[9-26] Note the following passage taken from a tribute to Sir Mellis Napier, "Chief Justice 1942-1967": "In referring to his career at the Bar, the paper added that aa good deal of his success has been due to his skill and ready discernment in the cross-examination of witnesses'". Refer to page 2 of (1967-70), 3 Adel. L. Rev. 1-6.

q) Counsel must always re-think the wisdom of the proposed approach

[9-27] In discussing the potential liability of an advocate for the decisions made while on his or her feet in the court room in the heat of the trial contest, Professors Belinda Baker and Desmond Manderson note at page 141 of their case comment "Counsel's Immunity: The High Court's Decision in Boland v. Yates", (2001) Vol 1 <u>Macquarie L.J.</u> 135-144 "In this way, Kirby J's formulation of the 'in-court/out-of-court' distinction aims to protect counsel for decisions made in the interests of the court, or in the interests of justice, or in making judgment calls as to the nature of their advocacy. Thus, for example, a decision by counsel not to pursue a particular line of cross-examination (<u>made, for example, because the counsel believes that the argument has little chance of success, and would likely waste the court's time</u>), is not subject to liability; whilst a failure to properly consider a particular line of argument when formulating pleadings would be subject to liability." [Emphasis added]

[9-28] Noteworthy as well is the unsigned case note on Rondel v. Worsley,[1966]3 All. E.R. 657 entitled "Negligence - Immunity of a barrister - Whether a solicitor acting as advocate is also immune" in (1964-67), 2 <u>U. Tas. L. Rev</u>. 315-319, especially at page 318.

[9-29] We should take from this obvious lesson that counsel are expected to think on their feet and to disregard a proposed line of cross-examination if it appears that it would not be advantageous given the unfolding of the trial.

r) Record of proceedings must reflect the success of cross-examination

[9-30] A fundamental point is that counsel must not be satisfied with obtaining a transcript in which it appears that success has been achieved in cross-examination. Counsel must also endeavour to ensure that the trial judge is not left in a situation in which the judgment will deny the essence of

what is consigned on the transcript by reason of a finding that the non-verbal responses negated the verbal ones. Reference to a lengthy passage from the next article will assist in making plain these concerns. As we read in "Cubillo v Commonwealth: Classifying Text and the Violence of Exclusion", by Alisoun Neville, (2005) Vol 5 Macquarie L.J. 31-56, at page 51:

> [...] O'Loughlin J does acknowledge some absences in the transcript, citing from an earlier case about receiving evidence by Aboriginal witnesses.
>
> > The difficulties courts face in receiving and dealing with evidence of Aboriginal witnesses is well known, particularly when English is at best a second, or lesser, language and the grasp of it is limited. A transcript cannot convey nuances of gesture, movement or expression that bear upon an understanding of the evidence received in such circumstances. Similarly, a transcript which presents as a seamless continuum of questions and answers may suggest more comprehension of the process by a witness than the court observes. [Footnote 142: Ward v Western Australia (1998) 159 ALR 483 at 497, cited in (2000) 103 FCR 1]
>
> Elsewhere, the process of reading an oral, embodied genre such as the hearings is reflected in O'Loughlin J's remarks, such as his comments on aspects of individual testimonies. For

instance, the statement that 'I found that segment of Mr Gunner's evidence very believable was contrasted directly with areas of Gunner's evidence 'where he was obviously guessing', for in the latter there was 'a discernible sadness in his voice and his appearance when he gave [his] answer'. [Footnotes omitted]

[9-31] Of another witness, Daniel Forrester, O'Loughlin J remarks:

> Mr Forrester was not an impressive witness. Because he strongly supported Mr Gunner's case and because he was firmly opposed to the role of the Commonwealth, there were several occasions when he answered questions with a heavy bias in favour of Mr Gunner's case. That may not be so readily apparent from a reading of the transcript as it was from listening to the way in which he responded to the questions asked of him. [Footnote omitted]

[9-32] In effect, it is wholly without profit if counsel obtains a "Yes" answer which is consigned on the transcript if the note by the trier of fact of that answer will doubtless be followed by an asterisk denoting that the bodily language was to the opposite effect.

s) Obtuse responses to cross-examination:

[9-33] Counsel will have gained some advantage if it can be shown that a witness demonstrated a measure of obtuseness in responding to questions in cross-examination. For example, at page 51 of "Cubillo v Commonwealth: Classifying Text and the Violence of Exclusion", by Alisoun Neville, (2005) Vol 5 Macquarie L.J. 31-56, the author observed: "[...]

O'Loughlin J. also cited a range of examples to support a contention that 'throughout his evidence, and particularly throughout his cross-examination, Mr Gunner showed signs of being quite obtuse'. [Footnote 146: (2000) 103 FCR 1, 925]

t) Confrontational attitude to counsel conducting cross-examination

[9-34] Counsel will have gained some advantage if it can be shown that a witness demonstrated a confrontational attitude in responding to questions in cross-examination. For example, at page 51 of "Cubillo v Commonwealth: Classifying Text and the Violence of Exclusion", by Alisoun Neville, (2005) Vol 5 Macquarie L.J. 31-56, the author observed:

> [...] O'Loughlin J. [...] insisted that, in one area, 'Mr Gunner told an entirely different and contradictory story under cross-examination'. There were other times, further, 'when he engaged in open confrontation with the cross-examiner for no apparent reason'.148 And, 'time and time again' Mr Gunner 'reacted with suspicion to questions that were asked of him in cross-examination. Simple questions that were capable of simple answers were converted into confused ramblings.' [Footnotes omitted]

u) About face in response to questions put in cross-examination

[9-35] The best that counsel may hope for is for a witness to provide an entirely different response in cross-examination from that which was advanced in chief. An example is seen at page 51 of "Cubillo v Commonwealth: Classifying Text and the Violence of Exclusion", by Alisoun Neville, (2005) Vol 5 Macquarie L.J. 31-56, wherein the author observed: "[...] O'Loughlin J. [...] insisted that, in one area, 'Mr Gunner told an

entirely different and contradictory story under cross-examination'." [Footnote omitted]

v) Simple questions should be answered in simple terms

[9-36] Counsel will have gained some advantage if it can be shown that a witness failed to respond to a simple question in simple terms. For example, page 51 of "Cubillo v Commonwealth: Classifying Text and the Violence of Exclusion", by Alisoun Neville, (2005) Vol 5 Macquarie L.J. 31-56, records the following: "[…] And, 'time and time again' Mr Gunner 'reacted with suspicion to questions that were asked of him in cross-examination. Simple questions that were capable of simple answers were converted into confused ramblings.'" [Footnote omitted]

w) "Let's not go on with suspicious minds"!

[9-37] Counsel will have gained some advantage if it can be shown that a witness demonstrated a suspicious attitude in responding to questions in cross-examination. For example, at page 51 of "Cubillo v Commonwealth: Classifying Text and the Violence of Exclusion", by Alisoun Neville, (2005) Vol 5 Macquarie L.J. 31-56, the author observed:

> […] O'Loughlin J. […] insisted that […] 'time and time again' Mr Gunner 'reacted with suspicion to questions that were asked of him in cross-examination. Simple questions that were capable of simple answers were converted into confused ramblings.' [Footnotes omitted]

x) Boundaries of cross-examination may be limited in certain cases

[9-38] It will be useful to note that legislative intervention may be desirable in certain cases in that little is gained from certain types of cross-examination and the process often leads to

serious acrimony involving the parties outside of the Court room, notably in Native title litigation. Note in this respect the following observations penned in Alexander Reilly's contribution, "How Mabo Helps Us Forget", (2006) Vol 6 Macquarie L.J. 25-48, at page 41:

> With historical evidence being admitted by the courts in exception to the hearsay rule, the main issue is the weight to be attached to it. In relation to historical evidence, there are several issues of weight that have commonly arisen in cases including, whether inferences and conclusions in historians' reports are supported by the archival material they purport to rely on, and whether historians have been even-handed in their appraisal of the archival sources. [Footnote 96: See eg, the cross-examination of the historian Christine Choo in Ben Ward and Ors v The State of Western Australia WAG6002 of 1996 and Clarrie Smith v The State of Western Australia, WAG72-75 of 1998.] Academic historians who have been involved in the native title litigation process have reported being subject to an unprecedented level of critical scrutiny of their work through the process of cross-examination. [Footnote 97: See Hal Wootten 'Conflicting Imperatives: Pursuing the Truth in the Courts' in Iain McCalman and Ann McGrath, Proof and Truth: The Humanist as Expert (2003) 15: Graeme Davidson, 'History on the Witness Stand' in Iain McCalman and Ann McGrath (ed), Proof and Truth: The Humanist as Expert (2003) 53, 62]

y) Cross-examination and hearsay

[9-39] Recall as well the contributions of Professor Roy Donnelly by means of his article "Gobbledegook, the hearsay rule and reform of Section 60, (2006), 25 <u>U. Tas. L. Rev.</u> 83-99 at pages 97-98: "[...] The rationale for the development of the hearsay rule was to protect the interests of the party against whom it was admitted. This incorporates protections in the form of the oath, testing of evidence via cross-examination and avoiding reliance on the witness's credulity. [Footnote 68: See, eg, E M Morgan, 'Hearsay Dangers and the Application of the Hearsay Concept.' (1948) 62(2) Harvard Law Review, 177]"

[9-40] Note as well these comments:

> The distinction between the testimonial and circumstantial use of an out-of-court act is not to be found in the ultimate conclusion which can be drawn from that act; rather, it relates to the manner in which that conclusion is reached. When a statement is used testimonially its cogency depends on the credit to be given to the speaker. The tribunal of fact is asked to conclude that a particular fact exists because the speaker has said so. They are asked to take the speaker's word' for it. Before concluding that the particular fact does exist, the jury will want to be satisfied that the speaker was neither insincere nor mistaken. This task is obviously much easier when the speaker is testifying in court: then the speaker's demeanour can be assessed and his or her evidence tested under cross-examination. Hence the hearsay rule's undoubted prohibition on the testimonial use of an out-of-court statement. [Footnotes omitted]

[9-41] Refer to page 47 of "Hearsay: A Definition that Works", by Andrew Palmer in (1995), 14 U. Tas. L. Rev. 29-62.

z) Fact-finding and cross-examination

[9-42] A simple expression is found at pages 7-8 of Sir Garfield Barwick's contribution, "Courts, Lawyers, and the Attainment of Justice": "[…] Our method of ascertaining the facts is by the production of witnesses and documents, and for the accuracy and veracity of witnesses and the authenticity of documents to be determined; by a process of examination and cross-examination; all followed by a discussion between counsel and the tribunal of fact, Judge or Jury as the case may be, as to the relative weight of the evidence, as to its meaning, and as to the inferences which ought to be drawn from it […]" Refer to (1958-63), 1 U. Tas. L. Rev. 1-19.

aa) Cross-examination of computers and other electronic instruments

[9-43] A superb discussion of the issue of hearsay and computers is found in R.A. Brown's article, "Computer-Produced Evidence in Australia", in (1984-86), 8 U. Tas. L. Rev. 46-61. Of note, page 50 provides direct guidance on the issue of cross-examining computers:

> Fundamental to acceptance of this approach, as with the computer as calculator, is that there be evidence that the computer was operating correctly and that the data recorder was accurate. Proof of 'independence' as defined above will be required, as will be proof that there were no relevant malfunctions in the recording process. Generally, such evidence will be available from experts, and hence will be subject to the usual testing via cross-examination.

bb) Cross-examination and the futility of ascertaining the truth

[9-44] Of course, it must be taken for granted that the trial process as a whole and in particular the engine for discovering the truth that is cross-examination are, in fact, capable of revealing the true state of affairs of any controversy. There are many who question this fundamental assertion. Perhaps the most interesting contribution of the scholars who doubt that such a feat is possible is that penned by Professor J. Neville Turner, "Dostoevsky – The Trial in Brothers Karamazov", (1984-86), 8 U. Tas. L. Rev. 62-73.

[9-45] Indeed, it will be most instructive to set out at length the instruction consigned under the rubric "(j) The Impossibility of Reconstructing the Truth", at page 72:

> One is led inexorably to the final query, which for most readers of Dostoevsky represents the key question about the judging of human affairs. Is it ever possible to know the truth? Can a human court ever be justified in coming to a conclusion?
>
> This problem may be discussed on two levels. First, on a mundane, factual plane - that the practical difficulty of reconstructing past events is so great that it makes the search for truth illusory. And, secondly, on a more metaphysical plane, that absolute, objective truth is an illusion anyway, a chimera. Pontius Pilate's equivocation stemmed from a genuine apperception of the impossibility of delineating material reality.

3) Conclusion: Trauma caused by cross-examination must be justified

[9-46] It is has been suggested in many quarters that the prospect of being subjected to cross-examination engenders such fears that victims of sexual violence refrain from bringing their victimization to the attention of the authorities lest they be compelled to testify and to be harmed again during the course of the trial. One representative example of the literature follows. Indeed, page 359 of "Criminal Proceedings: Obligation or Choice for Crime Victims?" by Chris Corns includes these observations:

> [...] Specifically, many rape victims refuse to report because of fear that they will not be believed by the police or the court, fear of the social stigma attaching to the status of 'rape victim', fear of reprisal from the offender, and <u>fear of trauma from cross-examination by defence counsel and other legal processes</u>. [Footnote 54: See Victorian Law Reform Commission, Rape: Reform of Law and Procedure, Interim Report No 42 (1991) [...]] [Footnotes omitted]

[9-47] Consider the insights gained from this insightful article by R.W. Betham, "The Bench and Bar in Ireland" (1958-63), 1 U. Tas. L. Rev. 209-230, at pages 225-226:

> Irish juries and witnesses, however, needed, and still need, a rather different approach. Rarely is it necessary for an English judge to appeal to an English jury for a conviction, sometimes he may have to appeal for an acquittal. In Ireland, however, the judges not infrequently had

to urge a conviction when public justice and safety demanded it. 'This was not merely true in political or agrarian offences, when fellow feeling might affect the jurors' minds, but in ordinary crimes where their own well-being and protection were at stake'. The famous case of highway robbery in Tralee is a well-known example. The evidence for the prosecution was overwhelming and yet the jury acquitted. The presiding judge showed his view of the case by requesting the High Sheriff to detain the innocent prisoners in custody until he had got a good start on his way back to Dublin! A certain irreverence for the law is to be found, too, in the Bench and Bar. Professor Dicey recounted how on a visit to Dublin he was invited to sit on the Bench in a criminal court. There was no doubt that the prisoner was morally justified in his conduct; equally there was no doubt that he was criminally responsible. The Irish judge, a Tory and a Protestant, told the jury that the prisoner had broken the Statute, but, he added, they would be a queer set of Irishmen if they could not find a way of getting round an Act of Parliament. Of course, the jury acquitted.

Maurice Healy, who himself had extensive experience of practice at both the English and the Irish Bar, sees the essential difference in technique between them as depending upon the personnel of litigation in the two countries. To him the English (witness) approaches a court of law unwillingly [...] especially apprehensive of cross examination. No doubt there are occasional witnesses of that kind in Ireland, too; but the vast majority go to give their evidence as a cricketer who walks to the wicket. Each is confident he will not be bowled until he has knocked up a good score […] This jaunty attitude is reflected by the Irish witness' reply to Lord Justice Darling when the judge turned sternly to him and said: 'Tell me, in your country, what happens to a witness who does not tell the truth?' 'Begor, me Lord,' replied the Irishman, with a candour that disarmed all criticism, 'I think his side usually wins!' [Emphasis added – footnotes omitted]

[9-48] I cannot reach any definitive views on this subject as a judicial officer, but I am hopeful that the foregoing discussion has been useful to guide the Bench and Bar as to future developments.

Chapter 10
Conclusion: Literature and the Art of Judging

[10-1] It is quite common for a newly-appointed judge to be advised, in the course of his or her swearing-in ceremony, that she should enjoy "… at least a bowing acquaintance with Acton and Maintland, with Thucydes, Gibbon and Carlyle, with Homer, Dante, Shakespeare and Milton, with Machiavelli, Montaigne and Rabelais, with Plato, Bacon, Hume and Kant …" in order to rule fairly and judicially on the various questions which will be submitted for adjudication.

[10-2] Indeed, speakers typically go on to point out that a judge's outlook must not be limited by parish or class: "They must be aware of the changing social tensions in every society which make it an organism; which demand new schemata of adaptation; which will disrupt it, if rigidly confined".[146]   This quote is from an article by Learned Hand, "Sources of Tolerance", (1930) 79 U. of Pa. L. Rev. 1-14, at page 12-13. The passage is quoted at page 488 of "Mr. Justice Cardozo and Public Law", 48 Yale L.J. 458 (1938-1939).

[10-3] The goal which I have pursued throughout this book has been to assist the members of the Bench, and especially those who are embarking upon their judicial careers, with a number of passages and references from the works of the greatest writers of the Western world on the issue of fact finding with particular emphasis on credibility, reliability and demeanour. It is my hope that this work will assist judges in gaining a full understanding of that most fundamental issue of all, human nature.

---

[146]   Learned Hand, "Sources of Tolerance", (1930) 79 U. of Pa. L. Rev. 1, at page 12, quoted at page 488 of "Mr. Justice Cardozo and Public Law", 48 Yale L.J. 458 (1938-1939).

INDEX

BIAS

    By witness
3-28 to 3-29
Reliability and bias
4-43 to 4-49

COUNSEL'S ROLE IN ASSISTING THE COURT
7-1 to 7-77

    Reversing the proposition
7-9 to 7-75

CREDIBILITY

    Accept all, part or none
3-14 to 3-15
3-83 to 3-89

    Capacity to perceive
3-90 to 3-95

    Common sense
3-17
3-114 to 117
3-122 to 140

    Consistency
3-42 to 3-46
3-66

    Contradictions
3-123 to 132